PRIME TIME ANIMATION

In September 1960 a television show emerged from the mists of prehistoric time to take its place as the mother of all animated sitcoms. *The Flintstones* spawned dozens of imitations, just as, two decades later, *The Simpsons* sparked a renaissance of prime time animation. The essays in this volume critically survey the landscape of television animation, from Bedrock to Springfield and beyond.

The contributors explore a series of key issues and questions, including: How do we explain the animation explosion of the 1960s? Why did it take nearly twenty years following the cancellation of *The Flintstones* for animation to find its feet again as prime time fare? In addressing these questions, as well as many others, the essays in the first section examine the relation between earlier, made-for-cinema animated production (such as the Warner *Looney Toons* shorts) and television-based animation; the role of animation in the economies of broadcast and cable television; and the links between animation production and brand image. Contributors also examine specific programs like *The Powerpuff Girls, Daria, The Simpsons, The Ren and Stimpy Show* and *South Park* from the perspective of fans, exploring fan cybercommunities, investigating how ideas of 'class' and 'taste' apply to recent TV animation, and addressing themes such as irony, alienation, and representations of the family.

Carol A. Stabile is associate professor of communication and director of the Women's Studies Program at the University of Pittsburgh. She is the author of *Feminism and the Technological Fix* (1994), editor of *Turning the Century: Essays in Media and Cultural Studies* (2000), and is currently working on a book on media coverage of crime from the 1830s to the present.

Mark Harrison is a Ph.D. candidate in communication and cultural studies at the University of Pittsburgh. His work has appeared in *Bad Subjects* and *Cultural Studies* as well as the anthology *Turning the Century*. He is currently working on a project tracking the figure of the e͏   th century to the present.

PRIME TIME ANIMATION

Television animation and
American culture

*Edited by Carol A. Stabile
and Mark Harrison*

Routledge
Taylor & Francis Group

LONDON AND NEW YORK

First published 2003
by Routledge
11 New Fetter Lane, London EC4P 4EE

Simultaneously published in the USA and Canada
by Routledge
29 West 35th Street, New York, NY 10001

Reprinted 2004

Routledge is an imprint of the Taylor & Francis Group

Typeset in Perpetua by Taylor & Francis Books Ltd
Printed and bound in Great Britain by MPG Books Ltd,
Bodmin, Cornwall

British Library Cataloguing in Publication Data
A catalogue record for this book is available from the British
Library

Library of Congress Cataloging in Publication Data
Prime-time animation / edited by Carol Stabile and Mark
Harrison. p. cm. Includes bibliographical references and index.
1. Animated television programs – United States.
I. Stabile, Carol, 1960– . II. Harrison, Mark, 1967– .
PN1992.8.A59 P75 2003
791.45'3--dc21   2002012968

ISBN 0–415–28325–6 (hbk)
ISBN 0–415–28326–4 (pbk)

CONTENTS

ILLUSTRATIONS

CONTRIBUTORS

Diane F. Alters completed her Ph.D. in media studies at the School of
Journalism and Mass Communication at the University of Colorado,
Boulder in 2002. She has taught at the Graduate School of Public Affairs
at the University of Colorado and previously worked as a staff writer at
The Boston Globe, the *Sacramento Bee*, and other publications.

Alice Crawford is a Ph.D. candidate in communication at the University of
Pittsburgh and teaches classes in visual rhetoric, web design, and media
criticism. Her dissertation investigates relations between spatial metaphors
embedded in information technologies and the rhetoric around them, and
the manner in which urban spaces are experienced and used. She has
published in *Social Epistemology*, and has forthcoming essays in *Eloquent
Images: Visual Literacy and New Media* and *Critical Perspectives on the
Internet*. Ms. Crawford worked in information design before her current
incarnation as an academic.

Rebecca Farley worked on animation at Queensland University between 1992
and 1999. She has published in *Media International Australia* and is book
reviews editor for *Intensities: The Journal of Cult Media and Social
Semiotics*. She is presently writing her dissertation on adventure at the
School of Journalism, Media and Cultural Studies at Cardiff University.

Joy Van Fuqua is an assistant professor in the Department of Communication at Tulane University. She teaches courses in television and popular culture and is the director of the cultural studies minor. Her current research project examines television and the rise of health consumer culture.

Mark Harrison is a Ph.D. candidate in communication and cultural studies at the University of Pittsburgh. His work has appeared in *Bad Subjects* and *Cultural Studies* as well as the anthology *Turning the Century*. He is currently working on a project tracking the figure of the extraterrestrial from the mid-nineteenth century to the present.

Wendy Hilton-Morrow is a doctoral student in the Communication Studies Department at the University of Iowa, specializing in media studies. Her research interests include media institutions, cultural theory and gender issues. Before attending graduate school, she worked in television journalism.

Allen Larson is a doctoral candidate at the University of Pittsburgh's Department of Communication. His dissertation is titled *Alienated Affections: Stardom, Work and Identity in US 20th Century Culture*.

David T. McMahan, Ph.D., University of Iowa, is an assistant professor in the Department of Communication Studies and Theater at Missouri Western State College. His research interests include media institutions, communication education, personal relationships, and the bridging of interpersonal communication and mass communication.

Jason Mittell is an assistant professor of American civilization and film & media culture at Middlebury College. He has published essays in *Cinema Journal*, *The Velvet Light Trap*, *Television and New Media*, *Film History*, and a number of anthologies. He is currently working on a book on television genres as cultural categories.

Kathy M. Newman is assistant professor of English/literary and cultural theory at Carnegie Mellon University. Her first book, *Radio-Active: Advertising and Consumer Activism, 1935–1947*, is forthcoming with University of California Press. Though she once tried her hand at animation with a hand-drawn cartoon (*Poor, Hungry and Desperate*) when at graduate school, today she writes a bi-weekly television column for the alternative press called "What's Left on Television?"

Brian L. Ott is an assistant professor of media studies at Colorado State University, where he teaches undergraduate and graduate courses in communication and popular culture, critical media studies, and virtual culture and communication. His essays have appeared in *Critical Studies in*

Media Communication, The Western Journal of Communication, and *Rhetoric and Public Affairs*.

Kevin S. Sandler is an assistant professor of media industries in the Department of Media Arts at the University of Arizona. He is the editor of *Reading the Rabbit: Explorations in Warner Bros. Animation* (Rutgers 1998), co-editor of *Titanic: Anatomy of a Blockbuster* (Rutgers 1999), and author of the forthcoming book, *The Naked Truth: Why Hollywood Does Not Make NC-17 Films*.

Carol A. Stabile is associate professor of communication and director of the Women's Studies Program at the University of Pittsburgh. She is the author of *Feminism and the Technological Fix* (1994) and editor of *Turning the Century: Essays in Media and Cultural Studies* (2000). Her published essays have appeared in *Camera Obscura, Critical Studies in Media Communication, Cultural Studies*, and *Monthly Review*. She is currently working on a book on media coverage of crime from the 1830s to the present.

Michael V. Tueth is currently an associate professor at the Department of Communication and Media Studies at Fordham University. He holds a BA in philosophy and an MA in English from St. Louis University and a Ph.D. in American civilization from New York University, where his dissertation was entitled *The Image of the Family in American Popular Theater: 1945–1960*. He has taught at Regis University (Denver), Santa Clara University, Loyola University (Chicago), Georgetown University, and University of Maryland. His primary interest in both teaching and research is in the areas of television and film studies, with particular attention to comedy.

Paul Wells, professor, is Head of the Media Portfolio at the University of Teesside, UK. He has published widely in the field of animation, including *Understanding Animation* (Routledge 1998), *Animation and America* (Rutgers University Press 2002), and *Animation: Genre and Authorship* (Wallflower Press 2002).

ACKNOWLEDGMENTS

Carol Stabile would like to thank the following people, without whom this volume would not have been possible. The oldest debt is to Rebecca Barden, who first suggested that I take on this project several years ago. My colleagues, Carrie Rentschler and Jon Sterne, watched many hours of *Beavis and Butt-Head* moron-athons with me – their critical eyes (and laughter) shaped this volume in ways that may be imperceptible at this point. My deepest and most loving thanks to some of the human members of my pack: Mrak and Tony Unger, Maria Magro, and Michael Stabile III, who picked up the slack as this volume lurched toward completion.

Mark Harrison wishes to thank the following groups and individuals: foremost Mom, for ongoing support and because I promised. Thanks to friends and fellow travelers from around the 'Burgh whose conversation and companionship nourished the thought that went into this book. You know who you are. Special thanks to Alice Crawford for always being there and to Laura Zimmerman who from the beginning was a constant source of sympathy and sage advice.

We are grateful to the following for permission to use images: Peter Coppin for "The TeleANT animated interface;" Remote Experience and Learning Lab for "Eventscope: interactive Martian data;" Hugh Hancock for "Barracuda Beach Bar" and "Hardly Working;" Klasky-Csupo for Duckman;

Minna Långström, Virta Animated Ltd. for "Character creation with wire-frame and texture mapping"; MTV for *Daria*; Justin Trevena for Sweeet.com; Turner Entertainment Group for *Scooby-Doo*, *Samurai Jack*, and *The Powerpuff Girls*.

PRIME TIME ANIMATION
An overview

Carol A. Stabile and Mark Harrison

During its five-year run (1992–97), *Beavis and Butt-Head* became the focus of a number of controversies over the effects of television on viewers: from accusations that the program caused a child to set fire to his trailer home, resulting in the death of a sibling; to rumors that frat boys were imitating some of the duo's more idiotic stunts. By and large, the mass media missed out on the fact that *Beavis and Butt-Head* was in many ways a protracted commentary about media effects and the role of media in late twentieth-century US society.

"The Pipe of Doom" (May 1994) is just one of many examples of this aspect of the program. In the episode, Beavis manages to wedge himself in a drainage conduit at a construction site. The media immediately converge on the scene, broadcasting images of Beavis' scrawny legs and posterior around the world. After being rescued from the pipe, Beavis is whisked off by emergency personnel and the media, leaving Butt-Head alone at the now-abandoned construction site. Envious of the attention that had been showered on his friend, Butt-Head wriggles into the pipe, and in one of those remarkable lapses in judgment so typical of these characters, he only gradually realizes that no one remains to hear his cries.

This episode illustrates the deftness with which this animated sitcom frequently functioned as a wider cultural critique. The media frenzy that follows from Beavis' mishap explicitly draws upon the Baby Jessica story from 1987, when an 18-month-old girl fell down a well in Midland, Texas. The major networks turned this unfortunate situation into an around-the-clock media event, broadcasting live from the site for more than two days. The final scene of "The Pipe of Doom," in which Butt-Head imitates Beavis, suggests that it is the media's fetishization of such incidents (rather than comedic representations of them) that encourage mimicry. This kind of self-consciousness was evident throughout the program's run, where it often took the shape of various warnings to viewers at the beginning of the program. One episode carried the statement: "Warning: If you're not a cartoon, swallowing a rubber full of drugs can kill you" ("Way Down Mexico," May 1993).

Beavis and Butt-Head, along with the renaissance in television animation inaugurated by *The Simpsons* in 1990, offers a rich site for understanding prime time television and the effects of cable television on the wider field of cultural production. That so little critical attention has been devoted to this genre attests to its doubly devalued status: as the offspring of a conventionally devalued medium (television) whose cultural products have only recently been considered worthy of scholarly scrutiny, and as the odd recombinant form of two similarly degraded genres – the situation comedy or sitcom and the cartoon.[1]

This volume provides readers with a framework through which to understand television animation in its cultural and historical context. Because of television animation's unique position in the field of television production, an investigation of the form has much to tell us about the nature of the television industry in the latter part of the twentieth century, as well as that industry's future. The volume itself is divided into two sections. The first section considers prime time animation within the context of the institutions that produce this programming, while the second features specific readings of prime time animated texts.

The essays that comprise these two sections cover a vibrant and diverse chunk of this inexhaustible form, ranging from Paul Wells and Jason Mittell's work on the history of cartoons to Allen Larson's political economy of children's programming to Brian Ott's essay on *South Park* cybercommunities. The animated television sitcom has an odd genealogy that mixes, as Jason Mittell puts it, a number of genres rather than hewing more strictly to a single genre. Unlike live-action sitcoms, which have their precedent in radio, animated sitcoms draw on both film and television codes and conventions. The remainder of this introduction provides a brief historical backdrop for the individual chapters that follow.

Cinematic animation

The history of animation might be imagined in terms of three primary epochs: cinematic, televisual and digital. The essays in this volume deal primarily with televisual animation, with the notable exception of Alice Crawford's contribution, which directly addresses the impact of digital technologies on animation. As several of the essays point out, however, there is a fair amount of overlap between the first two eras, both in the sense that most of early television's animation programming consisted of shorts originally created for the cinema and in the sense that the production of animation for the big screen, while greatly curtailed, did not cease with the 1948 Paramount Decision and the rise of television as a medium (on which, see Chapter 2 of this volume). Cinematic animation constitutes a pre-history for the animation that was to emerge in a televisual context. This pre-history will be treated here in brief, focusing on experimental, early commercial and industrial moments in the medium's development.

The advent of cinema per se was preceded by the development of various devices with such classically intoned names as thaumatrope, phenakistiscope and kinematoscope. In 1877, Emile Reynaud patented his praxinoscope, a modification of which (dubbed "théâtre optique") he would later use to project his animated drawings at the Grévin Museum – a wax museum which also staged variety programs. Beginning on 28 October 1892, Reynaud was to screen his *pantomimes lumineuses* for the next eight years, ending in March of 1900 when he was replaced by English marionettes and a Gypsy orchestra.

In the US, Stuart Blackton and Albert E. Smith stumbled upon the technique of stop-action animation, in which three-dimensional objects or drawings are shot frame-by-frame, slightly adjusting the position of the object between frames – thus creating the illusion of motion. Blackton and Smith used this technique to create a series of shorts, culminating in the live action film, *The Haunted Hotel* (1907), in which "haunted" effects were created via stop-action. It was this film that was to serve as the inspiration for the man generally considered to be the first "true" animator, Frenchman Emile Cohl, whose first animated film *Fantasmagorie* was screened at the Théâtre du Gymnase on 17 August 1908. "Worried about verisimilitude, Blackton was always careful to introduce or justify the presence of a cartooned world next to a real world. On the contrary, the Frenchman jumped into the graphic universe, animating the adventures of autonomous characters" (Bendazzi 1994: 9).

Blackton and Smith modeled their early animation after the chalk-talks of vaudeville, during which performers would quickly draw caricatures of audience members or modify drawings over the course of a monologue. As an example of the latter, the vaudeville act of Winsor McCay, an early American animator, often included a performance of *The Seven Ages of Man*, in which he sketched two faces and progressively aged them via modification. McCay serves as a transitional figure, from early independent animators-cum-inventors to the next phase in which the *business* of animation begins to take shape. This was a transition which McCay was later to lament – "Animation should be an art, that is how I conceived it. But as I see what you fellows have done with it is make it into a trade ... not an art but a trade ... bad luck" (quoted in Bendazzi 1994: 18).

McCay was based in New York, the home of the emergent businesses of both film and animation production. McCay drew on both of the primary sources of early American animation: vaudeville (in addition to McCay's use of the chalk-talk, he used his vaudeville act as the venue for early presentations of what is generally considered his animation masterpiece, *Gertie the Dinosaur*) and newspaper-based comic strips (McCay completed animated versions of both of his most well known, and still revered, strips – *Little Nemo in Slumberland* and *Dreams of a Rarebit Fiend*). His animated shorts were exhibited both in a vaudeville context and in movie theaters. The transition from newsprint to celluloid, initiated by McCay, was repeated by, among others, *Mutt and Jeff* and *The Katzenjammer Kids*, both of which were owned by the Hearst syndicate. Hearst went so far as to open the International Film Service in 1916, in part for the express purpose of producing cinematic versions of his syndicate's more successful strips. While the IFS was to close within two years, its creation was indicative of both animation's increasing commodification and its increasingly industrialized mode of production.

Over the course of the first two decades of the twentieth century, new technologies and studios emerged. As to the latter, perhaps the most notable were the Fleischer studio, which set up shop in 1921, and the Pat Sullivan Studios, which opened in 1915. Sullivan Studios is best remembered for its *Felix the Cat* shorts. Originally created for Paramount's newsreel, *Screen Magazine*, by Otto Messmer in 1919, the rights to Felix were acquired by Sullivan when *Screen* discontinued production. Felix (who reversed the trend of characters from the "funnies" moving from the page to the screen by appearing first as an animated character and *then* as a comic strip) was the first animated character to establish a highly lucrative half-life as licensed merchandise – appearing as and on toys, stuffed animals and other items.[2] This strategy of merchandising was later to be perfected by Disney Studios and continues today with the vast proliferation of *Powerpuff* and *SpongeBob SquarePants* paraphernalia (see Larson, Sandler, and Fuqua in this volume for more on merchandising and the related phenomena of "branding" and "synergy").

Fleischer Studios (originally known as Out of the Inkwell Studios), run by brothers Max, Joe and Dave, would later make their mark with *Betty Boop* and *Popeye*. In 1924, they formed Red Seal Distribution (which closed after two years with Paramount picking up distribution for the brothers) to circulate their catalogue of *Koko the Clown* shorts, documentaries, comedies, and live-action shorts. Red Seal also distributed the Fleischer's *Song Car-Tunes*. These shorts provided animated texts for audience sing-alongs, another vaudeville standby. With music provided by orchestra or pianist, these films introduced the "bouncing ball," a device destined to become a standard for audience sing-alongs in the cinema, to highlight the lyrics on screen. After the full arrival of sound film, the *Car-Tunes* were followed by Walter Lantz's color *Cartune Classics*, Ub Iwerk's *ComiColor Cartoons*, Warner Brothers' *Merry Melodies* and Disney's *Silly Symphonies*, all of which pursued an increasingly naturalized relationship between animation and music. Of them all, it was Disney's shorts that proved the most influential.

Walt Disney had started his animation career as an employee of the Kansas City Film Ad Company. Resigning in 1921, Disney formed Laugh-O-Gram films which, nearing insolvency, led to his Hollywood exodus in 1923. The series that he had begun in Kansas, *Alice in Cartoonland*, turned out to be a success and served to bankroll future endeavors. Disney Studios was to become immensely influential, shaping both the form and industry in ways that continue to reverberate. One of the fundamental changes brought about by the practices of the studio was the full industrialization of the production process. One element in rationalizing animation production was the creation of model sheets that fully and finally determined the physiognomy and kinetic style of each character, ending the restless morphology that previously accompanied a given character's passage through the hands of different artists and directors. Thus Disney standardized the presentation of characters. Disney further streamlined production by creating teams who served different functions in the process – with a primary demarcation between writers and artists. The element that most abetted the separation of the tasks involved in the animation itself was the adoption of the cel technique as standard practice. Patented by Earl Hurd in 1914, cel animation exploded one of the main barriers to rapid, assembly-line-style production. Prior to the advent of cel production, the animator had to redraw the whole of the background for each frame. The use of overlapping cellophane sheets allowed the artist to draw a particular background once, superimposing the character over that background. While cels had been in use for some time, it was Disney that established them as an industry standard along with an attendant division of tasks among colorers, buffers, "in-betweeners," and various other levels of animators.

The other primary innovation of Disney's was perhaps more subtle but just as far-reaching. Earlier animation had largely resided in a purely graphic universe, where any object might potentially become any other object – the teapot becomes alarm clock becomes a daisy, etc. By and large, animation did not strive for verisimilitude, but rather was characterized by a plasticity and mobility of graphic forms, a style that was reflective of the medium's native potential. In a filmic universe that is graphically rendered, anything is possible and this possibility is reflected by the anarchic sensibility operative in much early animation. Disney strove to create believable characters who behaved in believable ways in believable environments. In short, Disney brought the constraints and devices of drama and narrative to bear on the field of animation, containing the exuberance of earlier examples of the form by privileging story and character over the inherent plasticity of the form (Bendazzi 1994).

Thus the precedents set by Disney Studios all tended toward containment – the streamlining of the production process via compartmentalization, the standardization of characters' features and traits and the movement away from visual excess and toward narrative clarity. That such strategies were economically successful is obvious. Whether they were artistically successful or not, Disney's style of animation became the standard and is now synonymous with "classic animation" (see Wells and Mittell in this volume for more on the standardization of the Disney aesthetic).

Cinematic production of animation continued after the ascendancy of the Disney style. The contours of the industry were to change radically, however, in response to the 1948 Paramount Decision (which largely ended vertical integration within the film industry) and the rise of television. The art of animation and its mode of production necessarily responded to the emergent needs and economies of television. The preceding section of this introduction dealt with the details of the development of cinematic animation, a mode of production that constitutes the pre-history of the televisual mode. While the bulk of the present text deals directly with animation in the context of television, the following section looks specifically at the historical context of the rise of a genre central both to television and television animation: the domestic sitcom.

The cruelest cel

At the end of the studio era and the beginning of the television era, and despite the appearance of animated features such as *Fantasia* (1940), cinematic animation – as an art form – remained the poor relation of live-action film. Although as both Farley and Mittell observe in this volume, animation had yet to be inextricably linked to children's viewing and subsequently infantilized, it clearly was not in the same aesthetic league as live-action film. The end of the studio era, which dovetailed with the rise of television, pushed animation in different directions and ushered in a new age of animation. Animation's insertion into the genres then emerging on television was to shape prime time animation for decades to come, both in terms of form and content.

The Simpsons offers many excellent examples of the centrality of genre to understanding prime time animation, past and present. The Simpsons' setting, Springfield (a name that echoes the fictitious town where the ubiquitous Father lived in *Father Knows Best*), and the centrality of nuclear energy to the town's economy are just two ways in which the program has satirized its own generic foundations. Unlike the father of 1950s live-action sitcoms, Homer clearly does not know best, and the nuclear plant, rather than being a symbol of strength, power, and masculinity, invariably functions as a metaphor for insecurity, paranoia, and sheer stupidity. By toying with the codes and conventions of the earlier sitcom form, *The Simpsons* functions as an ironic commentary on the family values discourse prevalent when the series began.

The curious process whereby the 1950s was held up as a reality from which the present conjuncture (again measured in terms of televisual representations) sadly diverged is worth emphasizing. For it wasn't only aesthetic forms that were standardized in the post-World War II years, it was a politics of content as well. As noted by Wells in this volume, Disney's anti-union, anti-Communist labor policies certainly affected the technical production of animation, but these policies were signs of an ideological sea change that was to leave its imprimatur on television as a whole.[3] For the "domestic" or "family" sitcom is very much a Cold War product, born at the confluence of a shift in ideological priorities and the forcible imposition of those ideologies on the fledgling television industry. Although many media scholars have written about the ways in which the television industry took over genres that had developed via vaudeville and then radio, the domestic sitcom that emerged in the 1950s and the political mandate it served was arguably a rather different creature.[4]

Indeed, more than any other genre, the domestic sitcom served to institute a particular myth about the nuclear family in popular culture. Even today, when politicians and policy-makers describe the "traditional" family, their descriptions are invariably a pastiche composed of characteristics from a number of different domestic sitcoms. It's worth rehearsing some of the characteristics of this particular invocation. First, the traditional family includes a male dad, a female mom, and, ideally, a son and daughter. They are white, middle class and live in the suburbs rather than the city or country. African-Americans, immigrants of all ethnicities and races, and gay men and lesbians mainly do not exist within this vision. The father is the "breadwinner" (a word that did not exist before the latter part of the nineteenth century), the mom stays at home, the sons are strong, and the daughters are good. Within this kinship arrangement, the sexual division of labor is absolute, women's unpaid labor is taken for granted, and paternal authoritarianism guarantees the reproduction of strong "moral" values.

In addition, the traditional family is a safe haven in a cruel and unpredictable world. While Bud or Princess have their share of adolescent crises, and Eddie Haskell eternally taunts the Beaver, the family featured on domestic sitcoms is absolutely remote from violence, conflict, and the realms of labor and politics. These families were never homeless, hungry, prone to sexual abuse, discontent, or in any way unhappy. Although it might be argued that the comedic genre as a whole mitigates against treatment of more serious issues, live-action sitcoms such as *Maude* and later *Roseanne* have dealt with darker, more serious issues (abortion, unemployment, death, etc.). Indeed, as Kathy Newman persuasively argues later in this volume, animated domestic sitcoms such as *Daria*, *The PJs*, and

The Simpsons all manage to address topics not considered conventional comedic material. It might be more accurate to say that producers wanted the live-action format to be free of controversy in order not to alienate any portion of the mass broadcast audience they sought to deliver to advertisers.

The purges of the culture industries during the McCarthy era guaranteed that most television content would be uncontroversial, effectively silencing progressive voices capable of, and committed to, challenging the mythic traditional family and its reactionary politics – the voices of those who sympathized with the Civil Rights Movement, the voices of trade unionists, the voices of feminists.[5] What remained was a now unanimous support for a status quo that transformed the anomaly that was the fifties family into a transhistorical universal reality from which any divergence could be demonized as "communist" and "un-American." In a classic example of the machinations of hegemony, overt coercion was used against the agents of the struggle (radical, progressive, and even middle-of-the-road liberal cultural workers), while those remote from these events had only the official, reactionary representation of events, produced by a culture industry now unified against communist threats to "family entertainment." If the fifties family now appears as a shining oasis in contrast to contemporary realities, this is in large part an effect of the ideological homogenization of the culture industries that proceeded from the Red Scare. Thus, when the family is remembered in mass culture and political debate, it is represented in terms established by the culture industry.[6]

Given this history, no wonder the live-action domestic sitcom became the banal, worn-out workhorse of network television. The generic and ideological constraints of the genre have been stifling – the domestic sitcom has had to struggle within the "traditional" family structure, even when the living arrangements haven't quite lined up (*One Day at a Time*, *Alice*, *My Two Dads*, *Empty Nest*). As late as 1992, sitcom mom Murphy Brown, played by Candace Bergen, made headlines for ostensibly glamorizing the life of a wealthy single mom. The format of the sitcom, with its conflict–resolution plot line framed by the opening/credit sequence and the tag, is further limiting. The plot must center around some minor domestic conflict which must be resolved by the end of the episode. Thus, in one episode of *Father Knows Best*, Princess is mean to one of her classmates, but by the end of the narrative they've become fast friends. Having thus exhausted its narrative possibilities by the early sixties, the domestic sitcom was, with the possible exceptions of "dramedies" such as *The Days and Nights of Molly Dodd* and *Frank's Place*, as well as the inimitable *Roseanne Barr Show*, never permitted to comment on its own banality.

The re-introduction of animated sitcoms in the early 1990s changed all this. As Rebecca Farley observes in Chapter 8, earlier programs such as *The Flintstones* and *The Jetsons* contained an element of self-referentiality and irony lacking in their live-action counterparts. The field of television production oscillates between processes of imitation and distinction/innovation. As both Mittell and Farley observe in this volume, the networks rushed to imitate *The Flintstones* and *The Simpsons* and thereby to replicate their success. But imitation is no guarantee of success and, particularly in the case of sitcoms, a program must distinguish itself from other programs (remaining, of course, within certain bounds) in order to gain our attention. This process of distinction has certainly become more aggressive in the age of cable, although things certainly heated up, as Larson notes in Chapter 3 and Tueth in Chapter 7, with FOX's entry onto the scene.

What attracted viewers to *The Simpsons* was its ability to breathe new life into the near-exhausted genre of domestic sitcoms. The playfulness of its hybrid form – the cartoon sitcom – allowed the program to toy with, and in many cases destroy, existing narrative conventions.[7] In addition, its cartoon elements allowed it to address topics and issues that live-action sitcoms could not. Imagine, for a moment, Roseanne Connor's husband Dan working at a nuclear plant, where workers frequently fell asleep or unintentionally carried radioactive material home. This gag simply wouldn't be as funny, largely because we have been primed as viewers of television and consumers of other media products to equate animation with humor.

In addition to its playfulness, *The Simpsons* also capitalized on its audience's televisual literacy in largely unprecedented ways. Assuming that its audience had grown up on a television diet, *The Simpsons* offers a text rich with allusions to a body of popular culture history roughly equivalent to the history of television. At the same time, *The Simpsons* (as well as *South Park*) has created a dense, internal text that depends on a comprehensive knowledge of the program itself and its own history.

In a sense, then, prime time animated sitcoms have perfected the form of bimodal address considered so important to advertisers: at one level, its allusions to the history of television and its metacommentary on genre and media in general are believed to attract an older demographic, while its constant attention to its internal history and its sheer playfulness, as Farley puts it in Chapter 8, attracts a younger one (Stanley 2002: 16). We can see this dynamic at work in Diane Alters' ethnographic research in Chapter 9, where parents and children both enjoy *The Simpsons*, while Brian Ott describes how viewers of *South Park* help to document the program's internal history and to construct this process of documentation as a form of literacy.

Given this bimodal address and the satire characteristic of the animated sitcom – its pursuit of controversy rather than the live-action domestic sitcom's avoidance of it – it is not surprising that the animated sitcom was the source of so much dispute in the 1990s. After all, this was in large part the role it sought to create for itself. Yet it is interesting that while no one questions the effects of 1950s sitcoms on a generation of conservative politicians (which might include, but are not limited to sexism, homophobia, and stupidity), animated prime time sitcoms (like comic books before them) have been consistently demonized.

The longevity of *The Simpsons* suggests that prime time animation will remain a central televisual presence, as does the fate of other animated programs (*South Park* remains in production at this time; *Beavis and Butt-Head* were killed by creator/producer, Mike Judge, and not by MTV). As Alice Crawford and Allen Larson point out, moreover, there are a host of industrial and economic reasons for the continuation of new animated series, and such programs remain successful (like *The Flintstones* before) in syndication. Prime time animation, in short, has become as important a part of our cultural landscape as live-action domestic sitcoms were to a previous one.

Notes

1   See Mittell (2001) for an analysis of "genre mixing" and cartoons.
2   Felix was preceded by Outcault's *The Yellow Kid*, an earlier comic strip character who had also been the source of a merchandising bonanza.
3   See Michael Denning's *The Cultural Front* (1996).
4   For analyses of the relation between radio and television programming, see Lipsitz (1990), Hilmes (1997), and Spigel (1992).
5   For noteworthy accounts of the purges, especially as they affected the culture industries, see Griffin Fariello (1995), John Henry Faulk (1983), Ellen Schrecker (1998), and Bud and Ruth Schultz (2001).
6   What is excluded, or repressed, from these memories is revealing. Few are likely to recall that one-quarter of all Americans (some 40 to 50 million people) were poor in the 1950s, that the highest rate of teenage childbearing was in 1957 (when 97 of 1,000 women between the ages of 15 and 19 gave birth), that then, as now, children were more likely to be physically or sexually abused by family members rather than predatory strangers (Coontz 1992: 29, 202). Nor are they likely to remember that the 1950s suburban family, such as it was, was "in large measure a creation of the strong state" and that strong state's FHA loans, GI bills, and other federal programs which served a white middle class (Coontz 1992: 145).
7   *The Family Guy* has lately carried this disregard for narrative convention ever further, through its sometimes relentless pursuit of *non sequiturs*.

Bibliography

"Beavis and Butt-Head Guide". Available at: http://batcomputer.batcave.net/bnbguide.html/1, (accessed May 2002).

Bendazzi, G. (1994) *Cartoons: One Hundred Years of Cinema Animation*, Bloomington: Indiana University Press.

Coontz, S. (1992) *The Way We Never Were: American Families and the Nostalgia Trap*, New York: Basic Books.

Denning, M. (1996) *The Cultural Front*, New York: Verso.

Fariello, G. (1995) *Red Scare: Memories of the American Inquisition*, New York: W. W. Norton.

Faulk, J. H. (1983) *Fear on Trial*, Austin: University of Texas Press.

Hilmes, M. (1997) *Radio Voices: American Broadcasting, 1922–1952*, Minneapolis: University of Minnesota Press.

Lipsitz, G. (1990) *Time Passages: Collective Memory and American Popular Culture*, Minneapolis: University of Minnesota Press.

Schrecker, E. (1998) *Many are the Crimes: McCarthyism in America*, Boston: Little, Brown & Company.

Schultz, B. and R. Schultz (2001) *The Price of Dissent: Testimonies to Political Repression in America*, Berkeley: University of California Press.

Spigel, L. (1992) *Make Room for TV*, Chicago: University of Illinois Press.

Stanley, A. (2002) "Taking a Dip in TV's Wishing Well," *New York Times*, Section 4, 19 May: 16.

Part I

INSTITUTIONS

Chapter 1

"SMARTER THAN THE AVERAGE ART FORM"

Animation in the television era

Paul Wells

T HIS CHAPTER WILL PROVIDE A CONTEXT for the debates and issues that
have arisen about the development of animation for television, principally in
the American Broadcast arena. I will discuss how animation changed from its
"classic" configuration in the theatrical era to the "reduced" styling for television,
largely pioneered by Hanna-Barbera, but intrinsically related to work by United
Productions of America (UPA) and Disney in the 1950s. In privileging the
intrinsic "modernity" characteristic to the medium, I will challenge the prevailing
argument that this move towards reduced animation was to the detriment of
animation as an art-form, suggesting instead that the changes necessitated by the
much-reduced economies for production both created a new aesthetic for animation which foregrounded its versatility and variety, and re-introduced the public
to animation in a way which spoke to the ongoing "recombinancy" strategies in
programming for television per se. This, in turn, will lead on to an analysis of
how television animation has sustained this recombinancy strategy, and invoked
an intertextuality which is not merely concerned with the relationship between
previous forms and conditions of production in animation, but with other aspects
of social, visual and new media cultures.

Exhausting cartoons

The current prominence and omnipotence of the animated form at the beginning
of the twenty-first century has consigned the anxieties that once feared for the
very survival of the medium to the long-distant past, but it is worth noting that it

is the process of recovery and re-invention that followed the post-theatrical era that has created this position, and it is the nature of these changes that are the main preoccupation of this discussion. Writing in 1957, for example, Bernard Orna asks, "Are animated film script and character ideas exhausted; must cartoons disappear in an ever tighter circle of repetitions? After seeing the three most recent MGM cat-and-mouse and dog-and-cat set ups chase each other in familiar routine all over the wide screen, I went away with the thought that we had reached a dead end" – the proliferation of American cartoons – "cheap and mass produced affairs without regard to ideas" is blamed; non-American animation preferred, and "Cinemascope" productions viewed merely as cosmetic surgery on a corpse (1957: 33).

It is clear from these remarks that by the mid-1950s, the Hollywood cartoon seemed long past its "Golden Era" – arguably, the period between Disney's *Steamboat Willie* (1928) and Hanna-Barbera's Tom and Jerry classic, *Mouse in Manhattan* (1945) – but this is to neglect many important short cartoons made in the immediate post-war era, and indeed, perhaps the greatest of all animated cartoons, Chuck Jones' *What's Opera, Doc?* (1957), made in the year in which Orna anticipates that the end is nigh.

This is merely one example, though, of the way in which the American cartoon tradition resisted its own epitaph. Jones, one of the medium's key *auteurs*, consistently progressed the form by using its intrinsic malleability and the openness of its vocabulary in redetermining the very conditions of expression. The cartoon was in effect defined by the refinements of the *Silly Symphonies* and the deconstructive maturity of the *Looney Toons* and *Merry Melodies*, and characterized by popular characters, full animation, and a socially suggestive form of anarchy which was culturally acceptable. Terry Lindvall and Matthew Melton (1994: 47) have suggested that animation's particular form of anarchy is foregrounded in its self-reflexiveness, whereby in commenting about the film making process, cartoons demonstrate their own textuality, speak directly to their audiences, and crucially, reveal the presence of their creators as the deconstructive agents of deliberate artifice, and in doing so, promote animation as a singularly *auteurist* medium. Donald Crafton notes this "self-figuration" – the presence of the creator either literally or implicitly present in the text – right from the beginnings of the animated form, and flags it as one of animation's distinctive qualities (1993: 11, 347–8). This capacity for "self-figuration" results in the idea that animation may be seen as a self-enunciating medium, literally announcing its intrinsic difference from other visual forms and cinematic imperatives. In many senses, this also underpins the view that the cartoon operates as a potentially non-regulatory or subversive space by virtue of its very artifice, and the assumed innocence that goes with it. Animation always has the excuse that "it's just ink and paint."[1]

The fears for the end of the medium were clearly premature, and largely prompted by the economic factors that led to the closure of the main animation studios' production units, and the parallel emergence of television in the modern era. MGM closed their unit as early as 1957 – perhaps not surprising in light of Orna's comments – while Warner Brothers survived until 1964, by which time William Hanna and Joseph Barbera, the directors penalized by MGM's decision to close down production, had established Hanna-Barbera as the key production house for television cartoons. These cartoons were predicated on the idea of "limited animation" – essentially the reduction of animation to its most essentialist form: little animation, no complex choreography, repeated cycles of movement, a small repertoire of expressions and gestures, stress on dialogue, basic design, and simple graphic forms. While Chuck Jones sought to engage with and extend the form, he clearly objected to the animation of the television era, branding it "illustrated radio," because it prioritized the literalness of its dialogue and its soundtrack as the stimulus for a limited number of illustrative movement cycles, rather than emerging out of a purely visual concept of narrativization prioritized in full, traditional animation (Adamson 1980: 141). Jones could not accept that the new television aesthetic had any intrinsic value, and suggested that it merely regressed the art form. There is some irony in this, as one of the key aspects of the aesthetic change had been pioneered by Jones in his cartoon, *The Dover Boys* (1942), where characters appear to leap from position to position, and "smear" animation is used to "blur" the movement from the first point to the second. Jones' work, of course, is in the spirit of aesthetic enquiry, and not predicated as a consequence of economic restraint, and it was this factor that was actually the mother of invention elsewhere.

From the Disney aesthetic to minimalism

Hanna-Barbera realized that the economic conditions which dictated change could also be exploited artistically, but their experimentation was of a different order. Walt Disney, too, recognized that the television economy would dictate different approaches, but rather than defining the principles upon which animation for television might be understood, Disney used the medium for more commercial rather than creative ends, debuting *Disneyland* in 1954 as a vehicle by which to use the back catalogue of Disney material, but more importantly, to promote his theme park. Hanna-Barbera, in essence, had no competition in determining the new television agenda. As British-based animation director, John Halas, had anticipated in 1956, "Animation is bound to be greatly stimulated by television in the future. In the last two years, on both sides of the Atlantic, it has resulted in the number of personnel engaged on cartoons being increased by nearly 100 per cent," adding:

17

> [T]he technical requirements of television lend themselves well to anima-
> tion. The small screen and the necessity for keeping both the background
> and the foreground flat and simple is completely within the province of the
> cartoon medium…television films can be handled by very small units with
> every chance of retaining the original conception of ideas.
>
> (1956: 6, 13)

This more "minimalist" aesthetic – effectively one of the self-conscious principles
of modern art animation, as it had been adopted both by studios in Zagreb and
by UPA – underpinned the populist works of the Hanna-Barbera studio. This was
not conscious art-making in the spirit of modern thought, but a practical
approach which recognized the intrinsic versatility of the animation medium in
accommodating change, while remaining aesthetically engaging, and cost effective.

The deliberate interrogation of the possibilities of the form beyond its appli-
cation in the Disney-patented full animation style had characterized many
approaches in the US and elsewhere, in attempting work which offered a model
of "difference" aesthetically, and most importantly, ideologically, from that of the
Disney canon. The Disney aesthetic carried with it clear connotations of a "state-
of-the-art" achievement that was seemingly unsurpassable, and which was, and
remains, embedded in the popular memory as one of the key illustrations of a
conflation of self-evident artistry with a populist, folk, quasi-Republican, middle-
American sensibility. Disney had ensured that "art" seamlessly took its place
within popular culture, and created an aesthetic that was inextricably entwined
with intrinsically American values. This state-of-the-art identity ceased to be
progressive, however, and while acknowledged as an extraordinary and enduring
achievement technically and industrially, it was a model of art-making which was
essentially static and conservative, and arguably, diametrically opposed to the
inherent potential of the form itself. Disney essentially defined animation, and
having established this as the benchmark for the industry, was reluctant to
embrace other approaches. Walt Disney himself was clear that the potential
"modernity" available through new styles and approaches should not challenge
the established Disney aesthetic, and the classical definition of the form it represented. This was evidenced in his response to Ward Kimball's overtly modernist
production of the history and development of music in *Toot, Whistle, Plunk and
Boom* (1953). As Marc Eliot has noted,

> When Walt returned from Europe and screened [*Toot, Whistle, Plunk and Boom*],
> he was appalled at its unrepresentative, non-Disney visual style and lack of
> formal narrative. Walt and [its director, Ward] Kimball argued vehemently
> over the film. Frustrated by what he took to be Kimball's obstinacy, Disney at

one point considered firing his animator, and would have done so if *Toot* had not won the Academy Award for Short Subject (Cartoon) of 1953. Nevertheless, Walt explicitly banned all further stylistic experimentation by any animator and limited Kimball's participation in future film productions.

(1994: 218)

Disney's reticence is not surprising in light of his understanding of the Disney aesthetic not merely as the embodiment of ideological stasis and security, but most importantly, as a brand in an era which was less versed and sophisticated in the creation of such a key market concept. Disney wanted to diversify the company's work in the light of its tradition and the meanings generated by the classicism and Americanism associated with the cartoons, and any sense that the work might signify either a perverse version of the avant garde or a model of economic cutback that served as a measure of supposedly reduced quality and achievement as evidenced on the screen, was unacceptable. Such "cheap" aesthetics were to be the provenance of others.

Crucially, it remains important to stress that the reduced or limited animation that Hanna-Barbera employed in their early television cartoons was the direct outcome of financial constraint. Nevertheless, their work was still made with the kind of ingenuity that privileged different approaches to the very language of animation that insisted upon embracing the versatility of the form, and some of the fundamental principles that had characterized some of the work of the pioneering animators in the field, long made invisible by the success and achievement of the Disney studio. While Hanna-Barbera were inevitably reductive in their approach, this is only significant when the work is measured against the dominant aesthetic created by Disney, and finds more correspondent value when actually measured against some of the work that defined the medium in the period before Disney "classicism," which has been reclaimed and credited in recent years, particularly through the work of John Canemaker (1991) and Donald Crafton (1993). The early "primitive" works of animators such as Emile Cohl, Winsor McCay, and Otto Messmer were far more predicated on the graphic freedoms afforded by the simple use of lines and shapes. This is effectively what Hanna-Barbera returned to as its prevailing aesthetic, concentrating on producing simple forms in both line and form, but in color. In many senses there was less concentration on animation itself, and more on the ingenuity of visual joke-making and creating characters as graphic ciphers for specific ideas. The new television era recovered this principle, enhanced it through the greater concentration upon scripts and vocal performance, and most importantly, looked backward and outward to other ways in which animation could function and find productive influence, other than the seemingly oppressive artistry and history of Disney.

While it is clear that the Hanna-Barbera studio developed its own characters and situations to progress these ideas, it is quite useful also to look at a particular example of the way that the television era reclaimed a pre-Disney character as highly appropriate for the new medium. One might look at the ways in which *Felix the Cat*, the most popular cartoon character in the pre-Mickey Mouse era, created by Otto Messmer at the Pat Sullivan Studio, went through several periods of revival. In the television era, ex-Famous Studio animator, Joe Oriolo, a cartoonist on the *Felix* comics and a robust entrepreneurial spirit assumed the legal ownership of the character, recognizing that the minimalist aesthetics that underpinned aspects of Felix's construction and the execution of his cartoon stories might find a commercially viable place in the new market. As Canemaker has noted:

> Reviving Felix was not easy...Trans Lux became interested only after Oriolo put up his own money to finance a pilot for a TV series. On the strength of Oriolo's film, $1,750,000 in sales was appropriated to produce 260 *Felix* episodes. The format could run as four minute individual episodes or a continuing quarter hour, thus providing programming flexibility to stations.
>
> (1991: 150)

Oriolo had worked at the Fleischer Studios before it was taken over by Paramount and renamed Famous Studios, and consequently employed his former colleagues in the creation of the new Felix television material, each animator generating up to 150 feet of film per week by 1959. Oriolo knew that though this was not the working practice that facilitated the particular qualities of previous Fleischer animation of the 1930s and 1940s, nor, of course, work in the Disney industrial style, it nevertheless required speed and efficiency in its execution, and personnel who knew how to animate in this style quickly and simply. This need for a new *professionalism* in the maintenance of the *craft* of animation was important, even if it was seemingly at the initial expense of the *art*; but this was only in relation to the art as it had been previously understood. Animators had to go back to basics, and like Messmer all those years previously, make the most of the limitations of the design and the execution. Professional animators were essentially working to a new brief, and had to adapt to the requirements of what was essentially a new form. This was also the case for television programs which required competent directors, camera personnel, editors, sound crews, etc., and which inevitably drew these technicians from the film industry. Hanna-Barbera created a new model of animation for television which was immediately embraced by the new culture of animation professionals – largely veterans reconfiguring their role in the industry – and which formed the benchmark for economically sound practice in the late 1950s. Oriolo, equally recognizing the importance of this shift of emphasis, and the possibilities of recovering an established market, trained his workers in this style: "One of his dictums became well known within the industry: scenes that could not fit under his office door, said Oriolo, held too many drawings. Such fully animated scenes were considered a threat to the budget and were sent back to the animator for changes" (Canemaker 1991: 150).

New animation, new medium

In many senses, Hanna-Barbera's success was achieved with extraordinary speed, and the new aesthetic adopted readily. At first, suggesting new animation as "bookends" to the repackaging of old cartoons, Hanna-Barbera persuaded CBS's John Mitchell, Head of Sales at Screen Gems, to support the concept of limited or planned animation in the creation of new characters, "Ruff and Reddy," a cat and dog pairing allied against such villainous counterparts as Scary Harry Safari and the Goon of Glocca Morra. Premiering in December 1957 on NBC, *The Ruff and Reddy Show*, hosted by Jimmy Blaine and a number of puppet characters, was broadcast in black and white, but the cartoons were made in color in anticipation of the inevitability of color television, and the equally inevitable profits to be made from syndication. William Hanna and Joe Barbera had the foresight to recognize that animation had to respond to the conditions determined by the new medium, and the inevitability of its expansion. Though this was not at the same level as the technically adept and artistically progressive work that had characterized the cartoon at the zenith of its achievement at Disney, Warner Brothers, Fleischer Studios, and MGM, it was nevertheless a pertinent use of the medium which spoke to some of its distinctiveness, particularly in the relationship between sound and image, and crucially, in continuing to facilitate *non-realist*, comic scenarios. Cartoons still remained surreal and fantastical even in their simplest of forms – zany animals with obsessive or compulsive personalities in bizarre conflicts and pursuits remained the mainstay of animated shorts. This gave the work an intrinsic difference from the quasi-realist, neo-theatrical models of late 1950s television entertainment – *General Electric Theater*, *Father Knows Best*, *The Danny Thomas Show* – and consequently, it still operated as a competitive means of providing appealing forms of programming that while supposedly demeaning the art of animation, nevertheless established its credentials successfully within a new broadcast context.

Arguably, the repositioning of the cartoon on television merely chimed with the ways in which the form was necessarily changing in order to survive and develop following the success of the Golden Era. UPA had been established in

1945 by three ex-Disney artists, Stephen Busustow, Zack Schwartz, and Dave Hilberman, who left the studio in the wake of the 1941 strike, championing liberal and left-wing ideas thought suspicious and challenging within Disney's then non-unionized, right-leaning, working culture. The trio had formed the "Industrial Films and Poster Service" during the war years, and sponsored by the United Auto Workers they made a pro-Roosevelt election film called *Hell Bent for Election* (1944), directed by Chuck Jones. With the same backer, they made *Brotherhood of Man* (1946) about race relations, and it was clear that the imperative of the company was to wrest animation from the Republican conservatism of Disney and the comic bravura of the Warner Brothers studio to place it properly within the context of a visually obvious set of modern art sources, a seriousness of approach, and a politicized culture. UPA embraced a non-hierarchical structure that privileged and encouraged individual artists, and stood in direct opposition to Disney's industrial culture and its orthodoxies. Inevitably, this meant that artists displayed less loyalty to the company, and often worked for short periods on their own projects before leaving it. As Ralph Stephenson has argued,

> The UPA breakaway was undoubtedly a rejuvenating, fertilising influence whose value can hardly be overestimated. Even its offshoots, though they may have weakened UPA itself, established important creative artists in the animation field: Gene Dietch, Bill Sturm, [Ernest] Pintoff, [John] Hubley. The diversification of UPA also encouraged further diversification and made it easier for later avant garde experimental work by Carmen D'Avino, Robert Breer, Ed Emswiller and Teru Murakami.
>
> (1967: 47)

While Stephenson inevitably stresses the ways in which the art of animation survived through these self-conscious approaches in attempting to progress the form, it is still the case that this sense of progress was predicated on the notion of becoming more cost-effective, and it privileged a less-is-more approach to the work. Further, as with all models of cultural and artistic change, their repercussions did not merely affect specific areas in the field, and had wider implications and spheres of influence. UPA's minimalism had merely been embraced in another form by Hanna-Barbera, and translated from an "arthouse" context, still determined by a response to Disney, into a domestic context now responsive to the determining aesthetics of television itself.

UPA specialized in "Limited" or "Planned" Animation, which in the American idiom operates as a more economic form of animation by using fewer and less detailed backgrounds; creating fewer animated movements – often only the movement of eyes, mouth, and functional limbs on key characters; employing simple, repeatable movement cycles; and by stressing sound over some aspects of action. The design of the cartoons was radically different, and suggested a range of metaphoric meanings. The Zagreb School of animation used this minimalism – "Reduced Animation" – for more political purposes, preferring a more symbolic approach geared toward expressing metaphysical ideas rather than an indige- nously specific aesthetic innovation necessarily invoked by Hanna-Barbera or UPA in the US. It was highly influential upon the work of UPA, who also specifi- cally attempted to challenge the Disney hegemony in the 1940s and 1950s – both aesthetically and ideologically – with innovative works. These included *Gerald McBoing Boing* (1951), directed by Robert "Bobe" Cannon; *The Tell-Tale Heart* (1953), directed by Ted Parmalee, and *Unicorn in the Garden* (1953), directed by Bill Hurtz.

If Zagreb was concerned with symbolism and politics, and UPA was preoccu- pied with modernist aesthetics and a culturally specific challenge to Disney, Hanna-Barbera returned animation as a form to simple storytelling, drawing upon the distinctiveness of its language to differentiate the form from other tele- visual genres. More importantly, Hanna-Barbera had to necessarily re-invent the nature of personality animation, as well as graphic and iconic visualization, and crucially, move from the notion of a soundtrack as a set of aural signifiers, best exemplified by the work of composers Carl Stalling and Scott Bradley or the effects work of Treg Brown, to a model more in line with radio, and the primacy of the voice as a determining factor in the suggestion of movement and action. Chuck Jones lamented that Saturday Morning cartoons were little more than "illustrated radio" in which the dialogue had prominence over the visual and graphic elements, adding "the drawings are different, but everybody acts the same way, moves their feet the same way, and runs the same way. It doesn't matter whether it's an alligator or a man or a baby or anything" (Adamson: 140–41). Crucially, this emphasis on dialogue, and voice rather than sound, is one of the key determining factors in the way animation became subject to changing perceptions among its audience. The intonations and dynamics of Hanna-Barbera's voice artists, Daws Butler, Don Messick, and June Foray, in defining characters, supplanted previous models of largely visual encoding in cartoons, and specifically privileged the nature and quality of the script, and more readily allied the cartoon to the model of theatrical performance in early television drama and situation comedy. This is a significant difference in the sense that the supposed "demotion" of the intrinsic vocabulary of animation in its own right has determined that animation itself has been perceived differently by the generation who were ostensibly brought up on made-for-television cartoons, and those viewing generations thereafter, who use the Hanna-Barbera series from the late 1950s onwards as their point of comparison to new animation, and not the works of the Golden Era.

This inevitably provokes a whole range of issues about the status and achievement of animation on television since its own Golden Era in the US in the late 1950s and early 1960s. *The Huckleberry Hound Show*, sponsored by Kelloggs, debuted on 2 October 1958, featuring the "Droopy"-influenced Huckleberry Hound, once more recalling the backwoods folk idioms so cherished by Disney; Pixie and Dixie, and their persecution of the cat, Mr. Jinx, a more talkative variation of the conflict between cat and mouse in Hanna-Barbera's long established *Tom and Jerry* series; and the Sgt. Bilko-esque, nice guy-cum-con-man, Yogi Bear, who with his long-standing partner, Boo-Boo, raids the "pic-a-nic" baskets of Jellystone National Park. Huckleberry Hound emerged in a different guise in each episode, again echoing the multiplicity of roles played by Felix in his cartoon shorts, and Mickey Mouse in the *Silly Symphonies*. Television needed its "everyman" cartoon hero, and Huckleberry, working in the tradition of the endearing *idiot-savant*, combined accidental heroism with customary slapstick – his gags often were penned by Warren Foster and Michael Maltese, two of Warner Brothers' leading writers from the 1940s. The show won an Emmy in 1959 as the outstanding achievement in children's programming, the first animated cartoon series to be honored by the television industry. Pixie and Dixie – "This means War!" (a variation on Bugs Bunny's laconic call to arms); Mr. Jinx – "I hate meeces to pieces!"; and Yogi – "I'm smarter than the average bear," soon established popular catch phrases, and were soon augmented by a Cowardly-Lion variant, Snagglepuss, ("Heavens to Murgatroyd! Exit Stage Left!"), hero of Westerns, Quick Draw McGraw, cat and mouse private investigators, Snooper and Blabber, and sub-*Father Knows Best* family hounds, Augie Doggie and Doggie Daddy.

Recombinancy and genre

Despite being hugely popular, and initially standard bearers for animation on television, there was still concern that these programs misrepresented animation as an art. Leonard Maltin argued that "the cartoons produced by Hanna-Barbera and their legion of imitators are consciously bad: assembly line shorts grudgingly executed by cartoon veterans who hate what they're doing," adding that "the same canned music, the same gags, the same sound effects and gimmicks, and the same characters in different guises ... [most notably] the tall and a short sidekick wore out its welcome" (Slafer 1980: 255). It is clear that no animator sets out to make consciously bad work, and though there was inevitably some resentment that this was not the work such artists would prefer to do, it was nevertheless work which tested the versatility of the form, and its place within a comparatively new medium. The issue of quality, though, both in the technical sense, and in relation to content and its effects upon audiences, remains at the heart of the enduring debates about made-for-television animation.

Màire Messenger Davies has usefully articulated the issues raised by these debates as "concerns about corporate exploitation of children, cynical lack of attention to storytelling quality, effects on child audiences, the flooding of sched-ules with a majority of animation programs and the deceptively improvisatory nature of the genre itself, [which] are all conflated into one large, single area of concern" (2001: 228). While space prohibits me from addressing all of these issues, it is especially important to look at what Davies calls the "deceptively improvisatory nature" of animation as a key aspect in engaging with the other topics she suggests. Todd Gitlin has noted in discussing the "recombination culture" of American television that the recombination of elements of previously successful shows "is not simply a convenient if self-defeating way of concocting shows to exploit established tastes. It is part of the ground rhythm of modern culture," continuing that the object of the manufacturers and producers is "to generate novelty without risk" (1994: 77–8). This is an especially pertinent remark here because it enables me to view recombinancy beyond the obvious tenets of the recirculation of generic staples, but as a way in which the language of animation is used to reconfigure genre, draw cost effectively upon cultural resources, and progress its own definition and agenda.

Recombinancy effectively worked as the basic principle underpinning the production of cheaply made cartoons which sought to embrace cross-over audi-ences or already established demographics, and became an intrinsic approach within television animation in the US. In 1965, *The Beatles*, actually made by TVC in England, presaged series about popular music groups like *The Jackson 5ive*, which emerged in 1971 and was followed by *The Osmonds* in 1972. Crucially, the imitative iconographic quality of the animation in each case meant that the programs could gain credibility and popularity through their association with the groups, while not having to actually embrace the prohibitive costs of a group's involvement. This in turn benefited the group because their work was promoted to a young audience in a form which required little effort from them. Using a similar principle, in 1967, ABC broke new ground with the introduction of *The Fantastic Four* and *Spiderman*, animation based on popular comic books, which already had an established design strategy, narrative, and core themes, but more importantly, a committed fan base and market. Though CBS was partially successful in response with its comic strip adaptation of *The Archies* in 1969, their competitive edge ironically returned in the repackaging of classic Warner Brothers cartoons in the *The Bugs Bunny / Roadrunner Show* – a more explicit model of recombinancy as repackaging – but ratings success for the network was only properly achieved in the next season with the *Wacky Races* spin-offs, *Dastardly and Muttley* and *The Perils of Penelope Pitstop* – again a method by which the most popular elements of any one program could be recontextualized and re-sold – and the appeal of *Scooby Doo, Where are You?* Scooby survived on Saturday Morning television for over twenty years, and is still one of the most popular cartoon characters on Cartoon Network. Animated versions of popular prime-time series were also crucial to the advances in the Saturday Morning cartoon schedules. *The Brady Kids* followed on from the live-action *The Brady Bunch* in 1972; *The New Adventures of Gilligan*, *My Favorite Martians*, and *Jeannie*, based on the live-action sitcoms, *Gilligan's Island*, *My Favorite Martian* and, *I Dream of Jeannie* were made between 1973 and 1974; *The Fonz and the Happy Days Gang* based on *Happy Days* debuted in 1980; versions of *Laverne and Shirley* and *Mork and Mindy* followed; *The Dukes* based on *The Dukes of Hazzard* began in 1982, interestingly scheduled against *Pac-Man*, the first of the computer-game-inspired animation that reached its recent zenith with *Pokémon*.

If, in these instances, recombinancy is most obviously understood as the recirculation of materials and cultural resources which already enjoyed favorable dissemination and market acceptance, it is important to note that each version of the form, either as a vehicle for a pop group, or as a moving comic, or as a sitcom, still operates as a *re-interpretation* of the material and an echo of the primary developments that prefigured the Disney style. The early Warner Brothers cartoons were essentially primitive "pop videos" illustrating Warner Brothers' back catalogue of music and implicitly advertising to its concomitant sheet music market; the Fleischer brothers employed Cab Calloway and Louis Armstrong in their short films, and used their songs, often showing the cartoons featuring them as promotional vehicles for their forthcoming shows. Many early animations were based on comic strips – from Winsor McCay's *Little Nemo*, to Rudolph Dirks and Harold Knerr's variations on the *Katzenjammer Kids* to George Herriman's *Krazy Kat*. Disney's *Silly Symphonies*, themselves, were essentially comedies of situation, exploiting established characters in different scenarios. The "quality" in these works was not measured especially by the success or otherwise of the fledgling animated form as it translated these idioms into its own language, but rather the way in which animation facilitated the accessibility and affectivity of the entertainment.

History has rightly bestowed upon these works recognition of their art, and while it is unlikely that made-for-television animation of the 1950s, 1960s and 1970s will be viewed in that light, it is important that it is recognized as the method by which the art itself was maintained during a period of time when it was held with little esteem. Disney was in decline; high level stop-motion animation by key figures such as Ray Harryhausen in fantasy features such as *Jason and the Argonauts* (1963) was made invisible by its live-action context, and by the long-established difficulty with which animation was absorbed within an "effects" tradition; works such as *Yellow Submarine* (1968) seemed to offer a redefinition of the animation feature; and adult-oriented work such as Ralph Bakshi's *Fritz the Cat* (1972) and *Coonskin* (1975) was seen as almost unacceptably radical for such an "innocent" form.

Animation survived because of the recombinancy strategies that enabled it to re-invent itself in a populist idiom and context in the post-theatrical era. Crucially, though, one model of recombinancy has had an even more enduring effect than perhaps might have been anticipated. If appropriate cross-platform animated vehicles which promote popular music, use graphic narratives, and echo live-action sitcoms are still readily evidenced in contemporary television schedules, then joining them are animations informed by the profound influence of Japanese aesthetics. Post-war manga artists, ironically influenced themselves by American comic strips featuring Superman and Batman, created a new drawing style known as *gekiga*, and with it emerged a range of Japanese super-heroes, and models of animation which soon became part of the American schedules.

Astro Boy debuted in 1963, featuring a *Pinocchio*-esque robot boy, abandoned by his maker, and left to long for proof of his humanity, sometimes evidenced in his acts of life-saving and derring-do. *8-Man* (*Eighth Man*) debuted in 1965, and featured Tobor (robot backwards), an android with superpowers, who fights the global villainy of "Intercrime." Echoing the 1940s American comic hero, "Specter," but significantly differing in one key aspect, and one highly influential in the contemporary era, *8-Man* was "more honestly violent than standard American cartoons. If Tobor punches somebody, the character is obviously going to hospital – if not the grave – with a broken skull. In American cartoons, you can have frantic slugfests and nobody even needs a bandage"(Fred Patten quoted in Javna 1988: 106). *Gigantor* followed in 1966, emerging from the initially unpromising premise of being a story of a Japanese secret weapon made to aid the Nazis against the Allied powers in World War II, but later adapted in such a way that the robot, "Iron Man 28" was owned and befriended by a little boy, Jimmy Sparks, and used in the fight against would-be world dominating megalo-maniacs. *Gigantor* was probably a key source for Brad Bird's adaptation of Ted Hughes' *The Iron Man* (1999).

Most notable of these Japanese shows, however, was Tatsunoko's *Gatchaman*, which began in 1965, and rejected the robot-formulas of previous Japanese shows, instead privileging a team of transforming super-heroes. What is crucial from the perspective of this piece, however, is the way *Gatchaman* became subject to the most radical of recombinancy strategies in actually becoming *Battle of the Planets* in 1978, to cash in on the success of *Star Wars*. Characters were renamed, the show's trademark Bruce Lee and Sonny Chiba-inspired brutalities were removed, key story lines and episodes were excised, and what was left was rewritten and actually combined with footage created in the US of quasi-robots,

7-Zark-7 and 1-Rover-1. What Davies calls the "deceptively improvisatory nature" of the animated form is readily evidenced here in the ways that a text is literally transformed to accommodate indigenous economic and pragmatic needs, while facilitating a new model of programming. Casey Kasem, Janet Waldo, and Ronnie Schell, voice artists for the key characters, had experience at Hanna-Barbera, while writer and producer Jameson Brewer had worked on Disney's *Pinocchio* (1940) and *Fantasia* (1941), all of which was used to "Americanize" the already established animation and story lines. *Battle of the Planets* remained sufficiently influential, however, to prompt new fan bases to explore Japanese anime, as the sense of difference still extant in the program's style and outlook signaled a different quality in the work, and one that improved upon its American counterparts. *Gatchaman* itself inspired *Go Ranger*, the antecedent to the live-action *Mighty Morphin' Power Rangers*, and may be traced further in more recent series from *Sailor Moon* to *Jackie Chan Adventures*.

Animation for adults

The recombinancy strategy that involves Japanese work also acknowledges another key aspect that has underpinned the resurgence of animation per se in the contemporary era: the idea that animation was not only for children but also for adults, and further that "children" in the 1980s and 1990s were changing. It was becoming increasingly difficult for toy manufacturers and retailers, for example, to secure profitable margins purely in the market of traditional toys, which were being significantly challenged by the impact of computer games and PC applications. Major retailers, FAO Schwarz and Toys 'R' Us saw a rapid decline in toy earnings, and had to embrace the phenomenon now well known in the industry as "Kids getting older younger," and the consequent abandonment of toys by children at a much younger age (Gray 2000: 22–6). Industry figures assume that any child over age 8 will have already moved into the competing arenas of fashion, personal accessorizing, and new media entertainments, only to reactivate an interest in their childhood interests at age 17, and sometimes enduringly throughout adulthood. Consequently, producers, manufacturers, and marketers have a vested interest in creating artifacts which both move across platforms and have an appeal which reaches across ages and interests.

Robotech, known as the *Macross* series in Japan, which debuted on American television in the early 1980s, provides an example of the ways in which American television had to respond quickly to the ways in which animation *actually* attracted audiences, and how animation needed to be more specifically targeted at its appropriate demographic. *Robotech* was targeted at *Star Trek* fans, so as Fred

Patten notes, "the main complaints against the series – that it's too hard for kids to understand, that there's too much violence in it, and that it's controversial – aren't particularly valid. It is supposed to be geared to teenagers and adults, not children" (quoted in Javna: 109), and thus required different scheduling. Made-for-television animation in Japan always assumed a high degree of possible maturity in its audience as well as catering for its younger clientele, while in the US animation represented a problem if it transgressed an easy positioning in a taken-for-granted children's market. Significantly, the American agenda was inevitably market-led but in a way that often used animation as a graphic echo of live-action forms, extending the shelf-life of popular series by using what had become *the* visual language by which it was assumed children and young adolescents were addressed. The television generation essentially understood animation as the cartoon as it had been produced for television, and the children's demographic.

This was extended when television producers realized that the television generation was once again becoming a new movie generation in the 1980s with the rise of the multiplex, and that the line between fast-maturing children and "young people" was becoming increasingly blurred. Consequently, animated versions of *The Real Ghostbusters*, the Michael J. Fox vehicle, *Teen Wolf*, and *Beetlejuice* quickly followed on from their movie successes; the model continues in the contemporary era with animated features such as *Men in Black* and *Jumanji*. The final crossover area was inevitable. Will Vinton's *The California Raisins* graduated from their status as popular characters in commercials to secure their own series. Increasingly, the interface between a cartoon and its possible merchandising was effectively effaced in series like *Thundercats*, when concerns were raised by parents that series were only being created by and for toy manufacturers, working in their own interests.[2]

The "Saturday Morning" schedules were always highly competitive, and remain so into the contemporary era, but it was the innovation of animation in prime time that provided the model by which so much successful animated programming of the late 1990s entered the mainstream. In their heyday of the early 1960s, Hanna-Barbera cartoons were featured on over 100 stations and enjoyed circulation throughout the day, often being broadcast in early evening slots, anticipating a prime time scheduling position. Screen Gems' John Mitchell approached Hanna-Barbera and asked them to consider creating a half-hour series, using animated people rather than animals, which might have the potential longevity of a sitcom. *The Flintstones* (1960–66), directly predicated on the already successful series, *The Honeymooners*, featuring Jackie Gleason as Ralph Kramden, was essentially rooted in the suburban family narratives of the early 1950s sitcom (i.e. *I Love Lucy* and *Father Knows Best*) but enjoyed the comic incongruity of playing out the consumer artifacts of post-war modernity in the

29

context of the Stone Age. Equally incongruous were the show's initial sponsors – Winston Cigarettes (Reynolds Tobacco Company) and One-a-Day Vitamins (Miles Laboratories) – who recognized and invested in the originality of concept, believing it to have an intrinsic difference yet a culturally acceptable familiarity which made it commercially appealing. The intrinsic difference, though, essentially lies in the capacity for animation to embrace and literally illustrate this paradigm. While *The Flintstones* offered a mild critique of American consumer culture, and, unusually, offered a representation of working-class culture in a period when television privileged middle-class aspirant values, it ultimately reinforced the social status quo.[3] Though influential, it is a position that its 1990s relations have specifically rejected. *The Simpsons*, *King of the Hill*, *South Park*, etc., while all influenced by *The Flintstones*, have created a sustained satire on American mores, using animation as the vehicle through which to reveal contradiction, hypocrisy, banality and the taboo, which may be read, perhaps ironically, as a return to the fundamental anarchy of early cartoons, and later, both the Fleischer Brothers and Warner Brothers' response to Disney.

These quasi-sitcoms were not alone in their attempts to recall some of the more inherently disruptive and non-regulatable aspects of cartoon representation. Ralph Bakshi's *Mighty Mouse* series; Mike Judge's *Beavis and Butt-Head*; and John Kricfalusi's *The Ren & Stimpy Show* all looked back to the subversive aspects of cartooning, not merely to express personal perspectives but to critique the conservatism of made-for-television cartoons. Inevitably, all ran foul of the television regulators, but nevertheless, gained popularity and notoriety in a way that finally ensured that animation for television was recognized as a mature form, both in the service of art and entertainment, and in relation to its history as a televisual form, and as a classical cinematic form (Langer 1997: 145–50; Cohen 1997; Wells 2002).

Writing in January 2001, Harvey Deneroff noted

> the downward pressure on license fees due to the proliferation of new outlets, the limited amount of advertising dollars and increased Japanese competition are continuing to adversely affect domestic production of animated TV series. Compounded by a seeming collapse in the market for prime time animation, producers are being forced to pursue strategies aimed at reducing costs without – hopefully – affecting quality. These strategies often include exploring different styles and techniques, ranging from stop-motion puppets to the latest in computer technology.
>
> (2001: 14)

Such a prognosis, self-evidently, has a familiar ring. However, with niche markets both for children's programming and animation itself in the multichannel digital era, animated made-for-television programming will inevitably innovate its way into the twenty-first century, once more addressing issues of quality, history, affect, and influence. *The Powerpuff Girls, Roughnecks: Starship Troopers Chronicles, Samurai Jack, Braceface* and the *Rugrats* will no doubt be seen in the vanguard of recovery at this supposed moment of adversity in television schedules (Wells 2001c: 48–55; Davies 2001: 225–41). All possess the same degree of self-reflexive, self-enunciative, self-figuring "difference" which will once again refer to the antecedents and processes I have discussed. The concept of recombinancy in animation is not merely a mode of repetition and the tired recovery of a limited resource; rather it is an opportunity for the very re-interrogation and reposi-tioning of representational forms that is the intrinsic quality of the medium. Further, it is a context in which the comparatively insular field of animators can re-engage and reproduce variations on historically determined forms and approaches but with an inevitably fresh approach. Animation is the intrinsic language of metamorphosis, and the literal illustration of change and progress. It will underpin, not merely the television schedules of the future, but all visual cultures per se. One aesthetic may predominate – for example, "Classic Disney" – another may challenge – for example, CGI – but animation always enables alternative aesthetics and perspectives, the quality of much feature work and television material now sharing the same standard and style. Animation will converge, diverge, and re-invent itself. As a computer-generated Yogi might say, "It's smarter than the average art form."

Notes

1   This is explored more fully in Wells (2002).
2   For brief discussions of moral panics, cartoon controversies, and an overview of children's cartoons on both American and British television, see Paul Wells' essays (2001a: 105–7; 2001b: 102–5). See also Davies (2001).
3   For an extended discussion of the impact and influence of *The Flintstones* upon *The Simpsons*, see Wells (2002).

Bibliography

Adamson, J. (1980) "Chuck Jones Interviewed," in D. and G. Peary (eds.), *The American Animated Cartoon: A Critical Anthology*, New York: E. P. Dutton.

Canemaker, J. (1991) *Felix: The Twisted Tale of the World's Most Famous Cat*, New York: Da Capo.

Cohen, K. (1997) *Forbidden Animation*, Jefferson, NC and London: McFarland & Co.

Crafton, D. (1993) *Before Mickey: The Animated Film 1898–1928*, Bloomington: Indiana University Press

Davies, M. M. (2001) *Dear BBC: Children, Television, Storytelling and the Public Sphere*, Cambridge: Cambridge University Press.

Deneroff, H. (2001) "Tooning In," *Hollywood Reporter: Animation Special Issue*, January.

Eliot, M. (1994) *Walt Disney: Hollywood's Dark Prince*, London: Andre Deutsch.

Gitlin, T. (1994) *Inside Prime Time*, Routledge: London & New York.

Gray, R. (2000) "Toy Tactics," *Livewire*, October–November: 22–6.

Halas, J. (1956) "Not for Fun!" *Films and Filming*, Volume 3, Number 2.

Javna, J. (1988) *The Best of Science Fiction TV*, London: Titan Books.

Langer, M. (1997) "Animatophilia, Cultural Production and Corporate Interests: The Case of *Ren & Stimpy*," in J. Pilling (ed.), *A Reader in Animation Studies*, London: John Libbey.

Lindvall, T. and M. Melton (1994) "Toward a Postmodern Animated Discourse: Bakhtin, Intertextuality and the Cartoon Carnival," *Animation Journal*, Volume 3, Number 1, Fall.

Orna, B. (1957) "Blind Alley Cats," *Films and Filming*, Volume 4, Number 2, November.

Slafer, E. (1980) "A Conversation with Bill Hanna," in D. and G. Peary (eds.), *The American Animated Cartoon: A Critical Anthology*. New York: E. P. Dutton.

Stephenson, R. (1967) *Animation in the Cinema*, London: Zwemmer.

Wells, P. (2002) *Animation and America*, Edinburgh: EUP/New Brunswick, NJ: Rutgers University Press.

—— (2001a) "Children's Cartoons (Cartoon Controversies)," in G. Creeber (ed.), *The Television Genre Book*, London: BFI, 105–7.

—— (2001b) "Moral Panics (Teletubbies)," in G. Creeber (ed.), *The Television Genre Book*, London: BFI, 102–5.

—— (2001c) "Roughnecks: Reality, Recombinancy, and Radical Aesthetics," *Point*, 11, Spring/Summer: 48–55.

Chapter 2

THE GREAT SATURDAY MORNING EXILE

Scheduling cartoons on television's periphery in the 1960s

Jason Mittell

> If its rat-tat-tat formula is geared to a three-year-old's attention span, it can only give ma and pa the shakes.
>
> (*Variety* reviewer on *The Bullwinkle Show*, 1962)

ANIMATION UNDERWENT A DRASTIC TRANSFORMATION in the 1950s and 1960s. From the rise of film animation in cinema's early years to its establishment as part of the cinematic bill in the studio era, the first half of the twentieth century saw animation on a steady rise in cultural, aesthetic, and economic viability. But at the midpoint of the century, the animation mainstream was dealt a nearly-fatal blow – the Paramount Decision that broke up vertical integration within the film industry sent animation units into a steady decline over the 1950s. As longer theatrical bills gave way to single-bookings, animated short cartoons found themselves without an exhibition home on the large screen.[1] As the film industry retrenched, cartoons were relocated onto the medium that was often scapegoated for cinema's decline – television. Yet animation underwent a tremendous cultural shift from its introduction onto television in the 1950s to the establishment of certain central assumptions about televised cartoons that were in place by the end of the 1960s. This history has remained mostly untold, as the majority of animation scholarship regards television primarily as "the cartoon's graveyard" (Maltin 1987: 343). Television scholars have mostly ignored animation, and those that have examined the genre tend to focus more on recent works than on televised animation from the 1950s and 1960s.[2]

Yet this early period was the formative era for television cartoons, establishing most of the assumptions that the genre would adhere to until the 1990s boom of prime time cartoons and cable animation. This is especially true for industrial practices, as television networks linked animation explicitly with a scheduling time slot that would come to define the genre as a whole with a three-word phrase: Saturday morning cartoons.

The shifting fate of cartoons during this ten-year period is striking. In 1957, cartoons were scattered throughout television schedules, with occasional network prime time entries, like CBS's *Gerald McBoing Boing Show* (1956–58), and a vast number of syndicated afternoon and evening showings of *Popeye*, *Looney Tunes*, and *Krazy Kat*. Nearly all televised cartoons in this era were recycled film shorts, often presented by a live-action clown or cowboy host to serve as a framing device. ABC had no Saturday morning programming at all, while CBS and NBC featured a variety of live-action children's shows, adventure programs, and one cartoon each – CBS's *The Mighty Mouse Playhouse* (1955–66) and NBC's *Gumby* (1957) (Grossman 1981: 5–6). Cartoons, especially as syndicated programs, garnered quite high ratings with both children and adults, and often won their time slots against live-action original programming. As a cultural form, cartoons were still understood as they had been in the era of the studio system: as entertainment for mass audiences, but with particular appeal to children.

A decade later in 1967, the picture had drastically changed. All three networks now featured full schedules of Saturday morning programming from 9:00 a.m. to 12:30 p.m., showing nothing but animated programs like *Space Ghost and Dino Boy* (CBS, 1966–68) and *George of the Jungle* (ABC, 1967–70). Nearly all of these cartoons were produced originally for television, with the notable exception of Saturday morning stalwart *The Bugs Bunny Show* (ABC, 1960–69). Cartoons had virtually disappeared from other parts of the network time schedule, with the period of prime time cartoon experimentation ending by the mid-1960s. Cartoons still persisted in syndication across the schedule, but ratings were far weaker, especially among adults. Most importantly, cartoons were now culturally defined as a genre whose primary audience was children, and not legitimate entertainment for adults as part of a mass audience.[3]

How did the cartoon genre undergo these transformations? The industrial practices undertaken by television producers, programmers, networks, sponsors, and syndicators during this time period all worked to redefine the cartoon genre beyond the level of the text itself. As suggested above, production is not the primary agent of change in this case – many of the cartoons themselves were produced years before their television appearance, designed for a different medium and exhibition context altogether. Rather, the ways in which these texts, both recycled and original, were situated through scheduling and cultural circulation, demonstrate how these practices came to link the genre to a set of shared assumptions that have remained associated with the cartoon genre to this day. Specifically, I examine how what was once a mass-market genre with so-called "kidult" appeal became marginalized into the kid-only Saturday morning periphery, while exploring the effects this shift has had on our cultural understanding of the genre.[4]

There is no single causal factor for this generic shift. We will not find the titular character of the essay, "The Man Who Invented Saturday Morning" (Owen 1988).[5] As in most historical examinations, there are a variety of causal factors or generative mechanisms needed to understand this cultural phenomenon.[6] In order to understand the shift from 1957's broad distribution of cartoons to the emergence of 1967's Saturday morning enclave, I first chart a number of large-scale factors that are partially formative of this shift in the 1950s, aspects that provide cultural and industrial contexts for this transformation. Then I examine the story of the cartoon's move to Saturday morning in the early-1960s in greater detail, mapping out the stimuli that led to the genre's redefinition. Throughout I suggest that this shift was not culturally "neutral," but rather loaded with a number of assumptions in terms of cultural value, constructions of children's tastes, and industrial profit.

One crucial contextual development for the rise of television animation emerged from the transformation of cinematic animation units. Throughout the 1930s and 1940s, animated film shorts were a vital part of most film bills, with studios providing their own shorts (notably Warner Brothers and MGM) or distributing cartoons from independent producers (like Disney or Walter Lantz). This system flourished due to the vertical integration of the studio system, which guaranteed exhibition of animated shorts in studio-owned theater chains or through block-booking practices including cartoons within packages of feature films. Although cartoons were not profitable themselves, they were part of the whole package that film studios offered to moviegoers to fend off independent competitors. This situation was disrupted by the landmark Supreme Court anti-trust decision on the Paramount case of the late-1940s, which ended vertical integration and guaranteed exhibition of studio products in theatrical screens across the country. To maintain their dominance over independent rivals, studios reallocated their priorities toward large-budget A pictures throughout the 1950s, attempting to draw audiences to floundering theaters through spectacle and gimmickry (Balio 1990).

The demise of cinematic cartoon units was a gradual but direct reaction to the Paramount Decision. Since cartoons had traditionally not been a source of direct studio income, they were one of the primary areas studios could trim to remain economically viable. Independent exhibitors would not pay much for cartoons, as they did not appear to lead to greater box office numbers; studios could charge exhibitors little for these comparatively expensive short products.[7] As a

result of the declining theatrical market for cartoons, numerous studios dismantled their animation divisions: MGM in 1957, Warner Brothers in 1963, even
Disney all but ceased short production in the 1960s. Independent animators
were similarly withdrawing from the theatrical market, with Terrytoons selling
out to CBS in 1955 and Famous Studios ceasing production of its popular *Popeye*
series in 1957.[8] Not only did these shutdowns make film animation scarce, but
they also resulted in a number of out-of-work animators seeking employment
through the new avenue of television production.

One of the few profitable activities for animation studios in the 1950s was
selling vintage shorts to television. Disney pioneered the use of animation on
television through its prime time hit *Disneyland* (ABC, 1954–61). The show
mixed old cartoon shorts in with new live-action segments, all framed within a
promotional pitch for the company's forthcoming theme park (Anderson 1994:
133–55). Other cartoon studios followed suit by selling their pre-1948 libraries
to television in the mid-1950s, including Terrytoons, Warner Brothers,
Columbia, and Paramount's *Popeye* series. These shorts were primarily distributed
via syndicators like Associated Artists Productions (A.A.P.), a subsidiary of
United Artists that owned pre-1948 *Popeye* and *Bugs Bunny* libraries. These syndicated shorts soon entered daytime and early evening lineups in television stations
across the country, gaining favor with programmers as top-rated programs with
no production costs. Animation studios realized that their most profitable assets
were not new shorts produced for theatrical release, but old libraries made available for endless repetition on television, shifting the primary site of the
animation genre to the television screen (Erickson 1995: 13–16).

Although the move from theaters to televisions did not necessarily alter the
cartoons themselves, there were a number of textual transformations that helped
redefine the genre for its new medium. Cartoons were rarely programmed on
their own – since shorts were typically six to seven minutes, they needed to be
combined in order to fit into the half-hour matrix of the television schedule.
Stringing together three or four cartoons in a half-hour block significantly
changed the way audiences experienced the shorts – instead of working as an
amusing break before or between features, cartoons became the feature themselves, attracting audiences who found cartoons enough of a draw for their
viewing time. As I discuss below, this meant primarily (but not exclusively) children. Additionally, most of the recycled cartoons were presented within a
live-action frame. These programmatic contexts ranged from a host simply introducing the cartoons (such as Dick Van Dyke on *CBS Cartoon Theater* during prime
time in summer 1956) to a larger program with characters and live-action narratives, like the single cartoon within *Captain Kangaroo* (CBS, 1955–84) episodes
(program information from Erickson 1995; Lemberg 1991; Fischer 1983;
McNeil 1991). While the cartoon itself may have remained the same from the

film era, the way in which cartoons were presented on television altered their textual flow and relocated the texts within the realm of children's programming.

Not all cartoons migrated to television unchanged however. In addition to the selection process instigated by industrial maneuvers (like the union-mandated cut-off date of 1948 for television releases),[9] cartoon libraries were culled and edited for social reasons as well. While the visual style and humor of cartoons was celebrated for not aging, some of the cultural content was deemed troubling for recirculation. Most famously, a number of shorts with explicit racial stereotyping, such as Warner Brothers' *Coal Black and De Sebben Dwarfs* (1943), never made it to television due to concerns about their appropriateness a decade later, especially for children. While it is nearly impossible to identify exactly what cartoons were not imported to television, reminiscences of animators suggest that television sponsors and programmers were fearful of featuring any representations of black cartoon characters, whether explicitly racist or not.[10] Other cartoons produced during World War II were not shown on television, due to both their racist anti-Japanese content (like *Bugs Bunny Nips the Nips*, 1944) and their dated (and often brutal) references to wartime current events.

Some cartoons were edited in order to pare down or change questionable material as well. *Tom and Jerry* cartoons were regularly changed for television, transforming the character of a black maid, Mammy Two Shoes, into an Irish maid by re-dubbing her voice and recoloring her legs and arms (all that was seen of the character) white (Brion 1990: 29). Numerous racially suspect scenes, as well as images of violence deemed excessive, characters smoking or drinking, and representations of guns, were all edited from Disney, Warner Brothers, and MGM shorts when appearing on television.[11] While I do not wish to imply that the changing or censoring of racist or other images was inappropriate, it is important to note the effects of such practices. By eliminating references to blacks and other non-white (or animal) characters out of fear of complaints of racism, television programmers effectively created a white-only genre of programming. This policy was consistent with network live-action practices of the 1950s and 1960s – both to avoid accusations of racist representations and to placate racist viewers and sponsors who did not want to see "positive" images of blacks, television presented mostly white characters (MacDonald 1983). The elimination of racist representations from cartoons was performed under the common rubric of "protecting children," working to make cartoons a space free from controversial images (although the genre would come under fire in the late-1960s for its violent and commercial content). Finally by eliminating racist though highly sophisticated cartoons like *Coal Black*, programmers shifted the genre away from the cultural references that typically entertained adult audiences in theaters, and more toward repetitive visual humor and slapstick violence. The censorious practices of the television industry helped redefine the cultural content and associations of the pre-existing film cartoon genre.[12]

The reorganization of the film industry brought theatrical animation to television, albeit in somewhat altered form, but this was not the only reason for the rise of televised cartoons. A number of animators in the 1950s began experimenting with original animation for television, an option that had been long viewed as economically unfeasible. The production costs for typical animation were far too exorbitant to be justified for the still uncertain television market; for instance an average seven-minute MGM short in the 1950s cost between $40,000 and $60,000 (Mallory 1998: 24). The 1950s saw the rise of a new technique, called "limited animation," which minimized and repeated motions to decrease the number of drawings required and therefore reduce costs (Butler 1994: 272–73). This technique was most heralded in the work of theatrical animation studio UPA and their 1950 short, *Gerald McBoing Boing*. The earliest pioneer of limited animation for television was Jay Ward, who created *Crusader Rabbit* for syndication in 1949 (reemerging in more sophisticated form in 1957). *Crusader* was an extreme example of bargain basement production, as it reduced movements to an average of only one per four seconds, and cost only $2,500 per 20 minute episode (Erickson 1995: 10). More typical was Hanna-Barbera's debut program, NBC's first Saturday morning cartoon *Ruff and Reddy* (1957–64), which cost $3,000 per five-minute segment (Erickson 1995: 21). Both *Crusader Rabbit* and *Ruff and Reddy* exemplify a number of shifts in animated form that would become typical for television productions: minimal visual variety, emphasis on dialogue and verbal humor, and repetitive situations and narratives (Butler 1994: 278–81).

By 1957, there were two distinct forms of televised cartoons: endlessly rerun Hollywood shorts and low-budget original programs. Both modes of animation were primarily used to reach the children's audience. It is important to note that while the animated shorts of the theatrical era were regarded as mass entertainment, they were definitely skewed more toward children. As Warner Brothers producer Leon Schlesinger remarked in 1939, "we cannot forget that while the cartoon today is excellent entertainment for young and old, it is primarily the favorite motion picture fare of children" (quoted in Smoodin 1993: 12). Likewise, while the cartoon genre had not yet been designated as *just* for children, the industry did conceive of children as the *primary* audience for cartoons in the 1950s. Whereas other television generic offerings in the 1950s were invested in promoting associations with quality, prestige, and sophistication, cartoons were mostly seen as low-budget filler.

An exception to the cartoon's low cultural locale in the late-1950s was *The Gerald McBoing Boing Show*. CBS jumped on the limited animation bandwagon in 1956 by contracting UPA to produce a prime time program, consisting of both recycled *McBoing Boing* theatrical shorts and original material. The program tapped into the prestige of UPA's *McBoing Boing* series, which had been hailed as the savior of theatrical animation in 1951. UPA's graphic style was critically linked to modernist art, and the Dr. Seuss scripted premiere short was an upstart Academy Award winner in 1951. The television show combined UPA's high cultural associations with educational segments like "Meet the Inventor," all under the auspices of low-budget animation techniques that appealed to CBS. While critics and parents hailed the show as educational, cultured, and even "avant-garde" entertainment, the show never met CBS's expectations to compete against *Disneyland* in the ratings ("*The Boing Boing Show*" 1956, Phillips 1957). While prime time cartoons would get additional chances in the 1960s, television animation and cultural legitimacy seemed incongruous bedfellows from the beginning.

One reason for the low cultural value of the genre was the industry's initial disinterest in reaching children's audiences. While certainly television featured many programs for children, they were seen as a necessary component to serve a mass audience rather than a desirable niche. Television's industrial predecessor of radio reached out to children as a part of the mass audience, primarily with kid-friendly family programming. As NBC executive Fred Wile Jr. wrote in a 1954 memo concerning children's programming on Saturday morning, "all our experience in radio indicates that the Saturday morning audience is not exclusively a kiddy audience. If you recall, the highest ratings on Saturday morning used to be the all-family appeal show." He suggests "what we should strive for are all-family appeal shows with an emphasis on the youngsters" (Wile 1954). Nevertheless, networks were reaching out to sponsors to target children, such as in a 1954 NBC promotional piece highlighting the captive audience of "15,000,000 kids every Saturday morning." Featuring a boy holding a toy sword and the caption "the generals have gone AWOL," the brochure calls for sponsors to "give him his marching orders on NBC television" ("Promotional Brochure" 1954). However NBC's mid-1950s lineup of clowns and puppet shows failed to make much of an impact on either sponsors or Saturday morning audiences.

The industrial appeal of a predominantly children's audience grew during this time, as a number of sponsors began targeting children as primary consumers. In the early-1950s and before, toy manufacturers generally thought toys were not viable objects of advertising, as children were not active consumers. Some toy companies incorporated live advertisements into local children's shows, but in general there was little market for sponsors aiming directly at children. But in 1955, just as upstart ABC had successfully ridden *Disneyland* toward legitimacy as a network, a small toy company named Mattel decided to invest its entire corporate value in advertising by sponsoring ABC's new *The Mickey Mouse Club* (1955–59) children's program for a full year. The risk paid off, as Mattel's Burp Gun became the first nationwide toy sensation in 1955. Mattel broadened its customer base to girls in 1959, by using television advertising to promote their new doll Barbie, with obvious success. Through the phenomenal success of these two campaigns, the toy industry and other companies wanting to reach children, such as cereal manufacturers, dedicated themselves to reaching children's audiences via television (Schneider 1987).

By the late-1950s, the networks were primed to deliver children to eager sponsors, but the only surefire method was through the Disney name. CBS attempted to counter Disney by purchasing Terrytoons' studio and holdings, leading to a prime time anthology of shorts, *CBS Cartoon Theater*, and two Saturday morning cartoon retreads, *The Mighty Mouse Playhouse* and *The Heckle and Jeckle Show* (1956–60) (Maltin 1987: 147). While both Saturday morning programs were popular enough to enjoy long runs and solid ratings for General Foods, the Terrytoons material failed to produce the cultural excitement of ABC's two Disney programs. NBC was unsuccessful in finding an established animation studio to team with except for Columbia/Screen Gems, whose "cartoons were among the least appealing short subjects ever released" (Erickson 1995: 19). So in 1957 NBC took the risky step of contracting the production of original animation for the still undefined slot of Saturday morning, purchasing *Ruff and Reddy* from the new animation studio Hanna-Barbera. *Ruff and Reddy* was a hit, although NBC was not willing to jump aboard an animation bandwagon, maintaining their Saturday morning mix of cartoons with puppet shows, adventure serials, and educational programming.

This moment in 1957 was the calm before the storm of televised cartoons. While there were still few cartoon programs on television or Saturday morning by this point, we can see a number of central cultural assumptions linked to the cartoon genre. Television cartoons were still associated with their theatrical antecedents, as most televised animation was recycled or adapted from film sources. As such, the programs were still tied to notions of a mass audience with primary appeal toward children. Cartoons were considered "filler" and culturally devalued; they were often programmed into larger live-action contexts or relegated to the syndicated margins of the television schedule. The few cartoons that were able to gain cultural legitimacy borrowed their prestige from the cinematic reputation of their producer (Disney) or character (Gerald McBoing Boing). Yet the late-1950s would witness a transformation of the set of cultural assumptions comprising the cartoon genre, as sponsors looked to target children and producers brought more original animation to television. But before exploring the impact of Hanna-Barbera upon the genre, we need to consider some of the assumptions that the industry brought to bear upon this targeted audience of children.

As sponsors became more interested in reaching the children's audience, the television industry attempted to understand what this audience wanted to see and how best to sell them to sponsors. But as Ien Ang has argued, the television industry never merely accesses or targets pre-constituted audiences, but actually works to construct those audiences through their programming, marketing, sales, and measuring practices (Ang 1990). We can look at how the television industry constituted the children's audience during this era by linking together a number of associations under the rubric of what the trade press often called "kidvid" or the "moppet market." One notable assumption was that children did not mind the repetition of shorts found in recycled film cartoons like *Bugs Bunny* or *Popeye*. The President of A.A.P. suggested that children actually even preferred repeated material as they relish the familiarity (Hyman 1958). An NBC executive questioned the discerning taste of children, noting that syndicated shows of old recycled film shorts were doubling the ratings of NBC's stalwart *Howdy Doody* (1947–60).[13] The success of recycled film shorts, the industrial profitability of such textual reuse, and the assumption that children could not tell the difference all led *Variety* to predict in 1957 that original animation would never fly on television ("Cartons of Cartoons for TV" 1957).

Another vital assumption about children was that they could not discern levels of "quality" (which are usually held up as self-evident by adult reviewers). In discussing Walter Lantz's unpolished performance as host of *The Woody Woodpecker Show* (ABC, 1957–58), a *Variety* reviewer asked, "since when do kids need the kind of polish adults demand in adults?" ("*Woody Woodpecker*" 1957). Another reviewer suggested, "where the moppets are fixated by virtually anything on the TV screen, adult audiences are at least one notch more discriminating" ("*Top Cat*" 1961). Assumptions about children's lack of developed taste carried over to the rise of limited animation. While adult reviewers noted that the visuals in original television animation were far less sophisticated and nuanced than in classic theatrical shorts, the industry clearly believed that children could not discern (or simply did not care about) the difference between the two models (Erickson 1995: 21). Reviewers noted elements of animation that they assumed would appeal to children, including "noise and fast action" and unrealistic violence ("*King Leonardo and his Short Subjects*" 1960, Fox 1962). As original television animation emerged in the late-1950s, the industry's construction of the children's audience was an active assumption linked to the cartoon during this era. The subsequent rise of Hanna-Barbera and their model of television animation directly drew upon and revised notions of the children's audience, adult appeals, and cultural status of the cartoon genre.

The emergence of Hanna-Barbera was the catalyst that would eventually lead to the institution of Saturday morning cartoons, traveling through the unlikely detour of prime time. Bill Hanna and Joseph Barbera were former MGM animators who popularized the *Tom and Jerry* series, but found themselves out of work following MGM's animation shutdown in 1957. Seeing the potential of animation for the television market, they pitched their services by adapting UPA's style of limited animation. However instead of UPA's modernist graphic style, Hanna-Barbera offered a pared-down visual style, emphasizing dialogue, sound-effects, and repetitive motion. They followed *Ruff and Reddy* with a syndicated program owned by Kellogg's, 1958's *Huckleberry Hound* (1958–62). While Kellogg's was certainly aiming at a children's audience in lucrative late-afternoon time slots, the show transcended its targeted audience. One report suggested that over 40 percent of *Huckleberry*'s audience were adults, while another article described daily *Huckleberry Hound* watching rituals in a Seattle bar ("The Blue-Blooded Hound Who's in the Black" 1959, "Satire from the Animal Kingdom" 1960). Hanna-Barbera's next syndicated program was equally popular with adults, satirizing popular westerns with *Quick Draw McGraw* (1959–62). The breakout success of these programs led to the biggest boom of cartoons in television history.

The immediate success of Hanna-Barbera's original television animation led to an overhaul of what animation would look and sound like for years to come. The assumption among animation scholars and fans today is that this shift was for the worst – the limited animation style of television "killed off" the classic animation of Warner Brothers and MGM, with only Disney carrying the torch into their feature film work. We can see this hierarchy at work in interviews with canonized cartoon directors like Chuck Jones, who called Saturday morning cartoons "crap" and termed them "illustrated radio," dominated by dialogue without any visual vibrancy (quoted in Peary and Peary 1980: 140–41). Likewise cartoon voice artist Mel Blanc claimed that television animation "kill[ed] the cartoon industry" (quoted in Peary and Peary 1980: 165). Academics have reproduced this hierarchy by valorizing classic full animation from Disney, Warner, and Tex Avery's MGM work through detailed analysis, while only mentioning Hanna-Barbera as the commercialized nadir of the form (Klein 1993). Implicit in this hierarchy is that the classic animation of the studio era was better suited to a discerning mass audience, able to amuse and amaze all ages through its superior humor and vibrant visuals, while the television material of the 1960s was low-budget and low-brow filler, suited only to the unrefined taste of children.

While certainly this argument might be maintained on aesthetic grounds, the initial reception of these early television cartoons suggests that they were not objects of adult derision. Rather, the early Hanna-Barbera programs were held up as valued advances in animation that were more entertaining for adults and children than the studio shorts that we now regard as "classic." Critics hailed characters like Huckleberry Hound, Quick Draw McGraw, and Yogi Bear (who was featured on *Huckleberry Hound* before getting his own syndicated spin-off from 1961–63) for their adult wit and satirical content. The puns, malapropisms, and old jokes that seem stale today made Hanna-Barbera cartoons appear groundbreaking in their intergenerational appeal. This goal of reaching the "kidult" audience was achieved not through creating unified cartoons with universal appeals, but by specifically aiming the visuals and "wacky" sound-effects at the "moppets," and the dialogue at adults. As *Howdy Doody's* Bob Smith suggested in 1961, "Hanna and Barbera are creating children's visual shows and adult audio shows. Turn off the sound and children will enjoy what they see. Turn off the picture, and adults will enjoy what they hear" (quoted in Fleming 1961). A *TV Guide* reviewer similarly summed up the different appeals of *Huckleberry Hound*: "Children like the show because of the action and the animals.... Adults like the show for its subtleties, its commentary on human foibles, its ineffable humor" ("Review: *Huckleberry Hound*" 1960). Programs that have long been condemned for dumbing down animation were viewed at the time as actually broadening the genre's appeal through intelligence and sophistication.

Some critics explicitly compared Hanna-Barbera shorts with classic studio material. A *Parents'* magazine writer called the cartoons of 1962 "as far removed from the old animated cartoons of pre-World War II vintage as today's car is from a Model T" (Ardmore 1962: 43). One of the grounds for comparison was violence, a common object of discussion concerning animation. The same writer hailed the Hanna-Barbera material for relying upon character "rather than sadistic action," noting the violent content of most studio shorts seen on television. Of course we must note her article's celebratory myopia, as she hailed Hanna and Barbera's early work on *Tom and Jerry* as being appropriate for "family audiences," overlooking that *Tom and Jerry* was quite possibly the most excessively violent of all studio series. Besides this one article, most press accounts during this era did not castigate cartoons for their violent content, explicitly noting the difference between real violence and the fantasy actions in animation, a distinction that seems to have been lost in most discussions of television violence today. By this point in the early-1960s, cartoons were well-ensconced within what James Snead calls animation's "rhetoric of harmlessness," with cartoons regarded as culturally marginal enough to exist only in the world of innocuous fantasy, not "real-life" effects (Snead 1994: 84–85, Hendershot 1998: 216). Interestingly, although children's tastes and interactions with television were a site of parental and cultural activism in post-war America as documented by media historian Lynn Spigel, cartoons' assumptions of harmlessness exempted the genre from much of the anxiety that dominated this historical moment's construction of childhood (Spigel 1993).

While Hanna-Barbera's output was the most popular original television animation and certainly led the animation boom of the early-1960s, another producer made a series of important cartoons that fit a similar pattern of "kidult" appeal: Jay Ward. Whereas Hanna and Barbera were established studio animators who immediately created a popular formula for television, Ward was an industry outsider whose style never achieved mass appeal. *Rocky and his Friends* (ABC, 1959–61) played during early evening hours, reaching a decent-sized broad audience despite little network support. Ward's style matched the critical celebration of Hanna-Barbera, with bare-bones visuals, broad characterization, and pointed satirical references to contemporary America, especially Cold War politics. *Rocky* and its later incarnation of *The Bullwinkle Show* (NBC, 1961–64) form the primary exception to today's critical disdain for early television animation. However in the late-1950s, Ward's shows were far less successful than Hanna-Barbera's cartoons, even though most critics at the time regarded the work of both producers as equal in adult appeal.

Entering the 1960 season, the genre of television cartoons had acquired a number of revised assumptions: animation had established itself as having legitimate "kidult" appeal within syndicated late-afternoon and early-evening time slots. Cost-cutting techniques of limited animation had reduced production costs sufficiently to warrant network experimentation with original animated programming. Additionally the success of studio shorts in syndicated reruns suggested that the market for animated properties on television was potentially eternal; as one *Broadcasting* article suggested, "they never grow old, never depreciate" ("Cartoons Endure for UAA" 1959). Advertisers had begun showing interest in reaching young audiences, while animation had gained enough legitimacy to be viewed as more than just "kid's stuff." In 1960, ABC took a risk by programming three animated programs in their prime time lineup, including an original animated sitcom aimed primarily at an adult audience, *The Flintstones* (1960–66).[14] While ABC's innovation would be a huge popular success, leading to television's biggest boom in prime time animation, the end result of *The Flintstones'* success would be to drive cartoons out of prime time for almost three decades.

ABC was not on equal footing with NBC and CBS in 1960. Always the upstart, ABC was at a disadvantage in shifting from radio to television, as it both lacked the name programs and talent of NBC and CBS, and found itself highly disadvantaged by the FCC television license freeze from 1948 to 1952. Deficient in capital and market penetration, ABC established itself in the late-1950s by taking innovative programming risks, reaching out to audiences and producers that the other networks ignored. ABC reached the Nielsen top 20 for the first time in 1954 through a partnership to create *Disneyland*, and it similarly forged a successful alliance with Warner Brothers to produce a string of hit westerns in the late-1950s (Anderson 1994). Like FOX in the early-1990s, ABC's marginal status enabled – and forced – the network to follow less traditional paths, able to withstand many failed experiments in the hope of one breakout success. Its animation experiment of 1960 was thus not a radical move for ABC, but the outcome was certainly not what the network anticipated.

Two of ABC's three prime time cartoon entries in 1960 fit into established practices of television animation. *Matty's Funday Funnies* (1959–61) originally aired late Sunday afternoons, but was moved to Friday night in 1960 to reach a broader audience. The show consisted primarily of old shorts from the Harvey/Paramount studios, such as Casper the Friendly Ghost and Baby Huey, framed by new animated characters Matty Mattel and Sister Belle, designed by sponsor Mattel for merchandising purposes (Schneider 1987: 24, 112). ABC's second prime time cartoon was *The Bugs Bunny Show*, featuring both recycled and new animation from Warner Brothers. Since Warner's pre-1948 shorts had been saturated in syndication by A.A.P., ABC capitalized with its strong relationship with the studio to highlight Warner's post-'48 material on *The Bugs Bunny Show*. This program made television regulars out of classic cartoons from directors Chuck Jones and Friz Freling, featuring newer characters Pepe LePew, Foghorn Leghorn, the Tasmanian Devil, and the Road Runner and Coyote duo. Warner also contributed original animated bumpers and framing narratives to the program, sustaining the market for the studio's animation unit. *The Bugs Bunny Show*, moving to Saturday morning in 1962, provided exposure to Warner Brothers' animation for multiple generations to come and soon became synonymous with classic television cartooning.

The biggest surprise of the 1960 season was certainly *The Flintstones*, a Hanna-Barbera cartoon that defied nearly all established conventions of animated television. The show was formally structured like a sitcom, complete with single half-hour narrative episodes, suburban setting, domestic plots, and even a laugh track, deriving primary character and situational inspiration from *The Honeymooners*. The program was Hanna-Barbera's attempt to capitalize on the adult audiences for their syndicated programs, and ABC primarily targeted an adult audience as well. The show was initially sponsored by Miles Labs and R. J. Reynolds, until parental protests in 1961 that the show was selling cigarettes to children forced the latter to withdraw. The 8:30 p.m. Eastern time slot was later than typical for children-skewing programs, and the trade press clearly indicated that ABC and Hanna-Barbera were primarily aiming at adults with the show ("Animation Scores a Breakthrough" 1960). The show was a surprise success, finishing the season at number 18 in the overall Nielsen ratings and giving ABC a rare non-western hit.

Critics gave the program mixed reviews. Some enjoyed the show's satirical jabs at suburbia and the sitcom format, while others found the humor obvious and the situations contrived. Surprisingly, no reviewer that I found questioned the appropriateness of animation for an adult audience, suggesting that the genre had yet to develop a "kids only" stigma.[15] There is a degree of irony here, as reviewers of *The Bugs Bunny Show* assumed the show was solely aimed at a child audience, despite the fact that the shorts featured on the program were designed for mass consumption in movie theaters. *The Flintstones* was viewed as more adult oriented, primarily because it drew upon the cultural assumptions of the more adult, family-friendly genre of the sitcom. Through genre mixing, *The Flintstones* was able to establish more cachet and legitimacy than cartoon shorts.[16] Yet today our critical hierarchies have been inverted – the Warner shorts are seen as "classics," worthy of academic study and fan following, while Hanna-Barbera programs like *The Flintstones* are blamed for the death of classic animation and viewed as childish Saturday morning filler.

The success of *The Flintstones* led to television's first animation boom, bringing a variety of subject matters and settings to both prime time and Saturday morning cartoons. ABC tried to strike gold again with two prime time animated sitcoms during its next season, Hanna-Barbera's *Top Cat* (1961–62) and *Calvin and the Colonel* (1961–62). The latter program is an interesting footnote in media history, as it starred the voices of Freeman Gosden and Charles Correll, adapting the characters of Amos and Andy that had made them one of radio's biggest success stories. Since *The Amos and Andy Show*'s (CBS, 1951–53) television incarnation had been canceled under fire in the early-1950s, Gosden and Correll had been unable to translate their radio hit to the television screen. After their radio show ended its three decade run in 1960, they tried their hand at television once more, literally exemplifying Chuck Jones' pejorative phrase "illustrated radio." Gosden and Correll revisited some of their classic radio scripts with few changes in content, while animating their black face characters as a wily fox and dumb bear (without losing their stereotypical black dialects and malapropisms) from the South who moved up North to predictably "wacky" results. While animation studios were pressured to excise egregious racial representations from their television libraries, ABC felt comfortable recasting well-known racist caricatures as animated animals within *Calvin and the Colonel*. The show was canceled within a season due to poor ratings, although the show did survive further in syndication throughout the 1960s seemingly free of controversy.

The other networks tried their hand at prime time animation in 1961 as well. NBC signed *The Bullwinkle Show* after ABC had given up on moose and squirrel, placing it on Sunday evenings as a lead-in to *Walt Disney's Wonderful World of Color* (1961–81), which they had also lured away from ABC. CBS offered *The Alvin Show* (1961–62), based upon the 1958 hit novelty record by Alvin and the Chipmunks, on Wednesday evenings. ABC kept both *Bugs Bunny* and *The Flintstones* in prime time, renaming *Matty's Funday Funnies* in winter 1962 to *The Beany and Cecil Show* (1962–63) and retooling the program to focus on the show's most popular animated segment. Thus in the 1961–62 season, networks programmed seven animated series in prime time, a record showing for the cartoon genre. This boom is in keeping with a general programming trend of the 1960s. As networks gradually wrested control of programming away from sponsors in the late-1950s and early-1960s, they developed strategies for utilizing genres and formulas to spread success throughout their lineups. This led to a strategy termed "innovation – imitation – saturation," whereby one successful groundbreaker begets clones that eventually clutter the schedule to such a degree that the formula quickly dies through overexposure.[17] This pattern also played out for westerns in the late-1950s, documentaries in the early-1960s, and spy programs in the mid-1960s, and remains in effect to this day with reality programs and game shows.

The saturation phase of the cartoon boom was surprisingly quick in coming – the only prime time cartoon from 1961 which remained in prime time by 1963 was *The Flintstones*, which reputedly survived primarily because of a dedicated following amongst teenagers (Fleming 1961). Other cartoons attempted to take hold in prime time in subsequent seasons, including Hanna-Barbera's *The Jetsons* (ABC, 1962–63) and *The Adventures of Jonny Quest* (ABC, 1964–65), as well as UPA's *The Famous Adventures of Mr. Magoo* (NBC, 1964–65), but none lasted more than one season in prime time. All of these cartoons were met with the critical scorn typical for derivative clones of previous successes in all genres; as one *Variety* reviewer suggested, "with cartoon shows in boomsville, subject matter is getting harder to find" ("*The Alvin Show*" 1961). Importantly, reviewers suggested that the only way these shows would succeed was "in attracting the less critical moppet audiences," although success with children was not enough to sustain a program in the prime time lineup ("*The Jetsons*" 1962). *The Flintstones* lasted in prime time until 1966; the end of *The Flintstones*' prime time run marked the last network prime time cartoon until *The Simpsons* (FOX, 1990 – present) emerged. Cartoons disappeared from prime time because of their perceived inability to reach adult audiences. Although certainly the boom waned because of the typical effects of generic saturation, the industry took the failure to mean that the genre was inappropriate for adults. This assumption about the audience appeals of animation helped to form the shape of genre for decades to come.

The post-bust residue of other generic booms in the 1960s disappeared from the airwaves – the documentaries, westerns, and spy shows that lasted only one season generally were not to be found again in television schedules, at least until the rise of cable. This was not true for cartoons, however. Since the industry believed that the "uncritical moppets" would watch any cartoon that moved (however minimally), they looked for a way to capitalize on their expensive investment in prime time animation. CBS found the answer in spring 1962 – *The Alvin Show* had been a prime time bomb, but CBS had already paid the producers for a season of product (a typical arrangement for animation because of the extended production time needed to animate a program). Instead of merely cutting their losses in prime time as with other genres, CBS moved the program to Saturday mornings. In doing so, the network drew upon two assumptions that were linked to the cartoon genre – children did not mind watching repeats and recycled material, and children were uncritical viewers who would accept programs of any quality. CBS's move was considered a ratings success and other networks would follow suit, with nearly every prime time animated failure mentioned above finding a new home on Saturday morning in the 1960s. To understand the rationale behind this rescheduling, we need to examine how Saturday morning had evolved as a program slot in the early-1960s.

As mentioned previously, Saturday mornings still featured a mix of live-action programming and cartoons, with the latter mostly composed of recycled film shorts like *Mighty Mouse* and *Heckle and Jeckle*. Networks were generally reluctant to invest the money necessary to create original Saturday morning cartoons, as sponsors wishing to reach children were still most interested in late-afternoon and early-evening time slots with their superior overall ratings. NBC had programmed a few original Saturday morning cartoons, such as Hanna-Barbera's *Ruff and Reddy* and *King Leonardo and his Short Subjects* (1960–63), but they still scheduled these programs among educational programs, sitcom reruns, clown and puppet shows, and other live-action children's fare. ABC followed *Alvin*'s lead, moving *Bugs Bunny* and *Top Cat* from prime time to Saturday morning in fall 1962. CBS pushed animation further, creating the first cartoon-dominated lineup in 1963, programming *The Alvin Show*, *Mighty Mouse Playhouse*, *Quick Draw McGraw*, and the original *Tennessee Tuxedo and His Tales* (1963–66) in a highly-rated two-hour block, appealing to kid-seeking sponsors like General Mills and Kellogg's (Doan 1967).

The success of this block demonstrated the importance of niche marketing within television programming. Saturday mornings did not have strong overall ratings, especially compared with the late-afternoon slots that sponsors had been using to reach children audiences. The central difference, as illustrated by a graph of NBC's audience potential for different time slots in 1962, concerned not the number of children watching, but the relative density of age groups.[18] The weekday 5:00 – 7:30 p.m. time slot reached 41 million viewers, double the reach of Saturday morning's 20.5 million. This late-afternoon slot reached more children in all age groups than Saturday morning, including children under 6 (6.4 to 5.7 million), 6–12 years (10.0 to 8.5 million), and teenagers (4.7 to 2.1 million). Yet television stations and networks sold slots to advertisers, especially in the early years of demographic targeting, based on total ratings points and shares. Since adults were much more of a component of the late afternoon slot than on Saturday morning (19.9 to 4.2 million), advertisers who were aiming primarily at children would have to pay higher rates for the late-afternoon slots because of the high numbers of total viewers. While there were more children 12 and under among the late-afternoon audience than on Saturday morning, proportionally they comprised only 40 percent of the late-afternoon audience compared to 69 percent of Saturday mornings. Advertisers targeting children could spend less on Saturday morning ads, but reach a higher proportion of their target audience per dollar, making it a successful mode of niche marketing. This practice presaged the logic of narrowcasting that would predominate in the 1990s, as market segments were constituted both by appealing to core groups of children and by driving away undesirable adult audiences (Turow 1997).

The industrial logic of Saturday morning cartoons was motivated by this early example of television narrowcasting. CBS's line up in 1963 was highly successful in both drawing children viewers and child-hungry sponsors. More prime time rejects found themselves on Saturday morning schedules, including *Bullwinkle*, *The Jetsons*, *Beany and Cecil*, and eventually *The Flintstones*. As the genre continued to be dominated by theatrical retreads and prime time failures, production costs were negligible for most Saturday morning cartoons – networks and producers could maximize returns on their productions by endlessly rerunning one season of a program like *Top Cat* or *The Alvin Show*, making the generic time slot a comparatively low-risk venture with high potential for long-term profits (Turow 1981: 72–73). Saturation hit Saturday morning quickly, but it did not result in the typical generic decline; instead networks saw the time slot as a cash cow for toy and food sponsors looking to reach the "kidvid" audience and decided to raise the stakes by including more original Saturday morning cartoons. In 1965, the two biggest cartoons hits were ABC's *The Beatles* (1965–69) and NBC's *Underdog* (1964–66), as well as other modest successes like *Atom Ant* (NBC, 1965–67). Many of these subsequent original cartoons followed the structure of *The Flintstones*, featuring half-hour stories per episode rather than the compilation of shorts typical of older animation. New production continued through the 1960s, leading to the spate of superhero programs that caused a controversy over cartoon violence in the late-1960s and firmly established Saturday morning as the primary home for television animation (Hendershot 1998).

Another reason for the boom in Saturday morning cartoons in the mid-1960s stemmed from the pendulum swing within the regulatory climate of broadcasting during this era. Newton Minow made a historic splash in 1961, introducing his tenure as FCC Chairman by chiding broadcasters for their banal television programming. He specifically noted a number of offending genres in his "vast wasteland" speech, including game shows, westerns, sitcoms, and repeatedly cartoons (Minow 1964: 52–54). Minow, claiming that cartoons "drowned out" quality children's programming, challenged broadcasters to improve children's broadcasting by eliminating "time waster" shows and move toward more educational and "uplifting" programming. Networks responded by making modest offerings to appease Minow's calls for transformation, bringing educational children's programs to the air, such as *Discovery* (ABC, 1962–71), *Exploring* (NBC, 1962–66), and *1, 2, 3–Go!* (NBC, 1961–62). But when Minow left the FCC in 1963 and Lyndon Johnson endorsed a return to a hands-off FCC, the networks quickly swung back toward their profit-centered practices, encouraging the booming expansion of cartoons on Saturday morning and shuttling less lucrative live-action programs to more marginal Sunday mornings (Turow 1981; Watson 1990).

The syndicated market for animation dried up in these years for a number of reasons. Networks bought up some of the most popular syndicated programs for Saturday morning filler, including *Quick Draw McGraw* and *Yogi Bear*. Additionally the rise of color television in the 1960s made black-and-white reruns in many genres less desirable; monochrome animation such as *Popeye* and early *Looney Tunes* was viewed as comparatively inferior to the all-color output of Hanna-Barbera and newer Warner Brothers' material on Saturday morning (Kompare 1999: 79–80).[19] Finally, and perhaps most importantly, the late-afternoon slots were less effective at drawing only children, leading to comparatively inflated advertising rates because of more adult viewers. Syndicated animation shifted primarily to fringe network UHF stations, a site even more marginalized than Saturday mornings.

While certainly Saturday morning cartoons were successful at drawing the children's audience, we need to look for generic appeals outside the texts themselves. Many of the programs that helped create the Saturday morning cartoon boom of the mid-1960s were originally designed for mass audience appeal, either in prime time television or theatrical run – or both, in the case of *Bugs Bunny*. While certainly the bulk of the original animation created for Saturday morning was designed with kids in mind, most of the assumptions constituting the television cartoon genre were already established before the boom of original animation in the mid-1960s. The creation of the generic label Saturday morning cartoons was primarily the result of numerous industrial practices, including sponsor narrowcasting, the rise of limited animation techniques, and the reorganization of the film industry. Additionally the television industry, as part of a larger cultural context, drew upon and furthered cultural assumptions linked to the cartoon genre – that kids will gladly watch recycled and repeated programs, that kids cannot discern quality of animation, that cartoons should not address "adult" subject matter, and that cartoons are "harmless" entertainment. All of these factors coalesced in the 1960s to constitute the generic category "Saturday morning cartoons."

The most vital effect of establishing Saturday morning cartoons as a cultural category was filing the entire genre under a "kid-only" label. This was accomplished less through targeting a children's audience and more by driving away the adult audience. Cartoons had been on Saturday mornings since the mid-1950s, but it was only in the mid-1960s that they became difficult to find anywhere else in television schedules. Likewise sponsors moved to Saturday morning not because they could reach *more children* in that time slot, but because they could actually reach *fewer adults*, thus raising the percentage of children per rating point and advertising dollar. The appeal of cartoons for children was always considered a default – in the mid-1960s what changed was the assumption that adults could like cartoons too. Following the creation of the Saturday morning enclave, cartoons became stigmatized as a genre *only* appropriate for children, removing the traditional affiliations with a mass audience. This was accomplished partially by networks latching onto an existing phenomenon – adults watched the least amount of television on Saturday mornings. But the industry furthered this association by marketing Saturday morning cartoons solely to children, by foregoing the visual complexity and adult humor that marked earlier animation, by sponsors only advertising to children during the time slot, and by isolating cartoons from all other genres and time slots to maintain tight associations between all the texts within the generic category. The marginalization of cartoons also served to further its appeal among its target audience – one of the appeals of Saturday morning cartoons for children was the very fact that adults did not watch the shows and the programs (and ads) were aimed primarily at them. Parents accepted the generic time slot's role as "baby-sitter" and yielded media control to children, furthering the industrial commitment to defining the genre narrowly.[20]

What I have mapped out through this history of Saturday morning cartoons is how genres can be defined, interpreted, and evaluated outside the realm of the text (Mittell 2001b). Many of the programs labeled cartoons in both the 1940s and 1960s did not change, although their generic definition and assumptions did. The model of genre history I am offering does not chronicle the changing texts of a genre – *Crusader Rabbit* begot *The Flintstones* begot *Atom Ant* – but charts the evolution of the category itself. Cartoons shifted from a mass audience theatrical label to a "lowest common denominator" category, implying shoddy production values, formulaic stories and gags, hyper-commercialization, and limited appeals to anyone except children. The effects of this shift helped to define the debates concerning children's television that took hold in the late-1960s and 1970s, with groups condemning the genre's violent content and commercialization. Had cartoons not become isolated in the television schedule and defined as a kid-only genre, these complaints and controversies could not have occurred as they did. The assumptions constituting the cartoon as a cultural category were established in the 1960s through the institution of Saturday morning as a separate realm of programming and we must look carefully at the impacts this categorization has had on the genre to this day. While many of the categorical assumptions forged in this era still remain operative, cartoons underwent another transformation in the 1990s, one that has worked to redefine the genre and confound some assumptions concerning how media have shifted in the past. The rest of this anthology traces these changes.

Notes

1 I use the terms "cartoon" and "animation" somewhat interchangeably throughout this chapter. While I do not think that they are identical in connotation – cartoons have been tied more to children's audiences and short format, while animation is a more neutral formal delineator – I draw the use of these terms from the press discourses I use as my research material. "Cartoon" is certainly the more specific generic label for Saturday morning, and thus I try to use it to stand in for the genre as a whole.

2 The best historical account of television and animation is the introduction to Erickson (1995: 5–46). He provides much information and detail, but his history lacks detailed documentation or critical analysis. See Chapter 11 of Butler (1994: 261–86), for a strong overview of the formal evolution and construction of television animation. The best piece of cultural scholarship on television animation can be found in Hendershot (1998) and focuses on the 1970s, looking at how the categories of cartoons and children's television were impacted by production and regulatory practices.

3 I am focusing specifically on cartoons within the US – the history of animation in other countries, such as Japan, would tell a very different tale of the genre.

4 My approach to television genres is explored in further depth in Mittell (2001b).

5 Owen's "great man" is Mattel executive Bernard Loomis, although I find no evidence to suggest that Loomis (or any other single individual) was primarily responsible for this phenomenon.

6 The phrase "generative mechanisms" and its accompanying historical approach is drawn from Allen and Gomery (1985).

7 The direct results of the Paramount Decision on exhibition and film bills has not been sufficiently researched. This account is drawn from Lemberg (1991: 9); while this popular book is not the most reliable source, the argument is consistent with most work on the film industry in the 1950s.

8 See Maltin (1987) for an account of these studios. Both MGM and Warner would re-open animation units in the 1960s, primarily to supply television animation.

9 The film industry reached an agreement with the Screen Actors Guild, the Writers Guild of America, and the Directors Guild of America to pay residuals for television sales for all films made post-1948, effectively favoring pre-1948 product because of larger profit margins (see Balio 1990: 30–1).

10 The process of censoring cartoons is difficult to trace, as centralized standards and practices documentation does not exist, especially for syndication. Walter Lantz suggests in Peary and Peary (1980: 196) that none of his cartoons with black characters made it to television (quoted in Maltin 1987: 182).

11 Lists of edited scenes and cartoons appear on The Censored Cartoon Page (http://www.looney.toonzone.net/ltcuts, accessed 1 September 2002).

12 The censorship of cartoons on television is an area mostly underexplored. The only detailed examination can be found in Cohen (1997), although this in itself is frustratingly anecdotal and incomplete.

13 NBC Collection, SHSW, Box 369, Folder 6 – Charles Barry, *Howdy Doody*. In a letter from Adrian Sarnish to Barry, August 6, 1953.

14 The airdates listed for this and other prime time cartoons refers to their prime time runs; as I discuss below, these shows were rescheduled and rerun on Saturday mornings, although usually without generating new episodes.

15 For negative reviews, see "*The Flintstones*" (1960), Seides (1961), and Gould (1960). The most positive reviews came in subsequent years after the show's release ("Stone Age Hero's Smash Hit" 1960; Fleming 1961; "*The Flintstones*" 1961; "*The Flintstones*" 1962; Atkinson 1963).

16 See Mittell (2001a) for more on genre mixing and animated sitcoms concerning *The Simpsons*.

17 See Curtin (1995: 248) for a discussion of the innovation–imitation–saturation cycle and documentaries.

18 NBC Collection, "Children's TV Viewing Patterns," April 19, 1962, in Box 184 (NBC Research Bulletins), Folder 23. While I am certainly not in a position to judge the accuracy of the numbers represented in this graph, they certainly were considered "real" and accurate by networks making programming decisions. This numerical evidence is not "proof" of actual audience composition, but of the ways in which networks understood and constructed their audience, and therefore it is vital information in reconstructing the reasons networks shifted cartoons to Saturday morning.

19 Maltin discusses how Warner Brothers "colorized" black and white *Looney Toons* in the 1970s for the television market (Maltin 1987: 229).

20 Although I do not have space to address this further, this shift was probably also fostered by changing contexts of family politics and television's role within the home during the 1960s.

Bibliography

Allen, R. C. and D. Gomery, (1985) *Film History: Theory and Practice*, New York: McGraw Hill, Inc.

"The Alvin Show," (1961) *Variety*, 11 October.

Anderson, C. (1994) *Hollywood TV: The Studio System in the Fifties*, Austin: University of Texas Press.

Ang, I. (1990) *Desperately Seeking the Audience*, New York: Routledge.

"Animation Scores a Breakthrough," (1960) *Sponsor*, Volume 14, Number 26, 27 June: 43–5.

Ardmore, J. K. (1962) "TV Without Terror," *Parent's*, Volume 37, Number 7, July: 42–43.

Atkinson, B. (1963) "Critic at Large," *New York Times*, 4 October: 32.

Balio, T. (ed.) (1990) *Hollywood in the Age of Television*, Boston: Unwin Hyman.

"The Blue-Blooded Hound Who's in the Black," (1959) *TV Guide*, 10 January: 28–9.

"The Boing Boing Show," (1956) *Variety*, 19 December.

Brion, P. (1990) *Tom and Jerry: The Definitive Guide to their Animated Adventures*, New York: Harmony Books.

"The Bullwinkle Show," (1962) *Variety*, 26 September.

Butler, J. G. (1994) *Television: Critical Methods and Applications*, Belmont, CA: Wadsworth Publishing.

"Cartons of Cartoons for TV," (1957) *Variety*, 31 July: 33, 86.

"Cartoons Endure for UAA," (1959) *Broadcasting*, Volume 57, 10 August: 74–5.

Cohen, K. F. (1997) *Forbidden Animation: Censored Cartoons and Blacklisted Animators in America*, Jefferson, NC: McFarland & Co.

Curtin, M. (1995) *Redeeming the Wasteland: Television Documentary and Cold War Politics*, New Brunswick, NJ: Rutgers University Press.

Doan, R. K. (1967) "Where Did All the People Go?," *TV Guide*, 11 February: 10–13.

Erickson, H. (1995) *Television Cartoon Shows*, Jefferson, NC: McFarland & Co.

Fischer, S. (1983) *Kids' TV: The First 25 Years*, New York: Facts on File.

Fleming, T. J. (1961) "TV's Most Unexpected Hit," *Saturday Evening Post*, Volume 234, Number 48, 2 December: 62–6.

"The Flintstones," (1960) *Variety*, 5 October.

"The Flintstones," (1961) *Variety*, 20 September.

"The Flintstones," (1962) *Variety*, 19 September.

Fox, S. (1962) "TV Versus Children," *Television Quarterly*, Volume 1, Number 3: 40–4.

Gould, J. (1960) "TV: Animated Cartoon," *New York Times*, 1 October: 39.

Grossman, G. (1981) *Saturday Morning TV*, New York: Dell Publishing.

Hendershot, H. (1998) *Saturday Morning Censors: Television Regulation before the V-Chip*, Durham, NC: Duke University Press.

Hyman, E. (1958) "Cartoons: Child's Best TV Friend," *Variety*, 30 July: 43.

"The Jetsons," (1962) *Variety*, 26 September.

"*King Leonardo and his Short Subjects*," (1960) *Variety*, 2 November.

Klein, N. (1993) *Seven Minutes: The Life and Death of the American Animated Cartoon*, London: Verso.

Kompare, D. (1999) "Rerun Nation: The Regime of Repetition on American Television," unpublished Ph.D. dissertation, University of Wisconsin, Madison.

Lemberg, J. (1991) *Encyclopedia of Animated Cartoons*, New York: Facts on File.

MacDonald, J. F. (1983) *Blacks and White TV: Afro-Americans in Television Since 1948*, Chicago: Nelson-Hall Publishers.

Mallory, M. (1998) *Hanna-Barbera Cartoons*, New York: Hugh Lauter Levin Associates.

Maltin, L. (1987) *Of Mice and Magic: A History of American Animated Cartoons*, New York: Plume Books.

McNeil, A. (1991) *Total Television: A Comprehensive Guide to Programming from 1948 to the Present*, New York: Penguin Books.

Minow, N. N. (1964) *Equal Time: The Private Broadcaster and The Public Interest*, New York: Atheneum.

Mittell, J. (2001a) "Cartoon Realism: Genre Mixing and the Cultural Life of *The Simpsons*," *The Velvet Light Trap*, Volume 47: 15–28.

—— (2001b) "A Cultural Approach to Television Genre Theory," *Cinema Journal*, Volume 40, Number 3: 3–24.

Owen, D. (1988) *The Man Who Invented Saturday Morning and Other Adventures in American Enterprise*, New York: Villard Books, 158–91.

Peary, D. and Peary, G. (eds.) (1980) *The American Animated Cartoon: A Critical Anthology*, New York: E.P. Dutton.

Phillips, M. (1957) "Without Lisping Pigs," *New York Times*, 17 March: II:3.

"Promotional Brochure," (1954) NBC Collection, SHSW, Box 374, Folder 57, "Programming, Children's."

"Review: *Huckleberry Hound*," (1960) *TV Guide*, 25 June: 23.

"Satire from the Animal Kingdom," (1960) *TV Guide*, 23 January: 20–2.

Schneider, C. (1987) *Children's Television: The Art, the Business, and How It Works*, Chicago: NTC Business Books.

Seides, G. (1961) "Review: *The Flintstones*," *TV Guide*, 18 March: 15.

Smoodin, E. (1993) *Animating Culture: Hollywood Cartoons from the Sound Era*, New Brunswick, NJ: Rutgers University Press.

Snead, J. (1994) *White Screens / Black Images: Hollywood from the Dark Side*, New York: Routledge.

Spigel, L. (1993) "Seducing the Innocent: Childhood and Television in Postwar America," in W. S. Solomon and R. W. McChesney (eds.), *Ruthless Criticism: New Perspectives in U.S. Communication History*, Minneapolis: University of Minnesota Press, 259–90.

"Stone Age Hero's Smash Hit," (1960) *Life*, Volume 49, Number 21, 21 November: 57–60.

"*Top Cat*," (1961) *Variety*, 4 October.

Turow, J. (1997) *Breaking Up America: Advertisers and the New Media World*, Chicago: University of Chicago Press.

—— (1981) *Entertainment, Education, and the Hard Sell: Three Decades of Network Children's Television*, New York: Praeger Publishers.

Watson, M. A. (1990) *The Expanding Vista: American Television in the Kennedy Years*, New York: Oxford University Press.

Wile, F. (1954) "Memo from Fred Wile Jr. to Mike Dunn," NBC Collection, SHSW, Box 374, Folder 57, "Programming, Children's," 15 September.

"*Woody Woodpecker*," (1957) *Variety*, 9 October.

Chapter 3

RE-DRAWING THE BOTTOM LINE

Allen Larson

THE PROLIFERATION OF THE PRIME TIME, ANIMATED SITCOM in the 1990s often seems a particularly tangible sign of the broad economic and cultural challenges to the commercial broadcast network system (indeed, to traditional US notions of "television" itself) which confronted media producers in the last two decades of the twentieth century. At the very least, the increased prominence of animated sitcoms in this period can be linked directly to the context of broadcast network erosion and eventual dominance of cable signal transmission inasmuch as the well from which the prime time animation boom was drawn – *The Simpsons* – is very much a product of the cable age. The success of News Corps.'s FOX broadcast network, which *The Simpsons* is widely credited with having helped to build, was only made possible by the completed cable wiring of the national market.[1] Only cable signal delivery made possible the building of a "broadcast" network via the use of primarily UHF broadcast affiliates.[2] In the course of their expansion, the earliest cable networks usurped the programming strategies and undermined the audience base that had long been the mainstay of independent station groups (old movies, syndicated sitcom reruns, and daytime children's programming, in particular). The advance of cable also assisted the development of FOX and other upstart networks as increasingly anachronistic, independent broadcast stations became less profitable and readily available for purchase (specifically, the flagship Metromedia group, which Rupert Murdoch seized from a foundation of major market owned-and-operated broadcast stations) in order to build his network (Kaplan 1985: 34; "Foundation For 4th Network" 1985: 1).

Media critics would always do well to remember, however, that the onset of the cable and digital ages is not something that "happened to" television. It was, instead, the result of changes initiated and made manifest by media conglomerates themselves. The question of how content providers would effectively and more profitably deliver audiences to advertisers constitutes perhaps the most formidable "challenge" to television out of which the phenomenon of the contemporary prime time animated sitcom emerges. The cable age and the attendant era of corporate consolidation and conglomeration ushered in by federal deregulation in the 1980s and 1990s is not, in other words, one in which the cultural institution of television in any way shifted from its primary foundation as a business enterprise based upon audience commodification and advertising sales. Rather, this era is one in which that simple foundation became refined, re-imagined, and re-exploited to facilitate and work in concert with more complex and intricate systems of profit maximization. The significant increase in animated television programming that arose during this period is a particularly cogent case in point, exemplifying many of the ways in which discernible changes in the nature of media *content* in recent years might – the important sociocultural dimensions of such changes notwithstanding – be understood as emanating most directly from identifiable economic determinants and incentives.

First- and second-order television economics

At the onset of the prime time animation boom in the 1990s, production costs for animated television shows ranged from roughly $250,000 to $600,000 per half-hour episode, with prime time shows such as *The Simpsons* generally tipping the top end of the scale and syndicated production (typically, weekday afternoon kids' shows) the lower (Mallory 1996a; Karlin 1993b: 1). In keeping with industry tradition, typical licensing agreements would find networks paying slightly less (or sometimes slightly more) than the actual production cost to the supplying studio in exchange for limited airing rights, while the producing studio generally retained potentially lucrative syndication, international, and merchandising sales rights on the property (Hontz 1996: 48; "Film Roman" 1994: 40). At first glance, such fee ranges might thus seem to have provided an incentive for the traditional broadcast networks to dabble in prime time animation, since the average license fee for a sitcom or live-action drama was often well in excess of $1 million per half hour – or nearly double, at the very least, the going rate for animation.[3] But, by the beginning of the 1990s, audience erosion had already led the major networks to begin padding their prime time schedules with low-budget "reality" fare, ranging from *America's Funniest Home Videos* to the swelling glut of news magazines such as *Dateline* and *Prime Time Live*. Average production costs for these shows put them in the same or lower price range than animation (Landler and Grover 1992: 98; Hall 1991: 1). And, unlike animated fare, reality genres were less likely to provoke advertiser anxiety regarding program content while providing a more time-proven lure to the general, national "mass audience" which continued to be the primary business domain of the major networks even amidst the ever-increasing emphasis upon demographics and psychographics in the allocation of advertising dollars. These are among the reasons why the traditional "Big Three" broadcast networks did not provide the primary venue for the prime time animation boom.

The context of cable network programming economics, on the other hand, is not one in which animated production ever presented itself as an inherently thrifty alternative to standard fare. To the contrary, first-run animation has typically been a good deal more expensive, in terms of raw production costs and/or license fees, than the types of programming that cable networks have otherwise used to fill their schedules (Messina 2001: 20). To understand the economic incentives toward an increase in animated program production in the 1990s, we cannot, then, rely upon a simple model of cost-per-episode versus revenue, or, even, upon the assumption that the luring of demographically desirable audiences itself rendered animation more profitable than other forms of programming. This is an important point, as it is often misunderstood. Even today, advertisers rarely pay a significantly higher raw cost-per-thousand rate for viewers based upon their demographic characteristics alone. Attraction of a particular demographic makes the show's commercial time more sellable – more likely to be purchased – but does not necessarily raise the actual *value* of the time itself (again, cost-per-thousand remains more or less comparable across the range of most demographic categories).[4] For all of its arguable complexity, much of what we find on our television screens therefore still emanates from the decisions made in accordance with this first-order economic logic of the television industry: profits come from the difference between production and distribution costs versus revenue generated by advertising sales. These sales take as their basis a very simplistic currency (discursively constituted through ratings discourse) of "eyeballs" delivered.[5]

This first-order economic logic holds true even in the case of cable networks, despite the fact that most derive anywhere from 25 to 75 percent of their revenue from the subscriber fees paid out to them by cable service providers ("History Supports View" 1990: 2; Dempsey 1995a: 4; Motavalli 1989: 158). Our knowledge that the media environment is dominated by conglomerates with holdings in all areas of production and delivery – that the notion of a blood-thirsty competition between broadcast and cable is, for the most part, preposterous given that ownership of the respective television outlets is largely held by the same corporations – should not distract from the fact that within these conglomerate cultures individual executives and managers of respective outlets are still held to traditional performance models, and thus make their decisions based on the first-order logic of advertising sales profit. Much of what we see on television – including many broad-scale trends in programming formats – can be explained simply by knowing this.

But this first-order economic logic does not account for everything. The rise in "reality" programming, for instance, may indeed have a cultural dimension. It may in fact function as a tentacle of postmodern consciousness, confirming Jean-Louis Baudrillard's assertion that television's only logical end would be to turn itself entirely inside-out until the viewer and the fact of viewing had itself become "the star" of the entire enterprise (1983: 52–4). Nevertheless, an economic, materialist explanation also remains compelling. Reality fare is exceptionally less expensive to produce than other types of programming. Many of its forms eliminate altogether factors such as writers' and actors' unions and expenses, while also providing more easily exploitable opportunities to offset production costs by soliciting product placement deals with advertisers. Thus, the proliferation of "reality" formats has functioned as a fairly successful adaptive strategy for securing the survival of the broadcasting branch of media conglomerates. Even as those same conglomerates engineered the segmentation and fragmentation of audience markets, rendering the old business model of the broadcast networks (based, as it was, upon a national mass audience) anachronistic, reality programming has helped lessen the economic downside of the transition. As long as production costs are slashed at a rate higher than broadcast network audience dissipation, broadcast network *profits* can continue to *rise* even as audience share erodes: simple, first-order, media economics.

I have wanted to convey here, however, that this same order of economic explanation cannot be so easily applied to the concurrent phenomenon of increased animated programming. Unlike reality formats, animation is not – as a general category and mode of content production – cheaper than traditional live-action formats. Instead, an economic explanation for increased animation television production will have to be based in the larger question of where animation fits within the encompassing context of industry conglomeration and consolidation – that is, within a second-order of media economics.

Who's watching the kids?

The connection between animation and children's entertainment is made without contemplation. Further exploration of why and how this connection became historically naturalized occurs elsewhere in this volume. Suffice to say that animation's assumed, conventionalized appeal to pre-adolescent viewers has been the single most determining force driving the now nearly century-long evolution of filmed and televisual animation.

Often, commentary on the prime time animation boom proposes that this limiting, naturalized association of animation and children has been dismantled or "overcome" in recent years. The phenomenon represents, it has been claimed, a discernible shift in aesthetic values and cultural attitudes, the maturation of a popular art form marked by its increasing acceptance and recognition as a cultural practice which can be uniquely expressive of adult humor, desire, resistance, intellect, and pathos (Richmond 1996: 37; Schneider 2000b: 47). That cultural attitudes towards animation have significantly changed may or may not be so (and may or not be of any consequence, depending upon what stakes you are playing for). To attribute the increased presence of animated fare on television schedules solely, or even primarily, to a change in aesthetic attitudes would, however, dangerously obscure a more pragmatic view of the material conditions out of which the phenomenon emerged.

Although children have been the focus of intensive marketing efforts since well before the rise of the broadcast television system, media conglomerates only turned the full force of their attention towards maximizing the potential revenue streams provided by children-as-consumers with the onset of the cable age. Aside from the traditional broadcast networks' Saturday morning schedules, weekday morning and afternoon children's audiences largely remained the domain of the individual broadcast station or station group up until the late 1980s. Non-affiliate ("independent," generally UHF) broadcast stations once catered directly to kids with off-net syndication (reruns of old cartoons and other kid-friendly shows), while broadcast affiliates sometimes competed for the market by scheduling first-run, nationally syndicated children's programming in morning or afternoon fringe time slots. This remains a conspicuously under-remarked-upon turn of events worthy of restatement: it was not until the 1980s that *any* national, commercial television *network* began to significantly expand cultivation of the children's market beyond the borders of the traditional Saturday morning cartoon slot. In the 1990s, concentration upon children's markets became a veritable bedrock of the new conglomerate era.

At the center of this orchestrated, concerted corporate emphasis upon the full capitalization of children's markets was the same traditional association of children with animation that has always held true. A massive increase in animated production and the expansion of animation production facilities and capacities thus necessarily attended the industrial scenario within which the children's market emerged as one of the core components of the development strategies adopted by nearly all of the major media conglomerates. In varying ways, each of these companies actively explored the unique profit potentials afforded by animated feature-film production, animated children's television programming, and the plethora of ancillary products derived from franchised cartoon brands as they were repurposed across the full spectrum of media formats in the 1990s. To this extent, we may have – more so than any other factor – the increasingly efficient commodification of children to thank for the subversive pleasures afforded to viewers by shows such as *Beavis and Butt-Head* or *The Family Guy*.

Big screens/small screens: kids, buys, and videotapes

Inasmuch as television is now, more than ever before, merely one among many media in which our major media producers operate, a glance at the arena of *animated feature film* production is, in fact, the best place to begin further exploration of the intersecting financial interests which have fueled the television animation boom.

Throughout 1994 and 1995, the growing industry of feature-film animation was signaled repeatedly by trade publication headlines such as: "Dwarfs Tell Disney: Draw!; Rival Studios Get Serious About Animation," or "Disney Wannabes Play Copycat-and-Mouse" (Brodie and Greene 1994: 1; Brodie 1995: 1). Recovering from its nadir in the mid-1980s – when, one now strains to recall, Disney's feature animation division had failed to produce a hit for years, was consistently losing money, and was in danger of being shut down altogether – Disney had emerged, by 1990, as a veritable prototype for new media conglomerate strategy (Frook 1993: 1). In 1993, Chairman Michael Eisner acknowledged that "family entertainment from the Walt Disney label [represented] 80% of filmed entertainment operating income" and that film animation in fact drove "the entire company – providing rides for theme parks, products for the merchandising division...licensing revenues for the consumer products division, soundtracks for the fledgling record label Hollywood Records," and so on (Frook: 1).

Even before the acquisition of Capital Cities/ABC, *Electronic Media* observed that "Disney's mastering of the multi-tiered approach to maximizing return on investment" had already been demonstrated "by the fact that for every dollar a Disney animated film [made] in its premiere US theater run, the company [typically received] another $10 in revenues over the next three to four years from merchandising and exhibition windows such as home video and pay TV" (Mermigas 1995: 14). Such high returns on capital investment set formidable standards within an industry that operates under the watchful eye of Wall Street.[6] Never guilty of recklessly jumping forward with innovation where derivative imitation might otherwise do, competitors followed suit. The kid-driven cash-cow of feature film animation dominated by Disney henceforth became one of the 1990s' bloodiest competitive battlefields. By the end of the decade, *every* major conglomerate with a film division had either entered for the first time or greatly intensified its efforts within the animated feature film business (Klady 1996: 7; Karon and Klady 1998: 1; Klady 1997: 1).

Although film industry leaders will dutifully protest the claim at every turn, it was, however, the television set – not the multiplex – that would ultimately become the driving force behind kid-oriented feature film production in the 1990s. By 1991, the home video market exceeded the box office in terms of both revenue and profit within domestic and international markets alike (Sweeting 1992: 5). This so-called "ancillary" revenue from the home market was, in fact, at the core (along with other forms of merchandising) of Disney's recipe for earning exponential profits on feature film animation.

More specifically, Disney did the entire industry a favor with its aggressive cultivation of the once tentative video-sell-through (as opposed to rental) market (Stewart 1993: 6). Classic as well as new kid-oriented Disney titles provided the perfect stimulus to the emergent consumer predilection to purchase kid-oriented movies for keeps (Cohen 1986). In 1992, home video sell-through sales rose a staggering 30 percent from the previous year; and in 1993 they would rise another 20 percent, primarily due to the success of the Disney animated feature film VHS releases which accounted for 7 of the top 10 selling videos of the year ("Home Video Spending Up 5.3 Percent" 1994). Market research showed that consumers believed the purchase, rather than rental, of kiddie fare to be "good value," since children are predisposed to multiple viewings (Gelmis 1990: 2).

Anxieties over children's exposure to commercial broadcast and cable television also made the known entity of video cassettes attractive to parents, especially since young children's access would often remain dependent upon parents' ability to operate the physical machinery (although anyone with children may quickly learn that this is not necessarily an advantage). Ironically, the parents who had been the most reluctant to leave young ones propped in front of the television became the boon of sell-through marketing when offered the "wholesome" family fare associated with Disney. Observing this increasingly intimate link between big-screen and small-screen production, *Billboard* commented that "the coming of age of the sell-through video market…corresponded with a rise in the amount of family-oriented and children's product being churned out by Hollywood" (Sweeting 1992: 1; McCullaugh 1993: 1).

The fruition of video-sell-through also corresponded with broad, interconnected changes in the nature of retail marketing in the 1990s as warehouse clubs and mass-purchase discount chains predisposed to push a small selection of family fare over a wide range of diverse titles came to dominate the retail sector, further fixing the dominant emphasis upon children's products in home video production (Christman and O'Brien 1992: 6; Lerman 1995: A5). As that retail pipeline took shape early in the decade, industry observers appeared astonished to report, in 1993, that Disney's *Aladdin* sold "a record-breaking 10.6 million copies in its first three days of home video release," redefining, in *Variety*'s words, "the measurement of success for *feature-length animation*" [emphasis added] (Frook: 1).

Disney's rise to dominance in the home video market should not be misunderstood as emanating strictly from its library of legacy assets, although video issues of films such as *Sleeping Beauty*, *The Jungle Book*, *Cinderella*, and *Pinocchio* indisputably drew enormous amounts of cash into the organization to help support new animated production projects. But, to put "tradition" in its proper perspective: Disney released more feature-length animated films between 1987 and 2000 than it did during its entire six-decade history prior to that point. And, it was only the global relocation of feature film animation viewing to the privatized sphere of the home (through the establishment of pay cable and home video as routine sites of film consumption), along with the globally synergized landscape of media consolidation, that made this increased production profitable and, therefore, viable.

The centrality of the television set to the intensification of animated film production does not stop, however, with the importance of the home video release of successful movies (or, for that matter, "unsuccessful" movies that become profitable in their video afterlife, as is often the case). It has, for instance, become increasingly advantageous for producers, when dealing with the children's market, to blur entirely the line between traditional feature film and television animation. Only eight months after Disney's *Aladdin* broke home video sales records, the studio had enormous success with a direct-to-video sequel to the film, *Aladdin 2: The Return of Jafar* (Fitzpatrick 1994: 53). Since then, direct-to-video sequels for classic and new film titles alike (2002 saw *Jungle Book II*) became, along with the development of franchise titles never attached to any film at all, a staple of the studio's product line as it continued to dominate the home video market. Again, all other major conglomerates have sought to develop their presence in this animation-driven field as well. Echoing the language used five years earlier to discuss the feature film market, *Variety* observed in 1999 that "Disney's strong hold of the direct-to-video sell-through market" would "soon face some fierce competition" as "a growing number of studios hungry for non-theatrically based franchises – Universal, Paramount, FOX, Columbia Tri Star" began "turning to homevid and boosting production slates of sell-through titles." The goal of the developing trend, *Variety* succinctly observed, was not only "to compete with the Mouse House for family-friendly market share" but, perhaps more importantly, "to extend the life of brands and develop moneymaking sequels that perform long after the original pics have left theaters" (Graser 1999: 9).

The development of computer-generated image (CGI) animation technology also would play a prominent role in inspiring such trends. Although, as of yet, not less expensive than traditional cel animation on a raw cost-per-minute basis, CGI animation carries one great advantage: the re-usability of images. Backgrounds, settings, and characters can be stored on disc, allowing producers, in *Daily Variety's* words, to "amass a database of images that can be reused, amortizing the costs associated with CGI animation" while slashing by drastic proportions the production costs of the sequels and ongoing franchises upon which the industry has become increasingly dependent (Paxman and Klady 1998: 5; Spector 2002; Wolff 1995).

As fellow conglomerates sought to emulate Disney throughout the 1990s, Disney of course initiated its own further incursions into cable and broadcast content provision with its 1995 acquisition of Capital Cities/ABC, an even more productive way of putting television sets to work during the off-hours when they weren't busy replaying its video products to kids. Already a major supplier of animated television programs (through first-run syndication mostly) to various venues, the merger allowed vertical integration as Disney programmed ABC's available children's slots almost entirely with its own product – much of which was derived, again, from already established franchises (Levin 1997b). Above and beyond the increased income to be earned by the conglomerate's expanded collection of business enterprises, *Electronic Media* estimated, on the eve of the merger, that "$350 million in earnings synergies" would "be generated over the next five years from the cross-marketing, advertising sales and program distribution among the ABC TV network and its owned stations, The Disney Channel, ESPN, theme parks and Disney's retail stores" (Mermigas 1995: 14). Difficult to quantify, these earning "synergies" were likely perceived as not simply desirable but, rather, indispensable to the continuation of Disney's top-dog status, as supplier "branding" became increasingly central to the ways media producers approached the ever-expanding kids' market.

Indeed, branding strategy was, itself, simply another cornerstone of the Disney model to which competitors aspired. In 1991, one of the company's marketing vice-presidents bragged to *Billboard* that Disney was "already the third-best-known brand name in the US behind Coca-Cola and Campbell's Soup." Nevertheless, the company was then initiating a $40 million promotional blitz, nostalgically themed "The Magic Years," to bolster, in particular, a large slate of new and old home video release titles (McCullaugh 1991: 97). Again, by 1994, trade publications were observing that emphasis upon branding had become endemic to the "kid vid" sector as a whole. Of particular notice to Disney would have been the very successful Sony/Viacom partnership in marketing Nickelodeon brand video and audio products while CBS partnered with FOX for similar endeavors. Televisual – not theatrical – exposure (and by this I do not mean commercial advertising but, rather, exposure through program content) to both brand name and animated product increasingly became recognized as a necessary promotional tool for video manufacturing, further inspiring conglomerates to pull animation-pipeline assets into their fold (McCormick 1994: 67; Karlin 1993a: 9).

Networking children: keep the kids in-house

Needless to say, the latter-day placement of animated, kid-oriented product at the center of media conglomerates' business plans was not limited to ventures into feature film and home video. Branded and franchised animated fare increasingly preoccupied the broadcast and cable television branches of media industries in the 1990s as well (Lowry 1996: 23). Trade publication coverage of the television industry thus also echoed that of feature film by mid-decade. Under the headline "Everybody Into Kids' Programming Pool," *Variety* reporter Brian Lowry observed, in the fall of 1995, that "the children's television programming arena – often looked on as a wading pool when compared to the splashier world of prime time – is rapidly filling with sharks" (Lowry 1995: 36). As was the case with the increased competition in animated feature film production, this newly crowded field of children's television programming emerged not from a sudden new groundswell of advertiser interest in children's audiences but from the larger industry context within which virtually every major conglomerate made the development and expansion of in-house animated production capacities a top priority because of the ways that animated fare uniquely avails itself of the possibilities for thousand-fold returns on initial development investment (Flint 1996: 54).

Without a doubt, the reported $1 billion in revenue generated by FOX through ancillary sales and, more specifically, merchandising of *The Simpsons* helped inspire imitative forays into prime time animation by other major producers (Schneider 2000a: 1). But, as Heidi Beyer of *Daily Variety* observed in 1996, "the relationship between the licensing and animation industries has been crucial for as long as there has been animation." Perhaps even more innovative than the show itself, then, were the demands News Corp./FOX made upon producer Film Roman in forging their *Simpsons* relationship. Whereas merchandise licensing had more typically remained, in the past, the property and domain of the production company, News Corp. demanded most of that pie in exchange for giving the show life on its network, effectively rewriting industry standards for how networks dealt with program content-related merchandising (Diuguid 1997: 7; Levin 1996b: 35). And, at the same time as they were demanding shares of merchandise sales, the networks' license fees for first-run shows were declining, often leaving producers in a position where their only hope for profit resided in their remaining share of ancillary outlets such as toy sales or international sales if these were not, in fact, sold in advance in order to help raise initial production funds. In the bygone era of the Big Three networks, commented Film Roman president Phil Roman to *Variety*, "You could go to the network, sell them a show, and they'd give you the license fee to produce a whole show, and maybe even make a little profit on it. It doesn't work that way anymore" (Mallory 1996c). Under such pressure, merchandising would become, in *Variety*'s words, the lifeblood of the television cartoon industry: "the reality is that the licensing and merchandising of toys, clothing, school supplies, fast foods, etc., has become a 'revenue stream' that equals and often exceeds the TV income" (Mallory 1996c; Setlowe 1994).

The forms of merchandising discussed previously – the branding and franchising of content itself in spinoffs, sequels, and so forth – have ultimately been a more definitive force in shaping our media landscape than the licensing of consumer goods. A property that can become a library asset in perpetuity promises, after all, infinite potentials for later licensing. And, not inconsequentially, content brand and franchise marketing have remained peculiarly outside the purview of regulators and advocates responsible for the 1990 Children's Television Act, who sought to limit the use of commercial television as program-length commercials for toys but who seem not to notice or mind when programs serve as a promotional vehicle for other *entertainment* commodities (Lowry 1994; Goldman 1994: 33). However, inasmuch as merchandising would on average account "for at least 25% of a show's income" and an often much larger percentage of profit, producers began consistently to complain that the potential for merchandise licensing had come to dictate programming decisions. Despite the protestation of folks such as Disney's Michael Eisner that the merchandising tail would never wag the creative dog, most commentary and evidence contrarily confirms the complaint. In 1994, for instance, MCA/Family Entertainment & Universal Cartoon Studios president Jeff Segal told *Daily Variety*: "At Universal we look at a property for its potential value for all of our divisions...We look at our own programming with the hope that those shows, if successful, will develop into properties that would be exploitable in our theme parks" – and, therefore, in the theme-park gift shops, and on school notebooks and lunchboxes and on other sundries ad infinitum (quoted in Setlowe 1994).

As the corporate arts of branding, franchising and merchandising became increasingly well-refined, animated children's television programming burgeoned exponentially. By 2000, fifteen different networks and cable channels had blocks or entire schedules dedicated to children's and/or youth programming (Hall 2000: 36). Viacom's Nickelodeon cable network can most certainly be credited with blazing the trail that every other conglomerate would subsequently hope to traverse in kids' TV. Having set the industry model for narrowcasted cable network style/identity formatting with MTV, Viacom applied similar principles to its fledgling daytime kids' network (which originally shared a transponder and nights with the A&E Cable Network). By 1993, Nickelodeon claimed it attracted more viewers under age 12 than all of the broadcast networks combined, and its empire had begun to expand to international channels, movies, home videos, books, magazines, music, and a host of other licensing and merchandising deals for hit shows such as *Rugrats* (Zimmerman 1993: 41; Mallory 1996d). Although its schedule includes live-action shows as well, the majority of Nickelodeon's programming has been animated – and the majority of that has been developed and produced by the corporation's in-house animation studio, Nicktoons, from which, for example, the adult crossover favorite *The Ren & Stimpy Show* emerged (Goldman 1994: 33; Dempsey 1995b: 27).

Of those with major holdings in broadcast network ventures, only News Corp. moved quickly – largely at the request of its formerly independent station affiliates – to challenge Viacom's rising leadership in children's television programming (Mahoney 1989a: 1; 1989b: 3). The formation of the FOX Children's Network (FCN) in 1989 would mark the first time that a broadcast network successfully offered a full Monday-through-Friday afternoon children's block to affiliates (the service was also available to non-affiliates in some markets as well). Adopting an innovative approach which made affiliate stations profit-sharing partners in the venture, FCN was able to claim that it was beating both cable and broadcast competitors in kids' ratings in key day-parts by 1993 (Karlin 1993b: 1). In part, this success grew from direct imitation of Viacom with, for example, the marketing of the "FOX Kids' Club" and other forms of participant interpellation of children into the FOX Kids' brand. The infusion of cash and sudden increased demand for new animated television programming resulting from News Corp.'s" commitment to the network was subsequently among the factors most widely credited for helping to fuel the flourishing animation sector in the early 1990s. But, herein lay a problem: News Corp./FOX relied almost entirely on outside producers for the product it used to build FCN (Brown 1989; 1991).

Specifically, FCN relied most heavily upon Warner Brothers' television animation division, which at one point provided nearly half of all of FCN's shows. As Time Warner endeavored to build its own broadcast web, it let licensing contracts expire on many of these shows in order to relocate them onto its own children's program block. "Warner Brothers Animation was the creative foundation of the FOX Children's Network," WB Chief Executive Jamie Kellner somewhat ungraciously told *Variety* in 1994: "we're fortunate we can call upon these same talents and assets to build Kids' WB" (Flint 1994c: 1). As the rather risky move of recalling licensed shows indicates, when Time Warner jumped onto the networked kids' bandwagon it did so with full force, putting the formidable weight of its Warner Brothers' animation brand on the line.

Time Warner's infusion of resources into the formation of WB Kids is in fact a remarkable example of the extent to which conglomerates came to treat children's markets as the raw gold mine of media production in the 1990s. The creation of WB Kids emerged not simply from the obvious strength of WB's animation branch but directly from the ways that the specific nature of the children's market was believed to avail itself to upstart ventures in broadcast television (Mahler 1989: 6). "Kids," one industry spokesperson observed, "are the ones who find programming the fastest and have the least habitual viewing…They have no notions about the Big 3 networks, the little three networks, or the start-up network" (Tyrer 1995: 21).

By taking advantage of children's unique adaptability, "the animation-fed Kids' WB" would, one industry reporter assessed, "help take pressure off WB's struggling prime time shows" and "produce a financial windfall to Warner Brothers' vertically integrated pipeline" that would ensure the long-term viability of the broadcast network as a whole. Success for WB Kids would "increase ratings for WB affiliates and create more promotional flow for WB's prime time slate," not to mention fuel ancillary revenue generation through, for example, increased exposure for merchandise sold in the conglomerate's retail venture Warner Brothers stores in malls throughout the US. Profits from those revenues "would then be funneled directly to Warner Brothers' bottom line, helping to buy more time for the WB to entrench itself with [adult and teen] viewers" (Tyrer 1995: 21). Of course, Time Warner's merger with Turner Broadcasting and accompanying acquisition of Cartoon Network and Hanna-Barbera also provided valuable tools in the effort to claim a major portion of the kids' markets (Levin 1997a: 43). In 1997, *Variety* appropriately headlined one of its sidebar news items "WB Teaches Kids Synergy," reporting that the company would promote its Saturday morning WB slate by temporarily airing it on Cartoon Network during prime time viewing hours (Stern 1997: 34).

Both Time Warner and Disney's efforts to vertically integrate and fully synergize marketing platforms for their animation divisions via the direct ownership of broadcast and cable networks helped precipitate further consolidation of the industry as fellow conglomerates sought to create comparable earnings potentials through in-house animation (Mallory 1996c). Recognizing its disadvantage, News Corp.'s FOX attempted for two years, for instance, to acquire the premiere animation house Saban Entertainment before settling on a "strategic alliance" with the company that in 1996 resulted in the formation of a jointly owned subsidiary, FOX Kids Worldwide, which encompassed both Saban and FCN (Levin 1996a: 6; Flint 1995: 33). Commenting on the animation consolidation trend from the retrospective vantage point of 2002, and sounding more like F.A.I.R.'s *EXTRA!* than an industry trade magazine, *Hollywood Reporter* wrote: "More than a half-decade of shriveling license fees and superconglomeration have all but wiped out independent animation studios and distributors. Legendary firms ranging from Fred Wolf to Marvel and Hanna-Barbera have all been gobbled up by the voracious and ever-merging TV monster" (Callaghan 2002: S4).

Above and beyond the ways that the integrated animated children's market has provided conglomerates with a relatively still target and a playing field within which every capital investment seems almost infinitely exploitable through global distribution and merchandising, animation has carried the additional incentive of attracting large amounts of international co-financing investment. When not producing in-house, networks have increasingly come to demand and rely upon international partners in floating production costs. "The days when a US network would fully finance a show are long over," observed one Sony vice-president in 1999, also stating that while "getting a show onto the air in the US" was "vital for foreign sales," approximately "75% of [first-run licensing] revenues" for animated shows were "coming from the non-US markets" (Williams 1999: 16). Ironically, foreign reactions against US global culture actually helped propel this move toward joint ventures and further enhanced the attraction to international markets. As numerous countries – Canada, France, China, and others throughout Asia and the Pacific Rim – enacted laws mandating that specified percentages of programming be "home grown" (without typically specifying *how much* of the property the local company has to own) international co-productions have also proliferated (Hall 2001: M31). Conglomerate money helps generally cash-strapped local companies raise production funds while providing the conglomerate backdoor, under-the-quota access to foreign markets while also off-setting investment risks. Nickelodeon's animation/live-action hybrid *Blue's Clues*, for instance, has been globally distributed in a format which allows for insertion of a local host, thereby qualifying the show as a "local" production in foreign markets (Jensen 2000: 1).

Back to the "Magic Years"

Despite the complaints from independent animation houses that industry trends have cramped their ability to work creatively, the nostalgia Disney exploited to help jump-start the new age of animation in the 1990s has often been reflected – here, perhaps more in the style of a fun-house mirror – in trade publication discussions of shifting modes of production (Sheinkopf 1996: 1).

Prior to its merger with Time Warner, Turner Broadcasting acquired Hanna-Barbera Productions (and its library) in order to help build Cartoon Network. As

Turner's library-animation venue gained ground in the following years, the Hanna-Barbera division was commissioned to begin producing original animated shorts in what *Daily Variety* described as an effort "to replicate the atmosphere that led to the creation of classic characters at Warner Brothers and MGM in their heyday," when "franchises like Bugs Bunny, Tom & Jerry, and Daffy Duck were introduced" (Lowry 1993a: 8). Whereas standard television industry practice at the time had been to fund animated projects merely on concept – without any initial investment in the production of pilots or prototypes – the Hanna-Barbera shorts initiative, which aimed to produce 48 seven-minute shorts over a two-year span (to air in a bi-weekly showcase spot on Cartoon Network) both foreshadowed and helped set in motion a new animation economy in which the potential for long-term profits was seen to warrant large capital investment in an experimental "laboratory" production environment where much of what was produced would never be further developed. Dubbed the "World Premiere Toons" project, the venture begat *Dexter's Laboratory*, *Cow and Chicken*, and *Johnny Bravo*, the latter two of which were credited with producing "an immediate 45% spike in [Cartoon Network's] time period numbers among the kids' demo ages 6–11," therefore inspiring continuing investment in this form of development (Richmond 1997: 21). In 1996, *Variety* again perceived a return to the production modes of the oligopolistic Hollywood studio system when covering Viacom's infusion of $420 million into in-house animated production for its MTV and Nickelodeon networks. "Cartoon production at Nicktoons," observed reporter Michael Mallory, "is based upon a unit system, with each series' creator heading up his specialized team, much in the way the classic short cartoons of the 1940s and '50s were created" (Mallory 1996b: 31).

Much of the prime time animation boom has emerged directly from the production capacities of this latter-day, vertically *and* horizontally integrated, Hollywood studio system. Out of the aforementioned $420 million Viacom pumped into Nicktoons, the majority would go to kids' programming; but the bankroll also made possible the production of *Daria*, at one point imagined as an animation component for the evolving VH1 brand format (Mallory 1996b: 31). Ultimately unsuccessful ventures on the WB Kids such as *Pinky and the Brain* and *Baby Blues* emanated directly from the prolifically profitable Warner Brothers' television animation division. Beneath the tower of intra-organizational title credits for ABC's short-lived *Clerks* – Miramax Films, Miramax Television, Touchstone Television, View Askew Productions – resides the Walt Disney television animation studio.

Meticulously seeded and tilled throughout the 1990s, the corporate animation field has been developed to provide one of the most consistent and profitable revenue streams for major media conglomerates. Although labor intensive – and therefore still relatively expensive – animated production's status as a core commitment and established resource base within such organizations almost ensures continuing efforts to stretch the form beyond traditional genres and audience segments. Insofar as such efforts may also evolve in tandem with popular cultural sensibilities that covertly problematize – just as so much of our mass-mediated popular culture always has – the productive and ideological systems which give them life, television animation will also likely provide the fodder for continuing critical debate for quite some time. But, the simple fact of animation's increased prominence in program schedules cannot, unfortunately, tell us very much about actual social or cultural relations to television as such. Even within the irredeemably faulty paradigm of audience measurement from which executives fabricate notions of "audience demand," there is no justification for offering more adult-skewed prime time animation. The overwhelming majority of the endeavors following in the wake of, first, *The Simpsons* and then *South Park*, have been unmitigated ratings disasters. That the trend towards more television animation nonetheless continues is perhaps a surer sign than any that a new order of media economics is propelling the television industry. While on the surface the animation boom might seem to suggest a breakdown in the hegemonic authority that US network television's genres, conventions, and articulative structures ostensibly once held, a closer look finds the same phenomenon reflective of the arguable reality that, for all of their almost imperceptible vastness, the culture industries have never been more coherently organized, more unitarily orchestrated, or more efficiently harmonized than they are at present.

Notes

1   In 1986, it was estimated that between 70 and 75 percent of all households with televisions were passed by (able to receive) analog, coaxial cable. By 2002 this had reached 97 percent. Of homes passed by cable, the rate of those subscribing to at least basic cable was estimated to be 57 percent in 1987 and 70 percent in 2002 ("Cable Industry at a Glance" 2002; "Halprin Issues Call; VCRs, Backyard Dishes, Seen as Competitors to Cable" 1986: 3; "57% Cable Penetration Seen; High Growth Rate for Communications Predicted to 1992" 1988: 4).

2   In 1994, *Daily Variety* observed that with "65% of TV viewership in a given market [coming] from cable," the traditional concern about UHF "signal strength" was increasingly perceived as a "non-issue" in tabulating national clearance rates for network programs. Fox also used a relationship with dominant cable service provider TCI to bargain for carriage of UHF affiliates in the VHF 2–13 basic cable lineup along with using its own FOX Cable Network to supplement viewership for its network programs in markets where no affiliates were signed (Flint 1994b: 19; 1994a: 1; Lowry 1993b).

3   In 1992 the cost of the highest priced sitcom, *Cheers*, was reported to be $2.3 million per episode. In 1995, fees for brand-new sitcoms such as CBS's *High Society* were approximately $600,000 per episode. License fees for new hour-long dramas (such as *Central Park West*) averaged approximately $1 million per episode (Robins 1995: 1; Aho 1992: S22).

4   The exception is the 18–49 "demographic," insofar as the larger portion of advertisers are seeking audiences in this age range. Demographic distinctions within this age range on the

basis of, for example, gender or income level are not likely to alter substantially the price advertisers are willing to pay for commercial time (Umstead 2002: 11A).

5   For a discussion and critique of the ways audiences are discursively constituted through ratings discourse, see Ang (1991: 53–9).

6   Thus, Disney was picked by many analysts at the beginning of 1994 as the favored entertainment stock to hold (Noglows and Britell 1994: 120).

Bibliography

"57% Cable Penetration Seen; High Growth Rate for Communications Predicted to 1992," (1988) *Communications Daily*, 28 June: 4.

Aho, D. (1992) "Network Bugaboo: Getting Consistent Program Quality," *Advertising Age*, 11 May: S22.

Ang, I. (1991) *Desperately Seeking the Audience*, London: Routledge.

Baudrillard, J. (1983) *Simulations*, trans. Paul Foss, Paul Patton and Philip Beitchman, New York: Semiotext(e).

Beyer, H. (1996) "Licensing Remains Key to Big Deals," *Daily Variety*, 22 March.

Brodie, J. (1995) "Disney Wannabes Play Copycat-and-Mouse," *Variety*, January 2–8: 1.

Brodie, J. and J. Greene (1994) "Dwarfs Tell Disney: Draw; Rival Studios Get Serious About Animation," *Variety*, July 11–17: 1.

Brown, K. (1991) "Buena Vista TV Hikes Marketing Spending As FOX Kids Net Gains," *ADWEEK*, 17 June, Western Advertising News Edition.

—— (1989) "FOX Chases Kids With Program Network," *ADWEEK*, 19 June, Western Advertising News Edition.

"Cable Industry at a Glance," (2002) *Variety*, January 14–20.

Callaghan, D. (2002) "Fine-Tooning: The Cyclical Business of Small-Screen Animation is Slowly Making a Turn Toward the Independents," *Hollywood Reporter*, 22–28 January, Special Section: Animation: S4.

Christman, E. and M. K. O'Brien (1992) "Warehouse Clubs May Cool on Music Line, But Home Video Sell-Through Keeps Getting Hotter," *Billboard*, 18 July: 6.

Cohen, J. (1986) "Emotions Mixed, Say Studio Execs, Over Video Sell-Through Revenues," *ADWEEK*, 10 November.

Dempsey, J. (1995a) "New Nets Face Uphill Battle, Cablers Warn," *Daily Variety*, 10 May: 4.

—— (1995b) "Nick Takes Kid-Size Cut at Early Prime," *Variety*, October 16–22: 27.

Diuguid, C. (1997) "Marketers Armed With License to Sell," *Variety*, June 9–15: 7.

"Film Roman," (1994) *Electronic Media*, 18 July: 40.

Fitzpatrick, E. (1994) "Direct-to-Video's Image Brightens; Genre Now Considered Marketing Plus," *Billboard*, June 18: 53.

Flint, J. (1996) "Kidvid High Global Priority; Media Moguls Maneuver to Secure Programs," *Daily Variety*, January 5: 54.

—— (1995) "FOX, Saban Morphin Into Kidvid World," *Variety*, November 6–2: 33.

—— (1994a) "FOX Affils Climb to 42," *Daily Variety*, April 29: 1.

—— (1994b) "FOX Spikes Football," *Variety*, September 26–October 2: 19.

—— (1994c) "WB Sets Kids' Block," *Daily Variety*, 21 July: 1.

"Foundation For 4th Network; Metromedia Sells 7 Stations for $2 Billion to Company Formed by Rupert Murdoch and Oilman Marvin Davis," (1985) *Communications Daily*, 7 May: 1.

Frook, J. E. (1993) "Disney Changes Its 'Toon'," *Variety*, 18 October: 1.

Gelmis, G. (1990) "Honey, They Shrunk the Price," *Newsday*, 9 May, City Edition, Section II: 2.

Goldman, M. R. (1994) "Kids' Market Animated, Lively," *Variety*, September 26–October 2: 33.

Graser, M. (1999) "Ferreting Out Franchises For Direct-to-Vid Futures," *Variety*, February 8–14: 9+.

Hall, J. (1991) "And the Winner Is…News Magazines," *Los Angeles Times*, 24 December, Home Edition, Part F: 1.

Hall, W. J. (2001) "Riding the Shock Waves: Cash-Strapped US Outfits Look Abroad," *Variety*, March 26–April 1, Special Report: Spotlight MIP TV: Family Programming: M31.

—— (2000) "More TV Choices For Gen Z: Cable and Broadcast Co-Ventures Increase Branding Opportunities," *Daily Variety*, 8 September: 36.

"Halprin Issues Call; VCRs, Backyard Dishes, Seen as Competitors to Cable," (1986) *Communications Daily*, 29 April: 3.

"History Supports View: Analysts Call Basic Cable 'Resistant' to Recession, But Pay Could Be Hit," (1990) *Communications Daily*, 14 August: 2.

"Home Video Spending Up 5.3 percent," (1994) *United Press International*, 18 March: Financial, BC cycle.

Hontz, J. (1996) "Special Report: Kids & Teens TV; Animators Up Financial Ante in Studio Deals," *Electronic Media*, 11 March, Special Report: 48.

Jensen, E. (2000) "The Changing Face of International TV," *Los Angeles Times*, 27 October, Home Edition, Calendar, Part F: 1.

Kaplan, P. (1985) "Plan For a FOX Network Intrigues TV Industry," *New York Times*, 11 October, Section C: 1.

Karlin, S. (1993a) "Broadening Vid Sales is Part of the Package," *Daily Variety*, 18 October: 9.

—— (1993b) "Diversity Key to FCN Long Term Success; Net Bends Rules, Comes Out a Winner," *Daily Variety*, 7 September, Special Section: 1.

Karon, P. and L. Klady (1998) "High Noon for Toon Boon," *Variety*, June 15–21: 1.

Klady, L. (1997) "FOX Getting Set to Join Toon Platoon," *Daily Variety*, 10 October: 1.

—— (1996) "Studios Flog Family Values," *Variety*, July 1–14: 7.

Landler, M. and R. Grover (1992) "Why the Losing Network is Still a Winner," *Business Week*, 20 April: 98.

Lerman, L. (1995) "Sell-Through Booming as Video Rentals Linger," *Variety*, February 20–26: A5.

Levin, G. (1997a) "Cartoon Network Adding 10 Series," *Daily Variety*, 25 November: 43.

—— (1997b) "Consolidation Brings Isolation," *Daily Variety*, 24 March, Special Section.

—— (1996a) "FOX Seeks Kid Coin; FCN–Saban Teaming Plans Stock Offering," *Daily Variety*, 1 October: 6

—— (1996b) "Kidvid Loners Left to Pay the Piper," *Variety*, April 29–May 5: 35.

Lowry, B. (1996) "Muscle Tussle for Kid Coin; Industry Goliaths Tooning Up," *Variety*, February 12–18: 23.

—— (1995) "Everybody Into Kids' Programming Pool," *Variety*, November 6–12: 36.

—— (1994) "Changing Channels; Goals and Reality Don't Mix in Children's TV Act," *Daily Variety*, 15 June.

—— (1993a) "H-B Makes Short Work of Cartoon Net Deal," *Daily Variety*, 15 November: 8.

—— (1993b) "FOX Keeps Rolling in High Gear," *Daily Variety*, 7 September, Special Section.

Mahler, R. (1989) "Children's TV Rebounds With Help From Toyland," *Electronic Media*, 18 December: 6.

Mahoney, W. (1989a) "FOX Approves Children's Fare," *Electronic Media*, 19 June: 3.

—— (1989b) "FOX Stations Call for New Kids' Block," *Electronic Media*, 30 January: 1.

Mallory, M. (1996a) "Even Stick Figures Cost Six Figures," *Daily Variety*, 22 March, Special Section, Spotlight Animation.

—— (1996b) "Nicktoons Gears Up for Growth After MTV's Major Cash Infusion," *Variety*, November 18–26, Special Report: 31.

—— (1996c) "Hacking Through the Toon Jungle; Industry Swells, Field Crowds, Tactics Change," *Daily Variety*, 25 March.

—— (1996d) "Hit Series a Merchandise Phenomenon; Rugrats Taking Retailers By Storm," *Daily Variety*, 1 October.

McCormick, M. (1994) "Kid Vid: The Growing Market Challenges Manufacturers To Stand Out From the Crowd," *Billboard*, 19 February: 67.

McCullaugh, J. (1993) "Vid Retailers Value H'wood Emphasis on Family Films," *Billboard*, 29 May: 1.

—— (1991) "Disney Hopes to Keep The 'Magic' Alive with Brand-awareness TV, Print Campaign," *Billboard*, 18 May: 97.

Mermigas, D. (1995) "Setting Up a Knockout Combo, Analysts Say Disney-Cap Cities a Force to Be Reckoned With," *Electronic Media*, 6 November: 14.

Messina, I. (2001) "Reality Check," *Cablevision*, 25 June: 20.

Motavalli, J. (1989) "Marketing to the Year 2000; Media in the 90s," *ADWEEK*, 11 September: 158.

Noglows, P. and P. Britell (1994) "Wall Street Analysts Predict the Best of the New Year; Stock-picker Plums: Disney, Spelling," *Variety*, January 17–23: 120.

Paxman, A. and L. Klady (1998) "Battle of the Ant-imators," *Variety*, September 21–27: 5.

Richmond, R. (1997) "Cartoon Net Turns 5 Amid Animated Growth," *Variety*, August 11–17: 21.

—— (1996) "Toons Tune to Adult Auds," *Variety*, October 17–23: 37.

Robins, J. M. (1995) "Nets Spend Big on New Shows," *Daily Variety*, 23 May: 1.

Schneider, M. (2000a) "Nets Fear Viewer Toon-out With P'Time Animation Glut," *Daily Variety*, 4 February: 1.

—— (2000b) "TV Toppers Fret Over Toon Boom," *Variety*, January 31–February 6: 47.

Setlowe, R. (1994) "License to Draw Money Issued in Merchandising," *Daily Variety*, 24 March.

Sheinkopf, E. (1996) "Creator-Driven Toons on the Rise," *Daily Variety*, 1 October: 1.

Spector, J. (2002) "Studios Drawn to CGI Features," *Hollywood Reporter*, 2 January.

Stern, C., J. Flint, E. Guider, A. Paxman and G. Levin (1997) "Tauzin Tells Biz FCC Weather Will Change," *Variety*, January 20–26: 24.

Stewart, A. (1993) "'Beast' Topples but Disney Still Vid Sell-Through Star," *Daily Variety*, 16 February: 6+.

Sweeting, P. (1992) "Vid-Mmkt. Clout Not Film Focus," *Billboard*, 21 March: 5.

Tyrer, T. (1995) "Warner Brothers Putting Weight Behind Kids' Shows Committing Product, Brand to Service," *Electronic Media*, 24 April, Special Report: 21.

Umstead, R. T. (2002) "The Most Desirable Demo: Cable Networks Court the 18-to-49-Year-Old Viewer," *Multichannel News*, 25 February: 11A.

Williams, M. (1999) "Confab's New Toon: Biz Changing Amid Flood of Animation, Int'l Coin," *Daily Variety*, 4 October: 16.

Wolff, E. (1995) "CGI Revolution Hits Television," *Daily Variety*, 23 March.

Zimmerman, K. (1993) "Nick's Kiddie Empire Turns 15; Cable Television Network's Mix of Hits Remains No. 1 With Under-12 Crowd," *Daily Variety*, 20 December: 41.

Chapter 4

THE FLINTSTONES TO *FUTURAMA*

Networks and prime time animation

*Wendy Hilton-Morrow and
David T. McMahan*

A SCENE FROM THE 1992 HALLOWEEN EPISODE OF *The Simpsons* included a stroll through a darkened cemetery. Among the names on the tombstones were *Fish Police* (1992), *Capitol Critters* (1992), and *Family Dog* (1993), all of which were prime time animated series that premiered following the success of *The Simpsons* and which were subsequently canceled after extremely brief runs. Had we been able to read more of the tombstones, we may have noticed such names as *Calvin and the Colonel*, *Top Cat*, *The Bullwinkle Show*, *Jonny Quest*, and *Where's Huddles*, also all network prime time animated series. Of course, some of these shows were more successful than others, yet none generated much success in prime time. Others, such as *The Flintstones* and *The Simpsons*, provided a hit series for the networks on which they appeared. Significantly, both *The Flintstones* and *The Simpsons* appeared on fledgling networks that were trying to distinguish themselves through counter-programming strategies.

It has been over forty years since *The Flintstones* – the first animated series produced for prime time – premiered on ABC. Since that time, numerous animated series have aired during prime time, with varying degrees of success. Following the success of *The Flintstones*, a boom appeared in prime time animation. However, after the cancellation of *The Flintstones* in 1966, animated series were absent from prime time lineups until the premiere of *The Simpsons* on FOX in December 1989. Similar to the animation boom following the premiere of *The Flintstones* thirty years earlier, the success of *The Simpsons* led to a resurgence of prime time animation. Although this renewed interest originally appeared fleeting, as *The Simpsons* neared the end of its tenth season it was joined on air by a number of other prime time animated series.

The purpose of this chapter is to provide an historical overview of how television networks have used prime time animation. Specifically, we identify the two time periods during which prime time animation peaked on broadcast television. In doing so, we review the environment leading to the emergence of prime time animation in the early 1960s, factors leading to the subsequent absence of prime time animation, and the conditions leading to prime time animation's re-emergence in the 1990s. In order to better understand how networks have used prime time animation as a programming strategy, we then focus on a single network's use of prime time animation in a case study of FOX.

The original prime time animation boom

The two greatest boosts for animation came with the Paramount Decision in 1948 and the rise of television, both of which would set the stage for the emergence into television of two animation innovators. As a result of the Paramount Decision, the major film studios no longer had a guaranteed outlet for their product. Without the pressures of block-booking, which forced theaters to screen a studio's "B" and "C" films along with its hits, theater chains no longer accepted many of the "B" and "C" films produced by the studios. Studios soon began to look to television as an outlet for previously released movies and re-issued animation (Erickson 1995; Lenburg 1983). When television began luring patrons away, many theaters went to double features and eliminated the cartoons screened before the movie. Studios either curtailed production of animation or disbanded their animation departments altogether (Lenburg 1983).

Two animators who found themselves out of a job after their dismissal from MGM were William Hanna and Joseph Barbera. Rather than join another studio and possibly experience a similar fate, Hanna and Barbera opened their own studio. The name was determined by the flip of a coin (Hanna 1996). With Screen Gems as its distributor, Hanna-Barbera began producing *Ruff and Reddy* for NBC as well as *Huckleberry Hound* and *Quickdraw McGraw*. *Ruff and Reddy* was the first network series produced by the studio and was aired on Saturday mornings. Several local markets began airing *Huckleberry Hound* along with *Quickdraw McGraw* during prime time or shortly before (Erickson 1995). A survey conducted by the studio found that 65 percent of the audience for Hanna-Barbera cartoons were adults (Javna 1985).

John Mitchell, vice-president at Screen Gems, suggested that Hanna-Barbera develop a cartoon aimed at adults, and this soon gave rise to the development of

75

The Flintstones (Hanna 1996). The established networks CBS and NBC were unwilling to support the idea of animation in prime time and turned down the program as being too novel. However, for ABC, the fledgling third network, this program seemed to be something that would work. *The Flintstones* fit ABC's strategy of airing novelty and counter-programming such as Disney programs and Western series. On Friday 30 September 1960, *The Flintstones* premiered opposite CBS's *Route 66* and NBC's *The Westerner*. The show was greeted with mixed reviews but high ratings (Erickson 1995).

As is often the case, the success of one genre, format, or gimmick led to the placement of many similar programs on network schedules. The success of *The Flintstones* was no exception. Eight animated shows aired in prime time during the next two years. However, no other series matched the success of *The Flintstones*, and most lasted only a season before being moved to Saturday morning.

Following ABC's success with *The Flintstones*, CBS introduced *The Alvin Show* and its animated chipmunks for the 1961–62 season. Airing Wednesday nights at 7:30, *The Alvin Show* was up against *The New Steve Allen Show* on ABC and *Wagon Train* on NBC. The series was no match for *Wagon Train*, the number one program for the 1961–62 season, and was relegated to Saturday mornings where it lasted three more seasons. Not to be outdone by the other two networks, NBC introduced *The Bullwinkle Show*, airing in color on Sunday evenings at 7:00 in competition with the black and white *Lassie* on CBS. Although the program garnered acceptable ratings against *Lassie*, it was no match for the highly rated program and was moved to Sunday afternoons during its second season (Erickson 1995). ABC seemed to have found a niche during this period and included additional animated series in its prime time lineup. In 1961, ABC broadcast five prime time animated series, including *The Flintstones*, *Calvin and the Colonel*, *Matty's Funday Funnies*, *Top Cat*, and *The Bugs Bunny Show*.

This initial surge of prime time animation was to be brief however, with only *The Flintstones* returning for the 1962–63 season. Nevertheless, ABC was not quite ready to give up on prime time animation and placed *The Jetsons* on its 1962–63 schedule, where it too lasted only a year before being moved to Saturday mornings. Not to be deterred, ABC tried prime time animation once again during the 1964–65 season. *Jonny Quest* was the fourth prime time animated series produced by Hanna-Barbera and appeared to have potential against NBC's *International Showtime*, in its final season, and CBS's *Rawhide*, in its next-to-last season. On the other hand, *The Flintstones*, which had been moved to Thursday evenings at 7:30, was losing ground against CBS's *The Munsters*. Seeing greater syndication potential in *The Flintstones*, Hanna-Barbera switched the time-slots of the series, with the result that *The Flintstones* regained some of its previous popularity while *Jonny Quest* slipped in ratings and was ultimately canceled (Erickson 1995).

When *The Flintstones* left prime time in 1966, it marked the end of prime time animation for twenty-three years, with the exception of *Where's Huddles*, which aired briefly on CBS in 1970 as a summer replacement series. It appeared that animated series were no longer welcome in prime time. As Gitlin has noted, "sooner or later, the audience, having gone along with the fad, grows weary, bored, resentful – in its odd way, discriminating. It takes its revenge" (1983: 74). It would not be until *The Simpsons* premiered on FOX in 1989 that an animated series would once again appear during prime time.

The second prime time animation boom

Over a decade after its premiere, including *The Simpsons* as part of a prime time lineup seems like a sensible and lucrative decision. At the time, however, there were multiple factors working against the placement of animation during prime time. Despite the success of *The Flintstones*, no other prime time animated series yielded the same results for the networks. After getting burned by these programs, the networks had misgivings about using animation during this time-period. This is not to say that other types of programming had consistently lived up to network expectations, but rather that there were many variables in the production of animation that turned network executives away from this form of programming. The most notable distinction between animation and other programs produced for prime time is that with the former it takes at least six to eight months before network executives are even able to see a pilot episode. Quite simply, networks could not wait that long to see a pilot, and after the failures experienced during the seasons following the premiere of *The Flintstones*, network executives were even less likely to take a chance on a series they would not even be able to watch for six to eight months.

A second factor that impeded the development of animation for prime time was the relegation of animation to Saturday morning programming for children. Nearly all the animated series premiering in prime time were eventually moved to Saturday mornings where they became part of a lineup aimed directly at children. Saturday morning programming had never really received much attention until Fred Silverman was hired as director of daytime programming for CBS in 1964. Drawing from the counter-programming strategies he had observed at ABC and those he had personally cultivated while at WGN in Chicago and WPIX in New York, Silverman immediately placed animated programs such as *Superman*, *Space Ghost*, *Lone Ranger*, and former ABC prime time program *Jonny Quest* on the lineup known as "Superhero Saturday" (Erickson 1995). Advertising rates for these programs skyrocketed, and animation was once again an important commodity for the networks – but only as Saturday morning programming for a young audience.

77

The quality of animation had also seriously declined. By the 1980s, most animated programs were little more than poorly drawn, glorified half-hour commercials for action figures and video games. These shows included such notables as *Care Bears*, *My Little Pony*, *Challenge of the GoBots*, *G.I. Joe*, *Pac-Man*, and *Transformers*. In the past, writing for animated series was more complex, including occasional jokes for parents watching the program with their children. Animated series had become entertainment aimed solely at children.

By the late 1980s, prime time animation faced serious obstacles. Genres with episodes that could be written and taped in a week were to prove more resilient than prime time animation, since these genres could adjust to network expectations more swiftly. Also, animation continued to be seen as Saturday morning children's fare. The networks were still willing to use animation as long as it was in such a "throw-away" time-slot as Saturday morning. Eventually, through programming strategies such as those of Fred Silverman, networks began earning higher revenue from these animated programs, but this only served to strengthen their place on Saturday mornings. Finally, the quality of animation had significantly declined and could no longer be legitimately placed in a prime time lineup. However, a new network was about to premiere, and a second boom in prime time animation was about to take place.

In 1987, the FOX Network, the new kid on the block as ABC had been many years before, began running a program entitled *The Tracey Ullman Show*. Each half-hour show featured two or three sketch comedy bits starring Ullman. Shortly into the series run, animated shorts were included between sketches. Created by cartoonist Matt Groening, these shorts recounted the antics of a crudely drawn dysfunctional family.

The shorts soon became a cult favorite, and the producer of the *The Tracey Ullman Show*, James L. Brooks, approached Groening about turning them into a half-hour sitcom. The most difficult task was convincing the network to sign off on the project. As FOX chairman Barry Diller recalled, "[It seemed] a huge risk. We tried hard to say, 'Oh let's just do four specials. What do we need to rush so fast for?'" (Waters 1990: 61).

Teaming up with sitcom writer Sam Simon, Groening and Brooks began working on rough-cuts of the possible new series. Upon seeing the rough-cuts, FOX executives immediately believed they had discovered a niche to compete with the other networks as well as a likely hit series. As Diller describes the scene, "It's not often I've had this experience – the experience of watching something great and praying that the next minute doesn't dash it. And not only having that not happen, but saying at the end: 'This is the real thing! This is the one that can crack the slab for us!'" (Waters 1990: 62).

Groening believes the age of FOX executives had a great deal to do with the series being picked up by the network. "One of the reasons *The Simpsons* got on the air in the first place was that there were finally some executives who remembered watching *The Flintstones* and *The Jetsons* and *Jonny Quest* at night as children, so they could conceive of the idea of animation during prime time" (Solomon 1997: 22). *The Simpsons*, the first animated series on the air in twenty-three years, quickly became one of FOX's highest rated programs.

Like *The Flintstones* twenty-nine years before, the success of *The Simpsons* created a boom in prime time animation. The other three networks immediately started developing prime time animated series, although it was not until ABC premiered *Capitol Critters* in January 1992 that another animated series would appear. This would be followed by *Fish Police* a month later on CBS, *Family Dog* (CBS), and *The Critic*, premiering on ABC and eventually moving to FOX. As in the prime time animation boom of twenty-nine years before, none of the imitators would replicate the success of the forebearer.

Capitol Critters was Steven Bochco's first series following the failure of his *Cop Rock*. Premiering January 1992, the series centered upon rats, mice, and roaches living in the basement of the White House. Lasting just one month, *Capitol Critters* was quickly exterminated. It was now CBS's turn, premiering *Fish Police* exactly one month after *Capitol Critters* and the day before the latter was canceled. The animated program, in which all the characters were fish detectives battling fish crooks, was based on a comic book series created by Steve Moncuse. Looking at the cast, it seemed obvious the series would be a hit or at least have strong support. Among those supplying their voices were John Ritter, Ed Asner, Jonathan Winters, Buddy Hackett, Robert Guillaume, and Tim Curry. Ultimately, *Fish Police* lasted only three episodes before going belly-up.

Despite the disastrous showing of *Fish Police*, CBS decided to try its hand at prime time animation again the following year with *Family Dog*, a series that viewed family life from the perspective of a pet dog. Produced by Steven Spielberg and Tim Burton, a single episode had been broadcast in 1987 on Spielberg's NBC series *Amazing Stories*. *Family Dog* had drawn some attention, but nothing developed past the initial episode. Like the other series which premiered during this second prime time animation boom, *Family Dog* was put down after only one month on the air (Erickson 1995).

Two years after the initial surge, ABC debuted *The Critic*. Featuring the voice of Jon Lovitz, the series focused on a film critic named Jay Sherman and his program "Coming Attractions." Despite achieving a bit more success than its second-boom contemporaries, the program was used sporadically in ABC's lineup and subsequently garnered low ratings. Upon its cancellation by ABC, the program was picked up by FOX during the spring of 1995. Among the highpoints of its airing on FOX was an early episode in which the Jay Sherman character introduced himself to someone by mentioning that he used to have a show on ABC, at which point he turned to the television audience and dryly remarked, "…for about a week." The program would not last much longer on FOX, and *The Critic* was sent to "that big movie theater in the sky" four months later.

Much like the animated series debuting after the success of *The Flintstones*, which many perceived to be "mere pretenders to the throne" (Erickson 1995: 23), those which followed *The Simpsons* were doomed to failure. However, there are distinctions between the two prime time animation booms. One distinguishing characteristic is that the programs of the first boom lasted at least a season while series associated with the latter lasted only a month. If one thing had changed over the course of thirty years, it was that a program had to be an immediate success or face cancellation. A second feature that distinguishes the two booms is that programs of the 1960s were eventually moved to Saturday mornings. Due in part to high production values and changes in Saturday morning programming, the animated series of the 1990s were canceled outright. Finally, while the original boom in prime time animation lasted only briefly, the second boom continued past its initial surge. As we will discuss, the continued success of *The Simpsons* and its own network's need to distinguish itself from its competitors led to the emergence of additional prime time animated series on FOX. Yet, the question remains as to why prime time animation was able to re-emerge on broadcast television after a twenty-three-year absence.

The resurgence of prime time animation in the 1990s can best be approached by looking at the changing face of animation in general. Saturday morning animation had hit an all-time low by the 1980s, and both CBS and NBC eventually dropped their Saturday morning cartoons in favor of news programs and live-action programs geared toward teenagers. However, recalling the careers of *Quickdraw McGraw* and *Huckleberry Hound* years earlier, many animated programs were once again being syndicated and aired during the late afternoons and early evenings. Much of this trend can be attributed to the need of cable networks to compete with game shows and former prime time programs being shown on many network affiliates.

A second factor in the eventual resurgence of prime time animation was the new generation of network executives. The quality of animation was slowly beginning to improve, and new animated programs were suddenly being produced for times other than Saturday mornings, both of which can explain the eventual re-emergence of animation in prime time. However, the underlying factor in both these trends was the first generation of network executives who grew up watching cartoons. As Matt Groening explains, "Cartoons are invariably a celebration, the colors bright and simple. There's a whole generation of people in power at the networks who were exhilarated by great cartoons as kids and are trying to emulate them" (Kellogg 1992: 8).

Not only were many network executives fans of animation, so were many adult members of the viewing audience. According to Cartoon Network executive vice-president Betty Cohen, "We have the first generation of adults who grew up with television. There's a comfort level in the revisiting of shows, and people want something they can watch with their kids" (Kellogg 1992: 8). Eileen Katz, senior vice-president of programming for Comedy Central, proposed a similar explanation: "the adult audience that was weaned on cartoons and is comfortable with animation is telling us they want a product that just isn't aimed at their kids, and TV is responding" (Richmond 1996: 40).

On the other hand, there was also the fear that the long-held view of animation as children's programming would prevent even the biggest adult animation fans from watching such fare. Preparing for the first season of *The Simpsons*, Matt Groening recalled,

> My big fear was that adults would not give it a chance – that they would think it was just another kiddie show and never tune in. I knew kids would love it. There was nothing else like it on television at the time, and I remember what it was like being a kid and being bored out of my mind watching network TV, except for *Disney's Wonderful World of Color* on Sunday night.
>
> (quoted in Solomon 1997: 22)

As it turned out, more adults would tune in than children, with viewers aged above 18 constituting nearly 60 percent of the audience. It was also discovered that 44 percent of the general cartoon audience were adults (Kellogg 1992). However, there was one additional factor which would lead to the placement of *The Simpsons* and subsequent animated series in prime time.

Along with the enhanced quality of animated programs, the breaking away from Saturday morning programming, and the new generation of network executives and adult viewers, perhaps the most important factor in the resurgence in prime time animation was the introduction of a new network. *The Flintstones* had made it onto the air because ABC wanted to distinguish itself from the other two networks. Accordingly, much of the success of the series was based on its originality. Regardless of similarities between it and *The Honeymooners*, this was an animated series shown during prime time and audiences were drawn to it. Also, being placed opposite *Route 66* and *The Westerner* further highlighted the unique qualities of the program. Audiences had the choice of watching two men driving around in a new Corvette, Brian Keith wandering the Western plains, or an animated modern stone-age family riding around, courtesy of Fred's two feet. If *The Flintstones'* placement among the top twenty programs during its first season was any indication, audiences chose the latter. This type of programming enabled the fledgling network to compete with the established networks, and what ABC had done with prime time animation in the 1960s, FOX was going to do in the 1990s.

Prime time animation and the Fourth Network
– a case study

When FOX came onto the scene in 1986, it developed a very simple programming strategy – to be the alternative to the "Big Three" networks. Jamie Kellner, president of FOX Broadcasting, outlined the most important rule at the upstart network: "If it would work on one of the other networks, we don't want it" (Elder 1992:138). Instead of waging a seemingly unwinnable war for overall viewers, FOX instead targeted the very valuable 18–49-year-old viewers. It was a strategy employed by ABC decades ago, when it first competed with CBS and NBC.

It is not a coincidence that a former programming assistant at ABC in the late 1960s headed FOX Broadcasting's strategy. Barry Diller joined ABC in 1967, quickly climbing the network ladder and overseeing the development of made-for-TV movies and mini series such as the very successful *Roots* (Grover 1994: 36). Diller watched ABC compete with the other two networks by appealing to young, urban audiences. These often are the viewers less set in their ways and more willing to try something new. Diller was hoping this was still true three decades later as FOX tried to carve out its own market.

Television producers viewed FOX as a network that would be willing to experiment. James Brooks, producer of *Taxi* and *Mary Tyler Moore*, came on board after being guaranteed creative license. As Brooks recalled, "Diller told me that I could do anything I wanted, that there'd be no censorship" (Grover 1994: 36). Diller also promised to air whatever show Brooks developed, leading to the premiere of *The Tracey Ullman Show* and the animated shorts that would soon develop into *The Simpsons*.

The Tracey Ullman Show left the network in the spring of 1990, but this did not mean the end of *The Simpsons*, which had already aired as a half-hour prime time Christmas special in December of 1989. Originally, FOX executives were not ready to launch a regularly scheduled prime time animated show. Instead, Diller suggested airing four more *The Simpsons* specials in order to test the waters. After watching the show's first rough-cut, however, Diller quickly changed his mind about playing it safe.

On January 14, 1990, *The Simpsons* began airing on Sunday nights. Within just two months of its premiere, the animated program jumped into the Nielsen's top 15. This success came in spite of FOX's broadcast coverage reaching only four out of five homes in America. FOX's Sunday night lineup in 1990 teamed *The Simpsons* with two other successful programs, *Married…with Children* and *In Living Color*. By summer, as viewers channel surfed during reruns, FOX beat its three competitors on Sunday night (Stauth 1990). By its second season, *The Simpsons* became FOX's top-rated series, and any fears that advertisers would shy away from prime time animation were alleviated as *The Simpsons* commanded $300,000 from national advertisers for a thirty-second spot. FOX affiliates were equally pleased with prices for local spots. As Pat Mullen, station manager for WXMJ in Grand Rapids, related at the time, "I can get $2,000 for 30 seconds on *The Simpsons*. That used to be an entire Sunday night for me" (Grover 1994: 36).

The other three networks quickly took notice of FOX's programming strategies, but the fourth network still had problems of its own. During the same 1989–90 season in which *The Simpsons* became a hit, FOX had nine of the ten lowest ranked shows on network television (Stauth 1990). Also, FOX offered just three nights of programming, adding Monday night in 1989. The fall of 1990 was the year that FOX ambitiously offered five nights of programming, with *The Simpsons* again playing an important role in the strategy.

While with ABC in the 1960s, Diller pitted the tongue-in-cheek western *Maverick* against the highly rated *Ed Sullivan Show*. He was about to do the same thing at FOX, but this time it was *The Simpsons* against the top-rated *The Cosby Show*. In May of 1990, FOX announced that when it expanded programming to include Wednesday and Thursday nights, the dysfunctional Simpson family would go head-to-head with NBC's perfect dad. This was a strike at the establishment, since *The Cosby Show* had finished in first place for four straight years before dropping to second during the 1989–90 season (Zoglin 1990). This move proved FOX to be a serious player.

FOX owner Rupert Murdoch's suggestion to move *The Simpsons* to Thursday nights met with vehement opposition from executive producer James Brooks, but Murdoch and Diller voted their shares and forced the schedule change. Diller admitted he never expected to be able to beat *The Cosby Show*, but hoped to inherit the night when it finally went off the air (Grover 1994). It would take a season-and-a-half, but in March of 1992 *The Simpsons* scored its first weekly win against *The Cosby Show* (Freeman 1992). More important to FOX, however, was the fact that their animated show was reaching its target demographics. It ranked as the number two show with adults aged 18–34 and in the top five with men aged 25–54, the most difficult audience to reach (Freeman 1993).

After some success on Thursday nights, *The Simpsons* moved back to Sunday night, airing after newly acquired coverage of the National Football Conference in an attempt to keep young, male audience members from reaching for the remote. FOX believed a second animated series might perform well if sandwiched between *The Simpsons* and the male-oriented sitcom *Married...with Children*. Thus, in spring 1995, FOX began airing *The Critic*. FOX had picked up the series from ABC, hoping it could perform better on its network but dropping it before the next season. *The Critic* routinely performed a ratings point lower than its lead-in and lead-out programs. That fall *The Critic* was replaced by a live-action sitcom, *Living Single*. FOX was in search of a lead-out program that could re-invigorate its hit animated show, which was beginning to slip in the ratings.

By 1996 *The Simpsons* had dropped far from the Top 15 ratings list it had enjoyed during its first season and was now ranking in the 60s and 70s (Richmond 1996). Plus, the show had never in its history been able to improve on its prior season's ratings (Bierbaum 1998). However, during February of 1997, *The Simpsons* passed a milestone set by *The Flintstones* three decades earlier. Airing its 167th episode, *The Simpsons* became the longest-running prime time animated series ever.

As ratings for *The Simpsons* slowly slipped away, producer Greg Daniels teamed up with *Beavis and Butt-Head* creator Mike Judge to co-produce a new half-hour animated series entitled *King of the Hill*. The program, set in Texas, premiered in 1997, sandwiched between two FOX hits, *The Simpsons* and *The X-Files*. In its first year, the new animated program became a hit, named one of the best shows of 1997 by *Time*, *TV Guide*, and *Entertainment Weekly* ("Voter on the Hill" 1998). It also helped *The Simpsons* post its first increase over previous-season ratings (Bierbaum 1998). On nights when *The Simpsons* was teamed with a live-action comedy, it averaged an 18 share with the key 18–49 adult audience. With *King of the Hill* as its lead-out, *The Simpsons* averaged two shares higher. Further, *King of the Hill* not only outperformed *The Simpsons* in ratings (Nollinger 1997) but also brought more viewers to its own lead-out program, *The X-Files* (Bierbaum 1998).

FOX's four-year development deal with Judge, estimated at $16 million, appeared to have paid off. *King of the Hill* soon became the second-highest rated company program, finishing behind *The X-Files* and in front of *The Simpsons*. FOX also gained a double profit from *King of the Hill*, since Twentieth Century Fox Studios produced the show. Finally, *King of the Hill* also promised to be a syndication success. After the first month of sales during 1998, it had been purchased by affiliates representing 65 percent of the country. Sales at that time were on target to beat *The Simpsons'* off-network syndication price by $1 million per episode (Schlosser 1998).

With the hype following *King of the Hill*'s first season of success, FOX entertainment chief Peter Roth decided to take a scheduling gamble. Since expanding programming nights again in 1993, FOX had never assembled a successful Tuesday night lineup. Roth believed *King of the Hill* could be key in improving the night's poor track record. However, when *King of the Hill* initially made its move, going head-to-head with ABC's popular *Home Improvement*, it lost 50 percent of its 18–49-year-old audience (Freeman 1999). It appeared Roth's gamble was a losing one. Although it was only a short-term loss, Roth would not be around at FOX to be vindicated later in the season.

The beginning of FOX's 1998–99 season was a disappointment. Along with *King of the Hill*'s disappointing ratings, the network's stab at new live-action comedies also failed. By the third week of the season, FOX was down 11 percent in its target 18–49 demos, dropping to fourth place (Stroud 1998). Also, by this time, three of the network's four live-action comedies had been taken off the air. Roth paid the price for this programming disaster, losing his job as entertainment president.

FOX replaced Roth with Doug Herzog, the man responsible for bringing the animated hit *South Park* to Comedy Central. Herzog would oversee a plan to expand the number of animated programs airing on FOX, a plan that already had been in the works when Roth headed the network's entertainment division. FOX was planning to add three new animated series before the end of the television season. Herzog said the move toward more animation was unintentional, but the network was hoping to increase its appeal to younger men, which it had done with *The Simpsons* and *King of the Hill*. Programmer Mike Darnell explained the approach: "They can find live-action sitcoms everywhere else. They don't have to come here for them" (Krantz 1999: 92). Also, viewers had shown they were not going to come to FOX for live-action sitcoms.

When ABC announced the 1998–99 season would be the final one for *Home Improvement*, which had dominated on Tuesday nights, Herzog saw an opportunity to rebuild FOX's weakened schedule. *King of the Hill* would stay in its Tuesday time-slot, but the series would be followed by a new foamation program ('foamation' is not a standard aesthetic term, but is a variant on 'claymation,' used to refer to stop-action animation utilizing foam models versus clay models). *The PJs* (short for "the projects") starred Eddie Murphy as a housing superinten-dent in a primarily black and Latino neighborhood. Murphy teamed with two former *In Living Color* writers, Larry Wilmore and Steve Tompkins, who served as co-executive producers for the show. After a Sunday debut in January, *The PJs* settled into its Tuesday night time-slot and re-invigorated *King of the Hill*'s ratings. By February, *King of the Hill* had recovered most of its pre-schedule change ratings, and *The PJs* was outperforming by 59 percent live-action sitcoms that had previously aired in its time-slot (Freeman 1999).

After ten seasons focusing on *The Simpsons*, creator Matt Groening decided it was time to try for a second hit. FOX executives apparently agreed, ordering thirteen episodes of *Futurama* without even a presentation from Groening (Krantz 1999). The program, set in the next millennium, would feature a pizza delivery boy frozen in time.

Audiences eagerly anticipated the debut of Groening's new creation, evidenced by its record-breaking ratings. On its Sunday night debut in March, the animated series posted the biggest ratings of any show in FOX history premiering after *The Simpsons*. *Futurama* won its time period in most key demographic areas, including adults aged 18–49, adults aged 18–34, adults aged 25–54, men and women aged 18–49 and teens ("Futurama Breaks FOX Rating Records" 1999). After its successful premiere, the animated series was moved to Tuesday nights following *The PJs* to reinforce FOX's "Toon Tuesday" lineup.

For its final animated series debuting during mid-season, FOX looked to an animator they believed could appeal to their target demographics, in large part because he himself was one of them. Twentieth Century Fox TV signed a multi-million dollar deal with 25-year-old Seth MacFarlane for his show *Family Guy*, an animated series featuring the Griffin family. MacFarlane was just one year out of Rhode Island School of Design and was working at Hanna-Barbera when he made the deal with FOX, making him the youngest-ever executive producer (Krantz 1999).

Family Guy enjoyed a special preview following the Super Bowl in January, where it posted FOX's third highest debut ratings ever with a 21 share (Freeman 1999). Perhaps in an attempt to build hype around the new show, FOX waited until April to add *Family Guy* to its regular lineup. It settled into the time-slot after *The Simpsons*, which had been used to launch the network's other new animated series. Its official debut finished a respectable 22nd for the week, solidifying a second-place finish for FOX's 8:00–9:00 p.m. time-slot.

FOX's Tuesday scheduling strategy seemed to work. While FOX's 8:00–10:00 p.m. block finished fourth in overall ratings, it performed well with key demographic groups. According to Nielsen ratings for April 20, 1999, FOX narrowly edged out NBC for second place in adults 18–49, finishing behind ABC. However, it posted wins with adults 18–34, men 18–34 and men 18–49. The other networks were airing reruns, but this reinforced FOX's strategy of consistently rolling out new programming against the competition's weaker rerun programming.

The present and future of prime time animation

As the 1990s came to an end, the future of prime time animation seemed to hang in the balance. The promise of a record number of prime time animated series on the air failed to materialize as new series such as producer Kevin Smith's animated version of the movie *Clerks* aired only for a few weeks on ABC. *Sammy*, comedian David Spade's animated series, and *God, the Devil, and Bob*, featuring the voice of James Garner, both suffered a similar fate on NBC. FOX's Toon Tuesday lineup soon dispersed, with *Futurama*, *King of the Hill*, and *The Simpsons* all airing on Sunday evenings. *The PJs* moved to WB, and *The Family Guy* was removed from the air and placed on what appeared to be a permanent hiatus. At the same time, and despite the cancellation of *Futurama* in 2002, FOX's Sunday lineup continues to provide strong numbers in certain demographics for the now-established network. Airing opposite *60 Minutes* on CBS, the counter-programming strategy seems to continue. New networks such as UPN and WB also appear willing to use prime time animation in an attempt to compete against established networks, airing animated series such as *Baby Blues*, *Dilbert*, and *The Oblongs*.

Certain advantages exist for the current wave of prime time animation that may help prolong the existence of this genre. First, writers have chosen to take the humor of these shows to a new level. While shows such as *Top Cat* and *The Flintstones* "tossed in sophisticated little rewards for parents who paid attention" (Richmond 1996: 40), they were considered kids' shows. Current prime time animated shows are targeted at adults, with adult satire and humor. A second advantage is the ever-growing population that has been raised on cartoons. As discussed earlier, the baby boomer entrance into network executive positions has greatly contributed to this re-emergence of animation. Those same baby boomers are also potential Nielsen ratings numbers.

The number of media outlets for programming has grown significantly since the days of *The Flintstones*. No longer must shows succeed on ABC, NBC or CBS or be removed from television. Also, as audiences become more and more segmented, shows do not have to win in overall ratings to be successful. Instead, they must simply attract an audience that is marketable to advertisers, a strategy FOX has been using since its inception. With a number of broadcast networks and hundreds of cable channels, it is unlikely that prime time animation will disappear altogether. Accordingly, the history of prime time animation on broadcast television networks is far from complete. The next time we join the Simpsons for a stroll through a darkened cemetery, additional tombstones will have been erected, even as new prime time animation continues to emerge.

Bibliography

Bierbaum, T. (1998) "Retro Show Boosts FOX Sunday Schedule," *Variety*, August 31–September 6: 42–3.

Elder, S. (1992) "The FOX Factor," *Vogue*, December:138–42.

Erickson, H. (1995) *Television Cartoon Shows: An Illustrated Encyclopedia 1949–1993*, Jefferson, NC: McFarland & Co.

Freeman, M. (1999) "FOX Eyes Toon Tuesday," *Mediaweek*, 8 February: 9.

—— (1993) "FOX Denies any Simpsons Favoritism," *Broadcasting & Cable*, 22 March: 22–3.

—— (1992) "Stations Abuzz Over Off-FOX Bart," *Broadcasting & Cable*, 16 March:16–17.

"*Futurama* Breaks FOX Rating Records," (1999) *Ultimate TV News Daily*. http://ultimatetv.com/news/TVNewsDaily.html?1444 (accessed 29 March 1999).

Gitlin, T. (1983) *Inside Prime Time*, New York: Pantheon.

Grover, R. (1994) "See the Simpsons Run and Run," *Business Week Industrial Technology Edition*, 7 February: 36.

Grover, R. and S. Duffy (1990). "The Fourth Network?" *Business Week*, 17 September: 114–17.

Hanna, W. (1996) *A Cast of Friends*, Dallas: Taylor.

Javna, J. (1985) *The TV Theme Song Sing-Along Song Book 2*, New York: Hal Leonard/St. Martin's.

Kellogg, M. A. (1992) "The Toon Boom," *TV Guide*, 19 December: 6–9.

Krantz, M. (1999) "FOX Gets Super Animated," *Time*, 11 January: 92–4.

Lenburg, J. (1983) *The Great Cartoon Directors*, Jefferson, NC: McFarland & Co.

Nollinger, M. (1997) "Top Draw-ers," *TV Guide*, 12 July: 28–31.

Richmond, R. (1996) "Toons Tune to Adult Auds," *Variety*, October 7–13: 37, 40.

Schlosser, J. (1998) "King Poised to Beat Bart," *Broadcasting & Cable*, 22 June: 48.

Solomon, C. (1997) "Animation's New Wave," *TV Guide*, 12 July: 20–6.

Stauth, C. (1990) "In the Network Henhouse," *New York Times Magazine*, 15 July: 29.

Stroud, M. (1998) "FOX Hunting for More Viewers," *Broadcasting & Cable*, 19 October: 50.

"Voter on the Hill," (1998) *The Economist*, 25 July: 32.

Waters, H. F. (1990) "Family Feuds," *Newsweek*, 23 April: 58–62.

Zoglin, R. (1990) "The FOX Trots Faster," *Time*, 27 August: 64–6.

Chapter 5

SYNERGY NIRVANA

Brand equity, television animation, and Cartoon Network

Kevin S. Sandler

"'**G**OD' IS DEAD ON PEACOCK WEB." So read *Variety*'s headline in April
2000, a postmortem vigil for the controversial animated comedy, *God,
the Devil, and Bob* (Adalian and Schneider 2000: 72). After coming under fire
from several religious advocacy groups, the mid-season replacement about the
Almighty and the Prince of Darkness competing for control of the world and
the soul of a Detroit autoworker was canceled by NBC after only four airings.
Despite media pronouncements by NBC that *God* was not blasphemous and
that the network had several theological consultants on staff, Jerry Falwell,
the American Family Association, and the Council on American–Islamic
Relations found the show's portrayal of the "supreme being" to be tasteless
and offensive. Such protests adversely affected NBC's ability to sell advertising
time or guarantee clearance to advertisers, as 22 of its 220 affiliates pre-
empted *God*.[1] In its final week, *God* drew a 4.4 rating – under six million
viewers – down from the 14.4 million viewers who watched its premiere. In
fact, the last telecast of the show was the worst performance in the 8:30 p.m.
time period ever for NBC and about one-fifth the size of ABC's competing
Who Wants to Be a Millionaire? ("NBC Cancels *God, the Devil, and Bob*" 2000: D4;
Huff 2000: 122). It was evident that many affiliates felt the show did not serve
the public interest of their communities and that many viewers either found
the show inappropriate for broadcast network television or just not funny
enough.

God, the Devil, and Bob was part of a wider broadcast network renaissance in prime time animation at the end of the 1990s. Except for CBS and PAX, all the other networks dove into animated evening programming in the belief that the live-action sitcom had reached a saturation point, that animation had enormous ancillary potential, and that animation was an opportunity to restore viewers lost to cable and satellite television. Joining *The Simpsons* were *Clerks* (ABC), *Stressed Eric* (NBC), *Sammy* (NBC), *King of the Hill* (FOX), *Futurama* (FOX), *Family Guy* (FOX) *The PJs* (FOX, then WB), *Invasion America* (WB) *Mission Hill* (WB), *Baby Blues* (WB) *Dilbert* (UPN), *Home Movies* (UPN), *Gary and Mike* (UPN), and *The Oblongs* (WB). Many of these shows were more brazen and bolder than most other programs on the networks. It was believed that the animated form, more than live-action, was a safer way to push the envelope of acceptable television fare, a line continually being shattered and redefined by cable television series such as HBO's *Sex and the City* and E!'s *Howard Stern*. As Mike Darnell, FOX executive vice-president of Alternative Series and Specials, said at the time, "With animation you can get away with more. Because of *South Park*, we can go farther than ever before" (quoted in Hontz 1999: 65).

However, viewers failed to "toon" into this new cartoon crop. All of the above shows were canceled except for the FOX programming lineup, but even *The Simpsons* and *King of the Hill* are currently not getting the respectable ratings they once received. The broadcast networks have had no new animated shows on either their fall 2002 or fall 2003 schedules. Could an anonymous NBC executive be right when in 2000 he suggested, "I really don't get the feeling that viewers want to see cartoons on network television" (Braxton 2000: F1+)?

Not exactly. Overexposure and poor quality can partly account for animation's bust in prime time on the broadcast channels. For example, *Sammy*, reportedly, was one of the lowest-scoring pilots in NBC history and got delayed for a year before its premiere in August 2000 (Adalian 2000: 19). Despite its troubled history, *Sammy* still made it onto the air because of the networks' mad rush for animation. It was canceled after only two episodes, drawing a new record low 2.6 rating (3.5 million viewers) for NBC in the same time slot as *God, the Devil, and Bob*.

Thus, ratings do not fully explain the renaissance of animation that concurrently took place on cable television. Animation has thrived and multiplied not just in prime time but in all day-parts on the cable networks. In particular, Nickelodeon, Comedy Central, and Cartoon Network have successfully appropriated the form to help them survive in today's highly competitive, multichannel cable environment. Animation has proven to be a valuable addition to, and an essential component of, their distinct network identities – their brand images.

This chapter will argue that the contemporary practice of "branding" media properties is primarily responsible for the contemporary cartoon landscape, one that has unleashed a flood of animation on prime time cable television. Branding, the business of imbuing a generic product with an idea, attitude, or value, has transformed cable networks into one of the most powerful commodities in today's commercial marketplace. Solid brand equity is a new form of currency (together with ratings) that is exchanged between networks, audiences, and advertisers. The networks' mandate to build and maintain a brand profile, the audiences' thirst for programming tailored to their brand needs, and the advertisers' desires to be affiliated with strong brands with large niche audiences, has turned original animation series into a lucrative and hip programming option on cable.

This moment in American television history – what *The Simpsons*' creator Matt Groening calls the "golden age of animation" (Braxton: F1+) – can be properly understood by examining the relationship between branding and media conglomeration. The desire by conglomerates for synergy (the internally coordinated cross-promotion and cross-selling of its own media properties) has made branding an incredibly efficient and highly lucrative practice. I will first argue that corporate branding enhances consumer choice by catering to audiences not served by broadcast television. I next provide brand profiles of Nickelodeon and Comedy Central that lay the foundation for this chapter's primary case study: Cartoon Network. I then analyze how the manufacturing, marketing, and maintenance of Cartoon Network's brand essence across numerous different sectors of the media has made the network a global force for its corporate parent, AOL Time Warner. I conclude with a cautionary discussion of corporate branding and synergy and the role they play in media censorship.

Branding and cable animation

To fully comprehend the concurrent fall and rise of prime time animation and its relationship to branding, one needs to consider the very similar but quite divergent enterprises of broadcast and cable networks as each one subscribes to a different business model. The major distinction between the two competitors is that broadcast networks do not have the same programming freedom as their cable brethren. Broadcasters must serve the public interest, follow FCC guidelines, and appease hundreds of local affiliates. Program success is primarily measured by ratings, the number of people tuned to a show at a specific time. To attract large, undifferentiated audiences in prime time, which in turn attract powerhouse advertisers such as McDonald's and IBM, broadcasters try to produce entertainment and news programs that alienate as few viewers as possible.

Cable networks, on the other hand, have a different programming audience and bottom line. With cable viewership much smaller than broadcast numbers, networks measure success not only by ratings but by the type of viewer watching their show.[2] Cable networks aim to deliver a densely packaged, but modestly sized target audience to advertisers from Fortune 500 companies to local business owners. These advertisers subsequently are guaranteed an audience demographic predisposed to purchasing or likely to purchase its products. Since the FCC has no jurisdiction over the cable industry, cable networks have greater flexibility than broadcasters in shaping their content to fit the needs and desires of viewers and advertisers.

Like Nike or Pepsi, the brand of a cable network helps to attract specific target audiences, which in turn are sold to advertisers wanting to reach that demographic market. In contrast, broadcast networks, especially the "Big Three" – CBS, NBC, and ABC – are essentially brandless. Despite the broadcast networks' attempts to woo cable viewers back by imbuing specific day-parts with their own singular identity ("Disney's One Saturday Morning" on ABC, or "Must-See TV" Thursday on NBC), the fact remains that most of their shows are interchangeable. NBC's *The West Wing* could easily appear on CBS or ABC if its ratings were good. Even those broadcasters that position themselves as younger and hipper networks than the Big Three – FOX, WB, and UPN – would not hesitate to air *The West Wing*, although it is difficult to imagine this show on Comedy Central or the Sci-Fi Channel. FOX, the Big Three's most formidable competitor, rarely breaks the top thirty of prime time.[3] When an animated show not only has low ratings but also a high production cost and a less-than-desirable audience base for advertisers, why not replace them with new, low-cost, live-action programs, especially if the ratings stay the same?

Many broadcast networks did just that, replacing many animated prime time shows – even before all their episodes aired – with reruns of current network shows. Each cancellation was the result of different factors: the religious playfulness of *God, the Devil, and Bob* was found blasphemous by many of NBC's viewers, advertisers and affiliates; *Clerks* was perhaps too esoteric and obscenity-laden for NBC channel-surfers; *The PJs'* edgy social commentary may have turned off white audiences; and *Dilbert's* satirical look at office politics may have gone over the heads of UPN's younger viewers weaned on that channel's World Wrestling Federation matches. Nevertheless, had these shows premiered on cable, it is quite possible that many would have lasted an entire season or would still be on the air. It is not difficult to imagine *God, the Devil, and Bob* on FOX, *Clerks* on MTV, *The PJs* on BET, or *Dilbert* on Bravo. These animated programs would complement the brands of these cable networks that target smaller, but denser, niche audiences not served by broadcasters.

USA Network's efforts to strengthen its shapeless brand identity in 1996 is a case in point. The network felt that *Duckman*, the Emmy award-winning, but low-rated series about an acerbic, chauvinistic detective and his bumbling family, did not reflect the general-entertainment brand model that USA was trying to build in prime time (Dempsey 1996: 29). Banished to the Saturday midnight slot in its fourth and final year in 1997, *Duckman*, according to USA Network president Rod Perth on the day of its cancellation, had "been a great show for USA, but we need to take our programming in a different direction" (quoted in Richmond 1997: 3). In other words, *Duckman* could not help USA redefine its image as a competitor for adult audiences and advertisers drawn to demographic-compatible networks such as TNT, Lifetime, Family Channel, TBS Superstation, and Nickelodeon's "Nick at Nite" (see Figure 5.1). Instead, it attracted a youthful demographic attuned more to *Beavis and Butt-Head* than *Murder, She Wrote*. Terry Thoren, CEO and president of Klasky Csupo, *Duckman*'s production company, clearly understood the brand mismatch: "We were the right show on the wrong network" (quoted in Gelman 2000: 17). Four years later, *Duckman* found its brand match in reruns on Comedy Central.

Branding, it appears, is especially suitable for cable networks. Programs that may be unsuitable for one network may find their home on another. The adaptability and elasticity that branding provides for established and upstart cable

Figure 5.1 Duckman: a casualty of branding (Courtesy of Klasky Csupo)

networks mirrors the institutional, aesthetic, and audience changes undergone by American mass-market television in the 1980s. Content was no longer enough in a multichannel environment, a network needed a unique presentational mode, what John Thornton Caldwell calls a cool "televisuality," to draw highly discriminating viewers with multitudes of choice to their channel (Caldwell 1995: 4). As television veteran Fred Seibert put it, "with the coming explosion of choice, networks had to become more personalized, and if that personalization could be communicated, the network would become like a special club or a special place for its viewers" (quoted in Parisi 1999: S4).

Early cable networks such as Lifetime, TNT, and most notably, MTV, thus developed televisual techniques that reflected their brands. Although MTV previously used animation in videos and promotional ids to identify its aesthetic and identity, its sister station Nickelodeon became the first cable network to successfully mesh half-hour animated programming with the branding and televisual imperatives of narrowcasting. Nickelodeon borrowed MTV's aesthetics of flashy graphics, hand-held cameras, and logo ubiquity to create a televisuality unique to its brand. Wanting to establish emotional ties with children as MTV had with teenagers and young adults, Nickelodeon developed a brand that "put kids first." Family-friendly wholesomeness, not the kind that talks down to kids but "empowers" them, became the brand experience that Nickelodeon promised its viewers. Its characters were unique and non-violent, and targeted a 50:50 boy–girl audience. Nickelodeon's shows were a far cry from the "program-length commercials" such as *He-Man and the Masters of the Universe* of the early 1980s or the manic repartee of *Steven Spielberg Presents Tiny Toon Adventures* in the late 1980s. In fact, Nickelodeon was established as an alternative to the insipid and violent children's shows on broadcast television enabled by FCC deregulation. Nickelodeon, therefore, is an example in which branding made possible something not served by the other commercial television networks – a pro-social children's environment.[4]

When Nicktoons was launched in August 1991, Nickelodeon established itself as a network willing to use animation to build brand consciousness and brand preference. Its first two forays into original animation, *Rugrats* and *Doug*, clearly captured the "kidcentric" mission of Nickelodeon's live-action hit *Double Dare*. Its third Nicktoon, *The Ren & Stimpy Show*, violated the network's brand image and was cancelled quickly by the network. Despite its brand incongruity however, the licensing success of *Ren & Stimpy* and later *Rugrats* revealed that the profit potential of media properties, especially animated series, can be limitless when in the hands of synergistic media conglomerates. Animation, more than any other genre, could be logically exploited across a variety of retail outlets. Theme parks, toys, clothes, magazines, CDs, and musicals-on-ice are better suited for *Scooby-Doo*, for instance, than *Saved by the Bell*. These ancillary consumer products or experiences, known as brand extensions, are not just sound financial practice but are essential to a brand's survival. According to Naomi Klein, author of the anti-corporate book *No Logo: Taking Aim at the Brand Bullies*: "[it is] about pushing the envelope in sponsorship deals, dreaming up new areas in which to 'extend' the brand, as well as perpetually probing the zeitgeist to ensure that the 'essence' selected for one's brand would resonate karmically with its target market" (Klein 2000: 8). To bypass brand extensions in today's highly competitive market is a risky venture, suggests Nickelodeon chief operating officer Jeffrey Dunn: "One business brands are vulnerable. If you only have one business relationship with your consumers, that relationship isn't as strong as if you have a two-business relationship. Stronger still is if you can associate with your brand in three or four different ways" (quoted in Oppenheimer 1999: S-8).

Rugrats, *SpongeBob SquarePants*, and other Nickelodeon properties, therefore, are not just shows, but an endless parade of brand extensions that allow viewers to fully experience the meaning of the Nickelodeon mythology. There is the film *Rugrats in Paris* (2000), a *SpongeBob SquarePants* line of apparel, and Nickelodeon Studios at Universal Studios theme park in Orlando. These synergistic opportunities are simply the goal of every powerful brand: to develop a relationship with consumers that resonates so completely that they will remain faithful to the brand no matter what. The enormous mass-merchandising and cross-promotional possibilities of branded animated products also enables a company or network to disseminate one's brand meaning in partnership with other similar brands. Sometimes brand partnerships are a disaster (for example, *Batman Returns* and McDonald's),[5] but for the most part, when Nickelodeon aligns itself with Burger King, Target, Nabisco, and Campbell's Soup, among others, each corporation benefits from this cross-fertilization.

The strategy then for youth cable networks such as Nickelodeon is to deliver added value to kids through brand extensions and to responsibly persuade them to prefer their brand over that of someone else. Since broadcast networks only air children's programming in specific day-parts, they can not compete with the totalizing brand experience that cable networks such as Nickelodeon can provide. This explains why kids' programming on basic cable now attracts 74 percent of kid viewing ("Cartoon Network: Ratings and Distribution" 2001). This scenario pertains as well to animated programming targeted to teenage and adult cable viewers. Shows such as the edgy and violent *Spawn* on HBO or the female yuppie-centered *X Chromosome* on Oxygen are not constrained by FCC regulatory policies, syndication rules, "family hours," and other industrial pressures that make it difficult for broadcast networks to successfully tailor their content to niche markets. Language, violence, and sexual content have greater flexibility on cable television since the standards and practices department of cable networks are concerned more with regulating brand consistency for niche audiences, rather than monitoring appropriate discourse for mass audiences as do the broadcast networks.

To be certain, occasional profanity, nudity, and sexual discussion has crept into network and basic cable television over the past decade (ABC's *NYPD Blue*, ESPN's Bobby Knight film *Season on the Brink*, and MTV's *Loveline* and *Undressed* are prime examples). But Comedy Central differentiates its brand from other networks by gleefully dreaming up new ways to push the envelope of ad-supported television. *The Daily Show*, *The Man Show*, and *Strangers with Candy* are the cutting edge of basic cable, part of the reason why Comedy Central, by 2001, had quadrupled its revenues to $300 million in five years (Lawry 2001: 94). Its brand, states Bill Hilary, executive vice-president and general manager, "has always been about asking questions. It's been about challenging people's perceptions" (Huff 2001: 130). To become the lightning rod for attention and controversy that has become the network's brand philosophy, Comedy Central develops comedy programming involving satire, raunchiness, and shock value. Complementing this attitude is a hip televisual look attractive to their 18–49, primarily male, target audience.

Mature, original series such as *Dr. Katz: Professional Therapist*, *Bob and Margaret*, and *TV Funhouse*, and older syndicated castoffs such as *The Tick*, *Duckman*, and *The Critic*, comprise Comedy Central's animated lineup in Fall 2002. But primarily responsible for the network's success is *South Park*, an unexpected hit for the network in 1997 and now (together with *The Daily Show*) emblematic of Comedy's Central's brand profile. "Our whole deal is to poke fun at everything and everybody," says *South Park* co-creator Matt Stone, a mission that Comedy Central certainly embraces (quoted in Morrow 2000: Y10). Controversial plot lines (incest, bestiality, Christmas poo) centering on the scatologically-minded and obscenity-spouting grade-school kids Stan, Eric, Kyle, and Kenny, perhaps makes *South Park* the most iconoclastic show on the air. For example, in June 2001, the characters of *South Park* uttered the word "shit" 162 times. Before that episode, "shit," like most other profanity on the show, had been bleeped out except for its first two letters. Such insubordination, impossible (and unforgivable) for broadcast networks, is the commodity that Comedy Central sells to viewers.

Indeed, Comedy's Central risqué image does not attract as many brand extensions as Nickelodeon does in the US. *South Park* has become a stand-alone merchandising bonanza stateside with T-shirts, video games, and collectible figures, but in Europe it has attracted blue-chip licensees like Rossignol, Heinz, and Kimberly-Clark. Also successfully penetrating the domestic and global markets is Cartoon Network, which now broadcasts to 145 countries around the world. Its brand essence occupies the space between Nickelodeon and Comedy Central – one that provides yet another alternative programming sensibility on cable television.

The branding of Cartoon Network

To survive in today's multichannel terrain, cable networks cannot simply provide programming in a unilateral manner. They need to present programs in a value-added environment that is an attractive destination for viewers to hang out and revisit. How consumers feel about a certain network has profound implications for attracting advertisers and for developing brand extensions, because the ideas, feelings, and attitudes embodied by a network's brand image can translate into cold, hard equity – and lots of it. In a market flooded with animated programs – many of them mass-produced and indistinguishable from one another – cable networks must invest their cartoons with the unique identity they have already forged with their live-action series. Nickelodeon's animated shows helped to build their brand recognition of "Putting Kids First." Comedy Central's iconoclastic brand attitude for adults is noticeable in their animated series. But what about Cartoon Network, whose very name leaves no room for branding error when it comes to animation?

Fortunately for Cartoon Network, almost every original animated show greenlighted in a given year by the network brass has attracted a large, devoted audience.[6] Since Cartoon Network's launch in 1992, its popularity has led to record-setting ratings and delivery growth; as of August 2002, it had achieved cable penetration of 80.2 million US homes and 145 countries around the world. During this time, Cartoon Network has remained one of ad-supported cable's highest-rated networks, remaining in the top five for total day ratings seven years running and frequently appearing in the top three for prime time ratings. Although its entire twenty-four schedule is filled entirely with "cartoons," Cartoon Network appeals to people of all ages: 68 percent of its audience comprises children and teens (ages 2–17) and 32 percent of the audience are adults (ages 18+) ("Cartoon Network: Original Production Fact Sheet" 2001). While kids aged 6–11 remain the network's core audience, Cartoon Network continues to shape its brand to reflect its mass appeal.

Like Nickelodeon and Comedy Central, Cartoon Network prides itself on vision and creativity, exemplified by original characters, unique story lines, and brazen animation style. But even though Nickelodeon is Cartoon Network's prime competitor, their brands could not be any more different. Joe Uva, president of Turner Entertainment Sales & Marketing, puts it this way: "If Nickelodeon is about empowering kids, Cartoon Network is about the freedom to be wacky and zany" (quoted in Ross 1998: S-1, S-16). Unlike Nickelodeon, Cartoon Network neither attempts to make an emotional connection with kids' lives nor targets a specific age demographic. On the contrary, it is a place for kids of all ages, preferring to be irreverent and prankish, a Comedy Central-lite. Cartoon Network is like a wise guy that isn't mean, says former president Betty Cohen, kind of like Bugs Bunny ("The Queen of Cartoons" 1998: n.p.). The sassy humor and intergenerational appeal of Bugs perfectly captures the brand sensibility of the network, a mindlessly funny, oftentimes ironic, and playfully violent approach to animation. It is an eternally optimistic, all-ages network, which in the words of Linda Simensky, Cartoon Network's vice-president of original animation, reminds "adults, teenage girls – really everybody – that it's OK to watch cartoons" (Wilson 1999: 30).

"That something fun is always happening on Cartoon Network" has turned the station into the ninth highest-rated brand (out of 188) in kids' awareness (Craig McAnsh quoted in Wax 1997: 44). Once a member of Turner Networks and now a subsidiary of AOL Time Warner, Cartoon Network advertises itself as the "World Cartoon Headquarters," laying claim to the largest collection of animated programming. Its 8,500+ titles include the libraries of the theatrically released shorts of Warner Brothers (*Bugs Bunny*, *Daffy Duck*) and MGM (*Tom and Jerry*), and the television series from Hanna-Barbera (*The Flintstones*, *Scooby-Doo, Where are You?*). Cartoon Network also holds the rights to more recent television fare first shown on the syndicated broadcast franchise WB Kids (*Batman: The Animated Series*) as well as licensing many anime action series from Japan (*Dragonball Z*, *Gundam Wing*). Even so, almost 50 percent of Cartoon Network's schedule is devoted to their fourteen original series – its "Cartoon Cartoons."[7]

The Cartoon Cartoons are the principal conveyers of the network's demographic, attitude, and televisuality. "Our new cartoons were not developed for Saturday morning," says Cohen. "[P]rogrammers were thinking about 8 o'clock at night. And so we are looking to do things that have the same dual appeal for today's kids and their parents that *Rocky and Bullwinkle* had for me when I was watching with my dad" (quoted in "The Queen of Cartoons" 1998). Not as bawdy as Comedy Central, and less socially responsible than Nickelodeon, Cartoon Network's original fare like *Cow and Chicken* and *Courage the Cowardly Dog*, overall, is whimsically rebellious, undercutting seriousness at every turn. This approach is fully integrated into the highly exaggerated and self-conscious style of the Cartoon Cartoons themselves, each one visually bold and energetic in its own right: the stylized UPA meets Hanna-Barbera nature of *Dexter's Laboratory*, the anime and techno-influenced *The Powerpuff Girls*, the ever-changing surreal landscapes of *Samurai Jack*. And then there is the combination live-action/animation *Space Ghost Coast to Coast*, a droll parody of late-night talk shows airing at the 11:00 p.m. hour. The show features the late 1960s Hanna-Barbera superhero and a host of celebrity guests such as Charlton Heston, Jim Carrey, and Metallica. In this clever postmodern take, Space Ghost talks to live-action guests on Earth via a television monitor from his home world, Ghost Planet. Imprisoned on Ghost Planet are all his arch enemies from the original series, with two of them, Zorak and Moltar, serving as his band leader and show director, respectively. In fact, Hervé Villechaize (Tattoo from the TV show *Fantasy*

Island) was signed to be Space Ghost's sidekick before he committed suicide shortly after the show was announced in 1993 (Reboy 1995: 27).

Recontextualizing classic animated icons such as Space Ghost is the method by which Cartoon Network repackages its vast cartoon library to fall in line with the network's brand identity and to appeal to adult viewers. While the original Space Ghost and other older animated characters such as Porky Pig and The Jetsons may appear fresh and novel to kids, most adult fans of animation have seen these cartoons ad nauseam. There are only so many times that a grown-up can watch *Scooby-Doo*. But when Cartoon Network places the Great Dane in a new ironic and self-referential context, the classic character carries new meaning and an alternative, hip, glossy sheen (see Figure 5.2).

Take, for example, the numerous Scooby-Doo promotional interstitials or bumpers airing between the programs. There was "Behind the Scenes of Scooby-Doo" – reminiscences by the Scooby gang on their crime-fighting career. And "The Scooby-Doo Project" – a parody of *The Blair Witch Project* where the sleuths get lost in the woods and Shaggy, in one installment, weeps "I'm so hungry" in extreme close-up. Or how about the cross-generic pairing of Scooby-Doo in an episode of *Johnny Bravo* or even the *Speed Racer* parody in *Dexter's Laboratory*? Recontextualization is also visible in Cartoon Network's stunt programming, original specials featuring its library of characters. For every stunt featuring its Cartoon Cartoon characters (*The Powerpuff Girls'* "Papathon" on Father's Day), Cartoon Network also repackages its Warner Brothers, MGM, and Hanna-Barbera properties. These include "June Bugs" – an annual weekend marathon of Bugs Bunny cartoons; "Super Bowl Weekend Marathon" – a showdown between different arch enemies each year (Tom and Jerry, Sylvester and Tweety, Wile E. Coyote and Roadrunner) using old theatrical footage and hosted by football announcers John Madden and Pat Summerall; and the "13th Annual Fancy Anvil Awards Show Program Special," a parody of the Oscar ceremony featuring Scooby-Doo winning a lifetime achievement award.

Figure 5.2 Scooby-Doo: Cartoon Network's most ubiquitous brand extension (Courtesy of Cartoon Network)

All of these interstitials and stunts furnish vintage characters with an attitude they were never meant to have in order to build brand preference and strengthen Cartoon Network's brand identity. Rarely has Cartoon Network made an error in recontextualizing a classic animated star. Ironically, the biggest blunder occurred in 1999 and was created by the same man as Nickelodeon's *Ren & Stimpy*: John Kricfalusi. In "A Day in the Life of Ranger Smith" and "Boo Boo Runs Wild," Kricfalusi violated Cartoon Network's prescriptions and formula for brand recontextualization.[8] He showed neither reverence nor respect for Hanna-Barbera's *Yogi Bear* series. In place of celebratory homage, there is sacrilegious caricature. For example, "Boo Boo Runs Wild" is not about Ranger Smith thwarting the machinations of Yogi to steal picnic baskets or escaping from Jellystone Park. Instead, in what Kricfalusi calls "a fresh look at their original motivation" (quoted in Lucas 1999: 56), Boo Boo revolts against the oppressions of the forest by reverting back to his primal nature. Yogi brings back Boo Boo from the brink of insanity by the end of the cartoon but not until the following things have happened: Boo Boo turns rabid by moaning and drooling; Boo Boo and Yogi's girlfriend, Cindy, have sexual intercourse in some bushes; Ranger Smith tries to murder Boo Boo; and Ranger Smith makes a homosexual pass at Yogi. The indecent, tasteless, and sexual nature of these events may be appropriate comedy material for Comedy Central, but they are incongruous for Cartoon Network and incompatible with its brand image. In the end, Cartoon Network aired these Ranger Smith shorts only a few times; their odd time-length and low ratings make them even less likely to show again. In disavowing the Ranger Smith shorts, Cartoon Network returned to making cartoons that were irreverent without being vulgar.

When not showing stunts, Cartoon Network builds further brand loyalty by programming viewing blocks of cartoons arranged around a particular theme. These franchises, for the most part, are age-sensitive, fit to target a specific demographic segment of Cartoon Network's all-ages audience at different times of the day. *Small World* is an assortment of pro-social cartoons from around the world that targets preschoolers in the early morning hours. Cartoon Network's multiple-hour anime block, "Toonami", featuring *Dragonball Z*, *Gundam Wing* and others, plays after school to "tweens" (9–12 year-olds) and teenagers. *The Tex Avery Show*, *The Chuck Jones Show*, and *The Bob Clampett Show* play in the later prime time hours to teenagers and adults. In September 2001, Cartoon Network created a new franchise, "Adult Swim", to run twice a week from 10:00 p.m. to 1:00 a.m. EST. Featuring a rotating lineup of mature series such as *Space Ghost Coast to Coast*, *The Brak Show*, and the ex-UPN show, *Home Movies*, Adult Swim joins other around-midnight franchises such as *O Canada* (National Film Board of Canada animation), *Late Night in Black and White* (classic theatrical cartoons before color), and *Toonheads* (classic theatrical cartoons related by a single theme) aimed at adults aged 18–34. They all carry a TV-PG or TV-14 rating rather than the TV-G or TV-Y7 rating of Cartoon Network's all-ages programming.

However, programming is only the first step on the lucrative journey to brand consciousness for Cartoon Network. Disseminating one's brand by whatever means necessary is vital to brand survival, as less brand extensions mean less brand promotions which means less brand awareness. Cartoon Network is an industry leader in seeking out manufacturers and retailers, establishing sales partnerships, and developing consumer outreach events to infuse their brand with greater meaning beyond the television screen, which, of course, lines the pocketbooks of AOL Time Warner's shareholders. As Steve Heyer, former president and chief operating office of Turner Broadcasting states: "[Cartoon Network is] not just a network, it's become a brand. And it's not just a brand, it's a business with unlimited opportunities for brand extensions" (quoted in Ross 1998: S-16). Child, teenage, and adult viewers can fully experience the Cartoon Network brand in several, diverse cultural spaces, selecting those that match their consumer interests, lifestyles, and values.

In terms of merchandising, Cartoon Network usually allows a show to develop a following before licensing its characters to other companies. Such was the case with *The Powerpuff Girls*, a merchandising smash a year after its premiere since it attracts three distinct demographics – girls, boys, and adults (Flaherty 2000: 23). Whether one of Cartoon Network's newest series, *Samurai Jack*, will also capture this audience is too early to call, but the network broke protocol by licensing the property in the form of action figures, home video, and gaming even before the series' premiere (Burgess 2001: 21). These and other Cartoon Network properties are also branded with companies such as Subway, Radio Shack, and Kraft Foods, the latter a promotional partner in Cartoon Campaign 2000, an election to determine which cartoon character would serve as President (Scooby-Doo eventually won). To complement Cartoon Network's own on-air marketing, Kraft had widespread in-store and on-package advertising of Cartoon Network products targeted at kids. Other off-air brand extensions include a co-sponsorship with Discovery Zone of Dexter's Duplication Summer in 1998. Kids could try to secure the grand prize – the winner's bedroom converted into a Dexter-looking laboratory – by calling a 1-800 number scrolled across the television screen during a *Dexter's* episode, or by visiting one of twenty-five cities hosting the traveling "Dexter's Duplication Machine." Adults are not left out of Cartoon Network's joint ventures either. The lucky winner of the 1997 Space Ghost Haiku Contest (supported off-channel by Tower Records) earned a guest appearance on a special New Year's Eve episode of *Space Ghost Coast to Coast* ("Cartoon Network: Marketing/On-Air" 2001).

Brand building through external cross-promotions with Tower Records or Kraft Foods may indeed build brand preference for Cartoon Network. Yet, strong brands such as Cartoon Network are built by even stronger synergies with its corporate parent. While Nickelodeon is owned by Viacom, which also owns Paramount Pictures, Blockbuster Video, and CBS Television, Cartoon Network is a subsidiary of AOL Time Warner, which itself has vast holdings. In her statement about Cartoon Network's product development and marketing, Betty Cohen echoes the symbiotic relationship between branding and synergy: "It's important to Time Warner [now AOL Time Warner], as a content company, that the characters we create are ones we own for the channels of exploitation and distribution that Time Warner has. So it's incumbent upon us to develop characters that resonate now and in the future, characters that have the same resonance of Tom and Jerry or Bugs Bunny or Fred Flintstone. They all speak to people in our culture, and then all the commercial aspects follow" (Ross 1998: S-16).

The branded loop that circulates through AOL Time Warner's Cartoon Network reveals what Naomi Klein identifies as the blurring of sectors and industries, entertainment and retail, in the contemporary mediascape (Klein 2000: 148). The synergy available to Cartoon Network's series is endless. AOL Time Warner can guarantee distribution of Cartoon Network on all its Time Warner Cable systems. Turner Broadcasting Networks (a division of the conglomerate that oversees TBS Superstation, TNT, the WB, WB Kids, CNN, and Cartoon Network's new sister station for 1960s and 1970s cartoons, Boomerang) can cross-promote Cartoon Network shows, do feature stories on them, or swap programming among its networks. For instance, in an attempt to emulate Nickelodeon's success on CBS Saturday Morning, Cartoon Network and WB Kids are sampling each other's shows – what is known as "repurposing" – in order to cultivate what is largely an unduplicated audience and untapped cross-promotional source (Romano 2001). *Samurai Jack* (see Figure 5.3) has appeared on WB Kids and *Cardcaptors* has shown on Cartoon Network. The Time, Inc. publishing empire – over 64 magazines with a total of 268 million readers – can give favorable coverage and advertising space to *Samurai Jack* in the pages of *Time*, *Entertainment Weekly*, or *Sports Illustrated for Kids*. And Cartoon Network enlisted corporate sibling America Online for the *Samurai Jack* marketing campaign. AOL carried exclusive *Samurai Jack* content, an online sweepstakes, and tune-in banner ads on various AOL screens (Hogan 2001: 78). Perhaps *Samurai Jack* may one day be as popular as *The Powerpuff Girls* and its host of internal brand extensions. VHS tapes and DVDs are distributed through Warner Home Video, and CDs and cassette tapes are distributed by WEA/Rhino, all of them once available from the now-closed Warner Brothers Studio Stores. There is a DC Comics *Powerpuff Girls* comic book, a *Powerpuff Girls* movie scheduled for summer 2002 from Warner Brothers (which surely will appear later on HBO or Cinemax), and perhaps there may be a book tie-in with Time Warner Trade Publishing's Warner Books line.

Figure 5.3 Synergy at work: Samurai Jack (Courtesy of Cartoon Network)

The newest multimedia platform for AOL Time Warner companies, and certainly the channel that promises the most interactive brand experience, is of course the Internet (Klein 2000: 161). Since its launch in July 1998, CartoonNetwork.com has become the second most-visited site by kids (aged 2–17) on the Web with 2.5 million unique users a month in February 2001, trailing only Disney Online (Swanson 2001). It also has strong appeal among adults, who constitute 55 percent of users ("Jim Samples Named" 2001). Even though CartoonNetwork.com has unlimited on-air support from Cartoon Network to attract these "netizens," it does not simply act as a promotional tool for network programming. The site's creative integration of on-air programming with online enhancements demonstrates that Web content can produce editorial content consistent with Cartoon Network's brand philosophy.

Most Cartoon Network series, for instance, have their own personal Web sites within the CartoonNetwork.com kingdom. They feature an assortment of model sheets, screen savers, sound bites, video clips, pencil tests, music, and other raw elements from Cartoon Network and Boomerang series. Scooby-Doo's Web site contains a sound clip of Joe Barbera discussing the premise of *Scooby-Doo, Where are You?*, some character and storyboard art of Scooby-Doo, interactive games such as "Scooby Snapshot" and "Scrappy Stinks," and interactive cartoons such as "The Great Ghost Round Up." This latter Scooby-Doo brand extension constitutes part of "Web Premiere Toons," a collection of Internet-only animated shorts featuring Cartoon Network's classic series, Cartoon Cartoon characters, and Web originals. One can see *The Matrix*-inspired, re-interpretation of Hong Kong Phooey, of Ed, Edd, and Eddy in "Which Edd Rules?" or virtual one-shots such as *Hermann and Vermin*. There are also Total Immersion cartoons where television and online content are offered as a simultaneous, multi-tasking experience. In addition to content, CartoonNetwork.com offers destinations such as Cartoon Orbit, an online trading community (whose special codes are only available if one subscribes to the ToonFlash e-mail newsletter) and the Cartoon Network store, where visitors can purchase T-shirts, collectibles, and other goodies. Each of these environments is surrounded by sponsorships (Intel Play, Nintendo, Lego, and Kellogg's) and cross-promotions with AOL Time Warner's other properties. Products such as Warner Brothers' *Harry Potter* Trading Card Game, WEA's (Warner/Elecktra/Atlantic) Eden's Crush and Sugar Ray animated music videos, and Scooby-Doo Live on Stage banners appear repeatedly in banners, pop-up windows, and other links. No matter the content or advertising, CartoonNetwork.com reinforces the brand vision of its cable sister by presenting all its virtual material in the same hip and funny context for animation fans of all ages.

Conclusion: branding and censorship

Cartoon Network is not just a domestic channel with a Web component; it is a dominant global entity that adapts its programming strategies and brand marketing for all of its international networks. Cartoon Network India, for example, broadcasts indigenous-language animated programming, develops consumer outreach events such as Toon cricket matches (Scooby-Doo-led The Snackers versus the Dexter-led The Inventors), and maintains a CartoonNetworkIndia.com Web site. The checkerboard logo of Cartoon Network is an international language now recognized and understood around the world. The rise of global brand marketing (Cartoon Network) alongside the synergy of multinational media conglomerates (AOL Time Warner) means that worldwide consumer experience and media culture in the future will primarily revolve around a collection of "brand-extensions-in-waiting" (Klein 2000: 30).

This current "golden age of animation" took hold in the 1990s when media conglomerates realized that cable networks were a series of brand-extensions-in-waiting for their other properties that also had the potential to become brands themselves. With a richer pool of talent, wider access to computer tools, and greater audience demand for animation, cable networks quickly seized the opportunity to integrate the form into their brand identity. The imperative that an animated series must first exist as a brand concept and then as a creator-driven work has affected neither the quality nor the integrity of television animation. There is greater cultural diversity and programming choice than ever before; branding, synergy, and myriad channel space have made this possible.

However, the achievement of what Klein pejoratively calls "synergy nirvana" – a magical place where all of the conglomerate's subsidiaries are churning out related versions of the same product – does not come without a price (2000: 160–61). A branded economy has the power to erase the history of popular culture in the name of corporate enterprise. The machiavellians at the Walt Disney Company cunningly understood – decades before multinational corporations controlled the media universe and they themselves merged with ABC – the value and perils of brand equity. The financial success of Disney's theatrical films, television shows, theme parks, and other consumer products was inherently linked to a consistent brand image: that of wholesome family entertainment. Disney was also extremely aware that its brand iconography and mythology must change with time, continually reworked in response to new political, cultural, and social developments. Its animated heroines, from *Cinderella* (1950) to *Pocahontas* (1995), reflect clearly Western transformations in femininity and patriarchy. But these modifications in storytelling and characterization occurred alongside a contraction of past representations no longer compatible with Disney's brand status. Academy-award winning World War II shorts (*Der Fuhrer's Face*, 1941), racially problematic films (*Song of the South*, 1946), and moments of cigarette smoking (Pecos Bill in *Melody Time*, 1948) have been completely removed from cultural circulation. The public cannot view these texts on video, on television, or in archives. These past indiscretions by Disney the production company are now in brand violation of Disney the media conglomerate and therefore must be discursively and physically eliminated.[9]

Facing the same brand challenges – or demolitions – is AOL Time Warner. While not as egregious as Disney in censoring its past, AOL Time Warner has maintained the same pre-merger policies of Time Warner and Turner by editing for Cartoon Network most instances of gunplay, alcohol ingestion, Cowboy and Indian gags, and racist humor from Warner Brothers theatrical cartoons dating from the 1930s to the 1960s. Unedited versions of most of these cartoons had been available on video and laser disc from Time Warner prior to its merger with America Online. And at one time they also could be seen in syndication on Nickelodeon, TNT, or TBS, the three major broadcast networks, and various UHF stations including those airing WB Kids. But due to the economies afforded by branding and synergy, the Warner Brothers shorts are now all under one roof at Cartoon Network – many still in edited form – while, for reasons unexplained, AOL Time Warner has limited the release of the cartoons on video. Cartoon Network also selectively censored "The 50 Greatest Cartoons," a 1998 stunt program based on Jerry Beck's book of the same name.[10] Despite being selected by a poll of animation professionals and historians, the racist yet aesthetically fascinating *Coal Black and the Sebben Dwarfs* (1943) was omitted from the special as well as the violent conclusions to *The Scarlet Pumpernickel* (1950) and *Feed the Kitty* (1952). [11]

The interconnection between branding, synergy, and censorship on Cartoon Network was evident in the following statement made by Laurie Goldberg, the network's vice-president of public relations: "We're the leader in animation, but we're also one of the top-rated general entertainment networks. There are certain responsibilities that come with that." These words accompanied the controversy surrounding the 2001 "June Bugs" marathon, the forty-nine hour "rabbitfest" that was to originally feature every Bugs Bunny cartoon in chronological order. A month before the retrospective, Cartoon Network executives clashed with AOL Time Warner over twelve cartoons containing racial stereotyping of African- and Native-Americans. Cartoon Network was aware of the delicate nature of these cartoons. They had planned to show them out of sequence at 3:00 a.m. and to run a disclaimer at the bottom of the screen that read: "Cartoon Network does not endorse the use of racial slurs. These vintage cartoons are presented as representative of the time in which they were created and are presented for their historical value" (King 2001: 12). For Cartoon Network, "June Bugs" was an unprecedented and unparalleled stunt in television history that would be a big ratings grabber and plug some of the gaps in cartoon history for animation fans that had never seen any of these Bugs Bunny cartoons. For AOL Time Warner, on the other hand, "June Bugs" was a potential minefield that could lead to claims of corporate insensitivity and brand misrecognition by certain viewers. In the end, "June Bugs" was twelve rabbits less than a full bushel; Cartoon Network succumbed to the wishes of AOL Time Warner, to what in all likelihood, was a corporate ultimatum. In defense of the decision, former Cartoon Network president Betty Cohen said at the time, "I don't like sweeping things under the rug. I wanted to honor the intense interest that animation fans have for us, but I can't deny we're a mass medium" (quoted in Beatty 2000: A6).

It is unclear in these politically correct times whether Cartoon Network would have aired the notorious Bugs Bunny cartoons had it *not* been a subsidiary of a media conglomerate. What is evident is that branding will always cater to the needs of the corporation rather than the desires of its consumers. Even so, AOL Time Warner could not ignore a possible backlash and brand injury of Cartoon Network by its large adult fan base. Almost immediately after the "June Bugs" marathon, Cartoon Network made a "compromise" with its fans: the twelve Bugs Bunny cartoons would be shown in two upcoming documentaries in the long-running *Toonheads* franchise. This decision may have been a wise one, as animation commentator Martin Goodman noted, since "mixing controversial toons in with the general merriment [of June Bugs] was not the appropriate context" (Goodman 2001). The first special, "The Wartime Cartoons," showed on August 1, 2001 at 10:00 p.m. EST and contained *Herr Meets Hare* (1945) in its entirety and clips from *Bugs Bunny Nips the Nips* (1943). Mike Lazzo, senior vice-president of programming and production at Cartoon Network, said, "We always wanted to do things like this. But we didn't have much money to spend on specific demographic groups such as adult viewers and cartoon buffs. Now at almost 10 years old, we have more flexibility. We can address these audiences" (quoted in Rose 2001: 24). The second special, "The Twelve Missing Hares," has yet to air as of November 2002.

While the one-hour running time of "The Twelve Missing Hares" means that few, if any, of the twelve Bugs Bunny cartoons will be shown in their entirety, AOL Time Warner (via Cartoon Network) has demonstrated a willingness to confront and unveil the ignoble history of some of its animated properties, albeit in recontextualized and edited form. The same cannot be said for its MGM cartoons, and certainly not for most of Disney's output. While the present may only offer consumers a selective choice of cartoons past, it is not impossible to believe that as audiences become more fragmented in the new millennium and the cable landscape becomes even more cluttered with the arrival of broadband, all this will soon change for the better. Right now Boomerang plays only recycled material from Cartoon Network. But if video-on-demand (instant pay-per-view delivery) becomes a reality, as many industry pundits believe it will, the media giants will have enough available channel space to sell their entire animation libraries. For a price, viewers could purchase any Chuck Jones cartoon or even the "The Twelve Missing Hares." And without reliance on advertising support for these channels, AOL Time Warner will find another retail outlet for its products minus the branding imperative. Technology may be animation history's saving grace in this age of media conglomeration. The bottom line of capitalism will still remain shareholder profit, but sometimes – just sometimes – it could work on behalf of the fan.

Notes

1 Most of these affiliates were located in the heartland of the US. They included Boise, Idaho; Mobile, Alabama; Green Bay, Wisconsin; Paducah, Kentucky; Huntsville, Alabama; Joplin, Missouri; and several small cities in Texas. NBC, in fact, did give the show for free to rival stations in these cities' areas to make good on its national spots.

2 Obviously, this does not apply to pay-networks such as HBO or Showtime, who, in lieu of commercials, make their money by charging subscribers a monthly fee.

3 In terms of number of viewers in the 2001–2 season, *The Simpsons*, *Malcolm in the Middle*, and *Boston Public* were the FOX shows that occasionally appeared in the top 30 of Nielsen ratings for prime time.

4 Pro-social refers to actions that society deems appropriate for children. Pro-social content teaches actions that support interpersonal skills, such as helping others, negotiation, cooperation, sharing, and tolerance. Pro-social content also teaches children how to feel good about themselves, by teaching perseverance, honor, pride, and self-esteem.

5 Many parents, organizations, and media critics found the violent and sadistic PG-13 rated *Batman Returns* an inappropriate commercial tie-in for the family-oriented McDonald's restaurant chain (see Busch 1992; Peterson 1992: D1).

6 The two shows that failed to attract a large, all-ages audiences were *Mike, Lu, and Og* and *Sheep in the Big City*. They air infrequently now, and usually outside of prime time.

7 Although *The Real Adventures of Jonny Quest* is a contemporary series, it was produced by Hanna-Barbera prior to the creation of Cartoon Network.

8 For a more celebratory discussion of the cartoon, consult Amidi (1999).

9 For further discussion of the politics of representation in Walt Disney and Warner Brothers animation, see my article entitled "Introduction: Looney Tunes and Merry Metonyms," in *Reading the Rabbit*, 1–28.

10 Some of the cartoons in Beck's book were replaced by then Time Warner-owned properties since the corporation did not get the rights to air any of the Disney, UPA, or Fleischer cartoons (see Beck 1994; http://home.nc.rr.com/tuco/looney/50greatest.html).

11 *Coal Black and the Sebben Dwarfs* has not been shown on television for years or ever been available on video except in pirated form at www.coolstuffvideos.com and other e-stores.

Bibliography

Adalian, J. (2000) "NBC Pulls Plug on Spade's 'Sammy'," *Daily Variety*, 17 August: 19.

Adalian, J. and M. Schneider (2000) "'God' is Dead on Peacock Web," *Variety*, April 3–9: 72.

Amidi, Amid (1999) "Loose Floppy Dog Lips and Roughed Up Rangers," *Animation Blast*, 4: 3–7. Also available at the Animation World Network (www.awn.com)

Beatty, S. (2000) "Bunny in Blackface: Why Cartoon Network Won't Run 12 Bugs Pix," *Wall Street Journal*, 4 May: A6

Beck, J. (1994) *The 50 Greatest Cartoons*, Atlanta: Turner Publishing.

Braxton, G. (2000) "The Life Expectancy of Toons," *Los Angeles Times*, 22 April: F11.

—— (1999) "The Tube Turns Into 'Toon Town'," *Los Angeles Times*, 27 March: F11.

Burgess, A. (2001) "Cartoon Gives *Samurai Jack* a Sharp Merch Edge," *KidScreen*, 1 August: 21.

Busch, A. (1992) "Parents' 'Bat' Wrath May Change McDonald's Policy," *The Hollywood Reporter*, 2 July.

Caldwell, J. T. (1995) *Televisuality: Style, Crisis, and Authority in American Television*, New Brunswick, NJ: Rutgers University Press.

"Cartoon Network: Marketing/On-Air," (2001) Cartoon Network Public Relations, May.

"Cartoon Network: Original Production Fact Sheet," (2001) Cartoon Network Public Relations, May.

"Cartoon Network: Ratings and Distribution," (2001) Cartoon Network Public Relations, May.

Dempsey, J. (1996) "USA Searches for Brand," *Variety*, April 8–14: 29.

Flaherty, M. (2000) "Girl Power," *Entertainment Weekly*, 16 June: 23.

Gelman, M. (2000) "Prime-time Animation: The Ratings," *Animation Magazine*, April: 17.

Goodman, M. (2001) "June Bugged: Cartoon Network's Controversy," *Animation World Magazine*, July, www.awn.com (accessed 13 November 2002).

Hogan, M. (2001) "AOL Backs Cartoon's 'Samurai Jack' Premiere," *Multichannel News*, 23 July: 78.

Hontz, J. (2001) "'South Park's' Big Doo S-word Flies 162 Times," *Daily News* (New York), 22 June: 130.

—— (1999) "Tide of Toons Tips Sitcoms," *Variety*, March 1–7: 65.

Huff, R. (2000) "'God' is Dead as NBC Drops Series," *Daily News* (New York), 31 March: 122.

"Jim Samples Named Executive Vice President and General Manager of Cartoon Network World-wide," (2001) *Business Wire*, 22 August.

King, S. (2001) "Q & A; Bugs Bunny Takes Control of the Cartoon Network," *Los Angeles Times*, 1 June: 12.

Klein, N. (2000) *No Logo: Taking Aim at the Brand Bullies*, Toronto: Knopf Canada.

Langer, M. (1993) "Animatophilia, Cultural Production, and Corporate Interests: The Case of 'Ren & Stimpy'," *Film History*, Volume 5, Number 1: 125–41.

Lawry, T. (2001) "Life Beyond *South Park*," *Business Week*, 28 May: 94.

Lucas, M. P. (1999) "Yogi Bear Gets a Bit of the Ren & Stimpy Attitude," *Los Angeles Times*, 23 September: 56.

Matzer R. M. (2001) "Banned War-Era 'Bugs Bunny' Films to be Shown 'in Context'," *Los Angeles Times*, 29 June: 24.

Morrow, T. (2000) "No Killing 'South Park'," *The Record* (Bergen County, NJ), 21 June: Y10.

"NBC Cancels *God, the Devil, and Bob*," (2000) *The Gazette* (Montreal), 1 April: D4.

Oppenheimer, J. (1999) "Vision Quest," *The Hollywood Reporter*, Nickelodeon 20th Birthday Special Issue, June 15–21: S-8.

Parisi, P. (1999) "Piece of Cake," *The Hollywood Reporter*, June 15–21: S-4.

Peterson, Karen S. (1992) "The 'Batman' Flap; McDonald's Movie Tie-In Draws Anger," *USA Today*, 26 June: D1.

"The Queen of Cartoons," (1998) *TV Guide*, March 14–20.

Reboy, J. (1995) "'Live' from Ghost Planet," *Animato!*, 32, Spring: 27.

Richmond, R. (1997) "'Duckman' a USA Dead Man," *Daily Variety*, 10 July: 3.

Romano, A. (2001) "Toons' Sibling Duets," *Broadcasting & Cable*, 21 May.

Ross, C. (1998) "Cartoon Network: Cable TV Marketer of the Year," *Advertising Age*, 30 November: S-1, S-16.

Sandler, K. S. (ed.) (1998) *Reading the Rabbit: Explorations in Warner Bros. Animation*, New Brunswick, NJ: Rutgers University Press.

Swanson, T. (2001) "A Tale of Two Strategies," *Variety*, EVariety special supplement, February 26–March 4.

Wax, R. G. (1997) "World Cartoon Headquarters," *Animation Magazine*, March: 44.

Wilson, G. (1999) "That was Then; This is Now – New 'Toons at the Cartoon Network. An Interview with Linda Simensky," *Animato!*, 40, Winter–Spring: 30.

Chapter 6

THE DIGITAL TURN
Animation in the age of information technologies

Alice Crawford

AS THE TWENTIETH CENTURY FADED INTO THE TWENTY-FIRST, a broad shift has taken place in visual culture: the shift from analog to digital. As a technological and cultural transformation, the incorporation of the digital into every aspect of visual communications has been much remarked upon.[1] With respect to the practice of animation, the development of new digital technologies for image production and manipulation has affected everything from the creation of animated texts, to their distribution, reception, and aesthetic characteristics. In order to explain the variety and scope of the changes that digital techniques have brought about in the field of animation, it is necessary first to understand something about the nature of the technologies themselves. Accordingly, this chapter will proceed by explaining the basic function of a number of relevant technological developments. The technical explanations will then provide the foundation for an analysis of the impact of recent technological developments on animation as a practice of visual production, as well as its reception.

Previous chapters in this volume treat the development of animation in cinematic and televisual contexts. At this moment in time, "television" as a technology is no longer the device it once was (an extension of radio), which was based upon broadcast signals. Television is now increasingly based on direct cable signals, or used as a monitor for VCR, DVD, game consoles, or Web TV. This shift points to the convergence of various visual technologies. If we are to imagine the future of animation on "TV," we must do so with these technologies in mind.

Many commentators have dated the age of digital animation from the 1995 release of *Toy Story*, the first three-dimensional computer-animated feature film, made by Pixar and distributed by Disney. While *Toy Story* was in many respects a breakthrough film for digital animation, the film postdates by many years the period from which many practitioners and critics began making the claim that digital image-making would remake the world of animation from the ground up. Consider, for example, a relatively early textbook on the subject which begins with something of a manifesto on this new visual order:

> Today the animation love affair has exploded with such intensity that stars of movies are no longer actors and actresses, but rather behind-the-scenes complex computers and special effects technicians. To the new producers, the entertainment world has become a high-tech special effects race, with those having the best animation leading the pace...In fact, these days we can no longer go to a film and be sure that what we are seeing ever existed in physical space.
>
> (Fox 1984: 4)

In 1984, predictions of this sort had an air of the exotic about them. Today, they have become commonplace, even passé, however easy it remains to differentiate Dr. Aki Ross, the "star" of *Final Fantasy: The Spirits Within*, from a flesh and blood (or even flesh and silicone) actress.

While it has become widely accepted that digital technologies have infused current visual practice, the various implications of the digitization of visual culture are still being worked out. This chapter provides an overview of some key developments in image-making technologies which have enabled the "digital turn" in animation.

From analog to digital: new image-making technologies

Foremost among the technological developments that have affected animation in the past quarter-century is the merging of computing and image-making technologies. For many decades, animation was in large part a matter of generating a series of hand-made images. These images might be made of ink or paint on cels, or be painted on glass or made of clay or sand or paper cut-outs, as in the lyrical and groundbreaking *The Adventures of Prince Achmed*, arguably the world's first full-length animated film.[2] Thus we can say that earlier animation forms all had their basis in "analog" images; however wide the variety of media employed, each "frame" of animation was given visual form by reference to a physically existing image of some sort. Furthermore, while a wide variety of media were made use of as image material for animation frames, any animation that could be widely reproduced and appear on a screen (rather than in flip books or early devices such as phenakistoscopes, zoetropes, etc.) was the result of capturing these hand-made images in the analog media of film or, later, video.

Reliance on analog media limited the range of imagery that was possible in animation to that which could be produced through traditional image-making processes such as painting, drawing, sculpting, etc. Furthermore, analog media only allowed for a relatively limited number of viewing experiences. Making multiple copies of filmed animation is fairly expensive and, even when broadcast via television, the viewing experience is generally constrained to watching images on a screen. The introduction of computing technologies into the animation process has, while building upon earlier forms of production, allowed for qualitatively different techniques in the production and reception of animation. The following sections will describe some of the more significant ways in which the influence of computing technologies has redefined the creation and experience of animation.

Aesthetic transformations

As television became a central medium for the distribution of animation, video came to the foreground in the preparation of animated work. At first, this might only mean the transfer of animation previously produced on film to analog video for easy broadcasting. However, by the 1980s, new digital video tools became available for the production of high-end animation. These new, enormously expensive devices, such as the quaintly named "Harry," the "Ultimatte," or the "Paintbox," were at first used largely in the production of commercials. With these technologies, for the first time, animators were able to mix a variety of forms of animation into a single frame, layering, or "compositing" images from video, two-dimensional animation, and film them together, combining them all into a single image. This technological breakthrough not only allowed for a new method of production, but also brought about a shift in the visual style of commercial animation during this period.

As described by the animator and author Kit Laybourne: "cel animation, live-action video, motion graphics, and archival film merged in a new aesthetic that was named 'Blendo' by one of the cutting-edge studios involved in the innovations" (1998: 251). The studio Laybourne refers to here is Colossal Pictures of San Francisco, which produced works for, among other venues, the ground-breaking MTV series *Liquid Television*, which, in the early 1990s, provided a showcase for many early ventures into new animation techniques by smaller animation houses. The effect of the new technological capabilities of digital compositing on the aesthetics of animation could be witnessed in many of *Liquid*

Television's offerings. *The Blockheads*, for example, used intentionally blocky two-dimensional animation techniques, blended with faces of live actors captured from video, combining them into an aesthetic occupying a strange place between realism and crude two-dimensionality. Advertising of this period also offers a wide variety of examples of this new, technologically enabled aesthetic.

The collaging or "compositing" of images from a variety of sources, including live-action video, was an animation technique that would not have been feasible without the translation of analog images into data which could then be combined and transferred to video. While "Harry" and the "Ultimatte" made a new, multi-media form of animation technically possible, and signaled the introduction of computer programming into the production process, "Blendo" techniques still worked to combine a variety of images that were originally produced via analog media. The more significant shift from analog to digital arrived in the form of computer-*generated* imagery, or "CGI." With CGI, the keyframes in animation are produced through the manipulation of data within a computer program, and made visible through a combination of calculation-heavy procedures generally known as modeling, texture-mapping, compositing and, finally, rendering. In CGI, the convergence of computing and visual media has enabled truly unprecedented practices in production, distribution, and reception, as well as shifts in the aesthetic of animation. As these procedures provide the technical foundation for a variety of new production practices, and also create the possibility for a variety of unprecedented forms of reception, they are worth a brief review here.

The first step in the creation of computer generated imagery is modeling, which, significantly, can take place in two or three dimensions. In its three-dimensional form, computer modeling of animated actors, objects, and scenery takes a clear departure from analog techniques, which, in animated circumstances, are almost entirely made up of flat, two-dimensional images that are then transferred to film or video. The introduction of the third dimension, or "z" axis, to animation makes possible, among other things, the introduction of highly filmic visual techniques that are too labor-intensive in analog form. Because the actors and scenery have been mapped out in three dimensions, it becomes a simple matter to view them from any perspective, since this is a matter of quick, computerized calculations, rather than the production of a series of entirely new drawings. With the flexibility of three-dimensional modeling, some of the basic visual tropes of filmmaking that would be too time-consuming to produce in analog animation now become possible.

In some contexts, these visual tropes work to impart a sense of "realism" that would not be practicable to produce in earlier media, in which each frame would need to be drawn individually. For example, in a three-dimensionally modeled scene, it is relatively easy to create visual effects such as long zooms through a scene, smooth tracking shots, and "camera" motion which displays characters and scenery from a wide variety of angles. In analog production, to produce such an effect, each keyframe would have to be made individually, making such visual effects too labor-intensive to consider in most cases. Again, in CGI, once a scene has been modeled, it can be viewed from a limitless number of angles with the mere push of a button. As we will see later in this chapter, the introduction of camera-like motion to animation through CGI is only the beginning of the transformative effects on animation aesthetics brought about by the introduction of digitally modeled characters and scenes. First, let us continue with this brief overview of the basic processes of CGI.

The second step in CGI is to add or "map" textures onto the objects one has modeled. This process works by fitting surface textures onto wire-framed models, similar to how one would stretch upholstery over a sofa, or tile a bathroom. In the case of CGI, the "material" used to cover the frames are either predesigned textures such as glass, flesh, metal, wood, or stone, that come packaged with animation software, or image maps made from scanned images or images created through software such as Photoshop or Illustrator (see Figure 6.1). Through the addition of textures, the animator can produce a level of realism that, like the "camera work" described above, would be unfeasible in the analog production process. The amount of labor that would be involved in something relatively simple, such as the rotation of a wooden ball, would be fairly high using analog techniques, which goes far in explaining the popularity of large expanses of flat color in earlier animation forms.

In CGI, on the other hand, once the texture "wood" has been mapped onto the ball object, it can be viewed from any angle without any significant further effort. Once this wooden ball is immersed in a textured scene, with animated

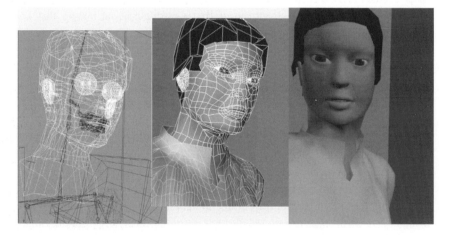

Figure 6.1 Character creation with wireframe and texture mapping using Maya animation software (Courtesy of Minna Långström, Virta Animated Ltd)

and texture-mapped characters, the amount of effort required for even minimal realism of this sort in analog production goes right off the chart, while all the digital animator needs is to be sure that his/her computer has the processing power to run the calculations required. For the first few decades of CGI, this was a major obstacle for most animators, as only huge, expensive machines could perform the massive number of floating-point calculations that the rendering of such scenes requires.[3] In the early years of CGI – basically from the early 1980s until the late 1990s – such processing power was available only to the larger production houses, such as Disney, Industrial Light and Magic, or Pixar, and even then the rendering of a single frame could take hours, or even days, depending upon the level of complexity.

The enormous expense of the machines needed to render CGI led, at first, to an increasing divide between the capabilities of independent animators or small production companies to produce the kind of animation possible in larger companies. The cost of producing a feature-length film including extensive CGI (let alone rendered entirely as CGI), such as Disney's 1982 CGI breakthrough, *Tron*, or even Pixar's 1986 short, *Luxo Junior*, was prohibitive for smaller operations, keeping such realistic animation strictly within the bounds of major studio releases. However, since the late 1990s, with processing power continuing simultaneously to increase and become cheaper, the same procedures the major animation companies have been using have become available to a much broader array of animators. Developments in computing technology have, among other effects, put an unprecedented capacity for realism within the reach of many animators.

Realism, or even what has been referred to as "hyperrealism," has been the most noteworthy of the aesthetic shifts made possible by the enormous increase in processing power. A widely cited benchmark of realism has, "historically," been that "80 million polygons per second = reality." This figure, like so many others in the computing world, has quickly been outrun, with new systems boasting performance in the range of over one hundred million polygons per second.[4] What is the significance of these rapidly inflating numbers? CGI is rendered in polygons, which break down the surface of objects and determine how light is reflected from them. The more polygons you are able to render, the more detailed and polished your animation will be. Over the past decade there has been a race among animation studios to successfully render certain hard-to-capture textures and movements, with each step toward this goal analyzed in depth in trade magazines and online forums. For example, *Mighty Joe Young* (Disney, 1988), an otherwise unremarkable movie starring a giant computer-generated ape and Charlize Theron, generated a good deal of buzz through its unprecedented rendering of fur, one of the holy grails of animation realism. Likewise, one of the more remarked-upon aspects of the movie version of *Final*

Fantasy was the lifelike rendering of Dr. Aki Ross' hair, which, the animators noted with great pride, even included flyaways (*Final Fantasy* DVD interview, 2001).

Of course, the "realism" that has arguably become the dominant aesthetic of CGI is a relative quality. The same animation textbook that brought us the enthusiastic quotation about the explosion of the "animation love affair," and claimed that "we can no longer go to a film and be sure that what we are seeing ever existed in physical space," (Fox 1984: 4) includes a screenshot from an early character animation, *The Juggler*, in which an eerily mannequin-like figure in a top hat and tails juggles various simple solids. This image is accompanied by the claim that computer animated characters are now poised to pass a "Turing Test" of realism.[5] To our now-refined CGI palates, the character is laughably synthetic, with a face more likely to pass the Ken™ Doll test than anything else.[6] However, this is not to discount the effects of increased computing power (that which allows for ever-higher numbers of rendered polygons) on the ruling aesthetic of CGI.

The difficulty of rendering moving, organic textures such as skin and muscle and hair provides another technical foundation for the look of current CGI. The smooth, generally non-elastic and static surfaces of machines are vastly more simple and economical in terms of the number of cycles that need to be burned to render them. The relative ease with which mechanical objects can be animated in this medium has intersected with a broader cultural shift in which the styles of the Pacific Rim, specifically Japan, have become influential across a broad array of artistic practices. The "anime" style of Japanese comics or "manga," in particular has had enormous influence on the graphic styles of popular culture in the past decade, which can be observed in such disparate arenas of visual culture as the wild popularity of "Superflat" artist Takashi Murakami, to the anime-influenced styling of *The Powerpuff Girls*. At the same time, the oft-noted hardware fetishism of anime is ideally suited to the strengths of computer-generated animation. Furthermore, Japanese animation houses have created some of the more ambitious animated features of the past decade, such as *Akira* (1988), *Ghost in the Shell* (1988), and *Princess Mononoke* (1997), and 2001's anime version of *Metropolis*, providing a wide array of compelling models for the hyperreal style.

This combination of technical developments which allow for an unprecedented level of realism in animation, along with a highly imaginative, sci-fi-influenced visual vocabulary has paved the way for a distinctive aesthetic in CGI. This aesthetic, which might fittingly be named an "algorithmic aesthetic," works to create a heightened sense of reality, in which the details of scenery and objects are on the verge of being rendered in even more detail than the depth of field of a film camera is capable of capturing. At the same time, the scenes and characters that are created in this medium are for the most part highly fantastical, even surreal, and the human and animal elements are consistently less realistically rendered than their machinic and synthetic counterparts.

The effects of this aesthetic will likely become rather more uncanny as a combination of technological procedures promise eventually to break down the final barrier to realism in CGI: the convincing rendering of animal motion. The techniques known as "motion-capture" animation[7] and the refinement of "inverse kinesthetics" continue to bring the look of animated characters closer in line with how we expect human and animal actors to move through space. Earlier in animation history, a fairly accurate and compelling approach to realistic rendering of animal motion was made possible through the practice of "rotoscoping" or drawing animated figures over the outline of figures captured on film. The techniques of motion-capture skip over the filming process and "capture" motion directly from a human actor. Here an actor wears a suit with electromagnetic sensors attached to a number of key points on the body, defining the major joints and limbs of the figure. As the actor moves through a magnetic field, a computer records the relative positions of the potentiometers within the field, and translates the data gathered in this fashion into parallel movements in an animated character onscreen.[8]

While expensive and labor-intensive, motion-capture allows for a higher degree of realism in animal motion than previously possible. "Inverse kinesthetics" also seeks to provide this final step in CGI realism, only by the means of complicated formulas which mathematically calculate the relative positions of limbs in motion, creating a set of scripts with which animators can build complex series of motions without having to work out the details of limb position, relative velocity, and gravity effects each and every time they want to move a character through space. For example, an "inverse kinesthetics" script will allow an animator to move the entire arm of a character from position A to position B in a fairly lifelike fashion without having to painstakingly move the hand, forearm, and upper arm separately, and render each step in between. Instead, inverse kinesthetics relies on sophisticated computer programming to calculate and render the range of motion between positions A and B, and then stores that information to be applied to the character at any time the animator requires it. This technique is used extensively by large production houses in creating animation such as *Toy Story*, which contained extensive, multi-character motion which would have been impractical to animate in such a lifelike fashion without this technology. Clearly, these technological developments have played a decisive role in shaping the current look and feel of animation, as well as the constitution of animation as a business, which is now much more integrated with computing and gaming industries than ever before.

I have argued in this chapter that the particular strengths and weaknesses of the CGI process have worked to mold a certain aesthetic, which might be mistaken for a strictly cultural, rather than deeply technological affair. This aesthetic development points out the significance of the merger with computing for the future of animation. However, it is the intersection with the specific technologies of computer gaming that has been the most transformative of the field of animation, and promises to be the most influential in the decades to come.

Gaming technologies: new narrative forms

Computer games are, of course, a form of animation. Even the very first computer games, such as Pong or Breakout, engaged the user through the combination of interaction and animated graphics, however simplistic. Soon to become even more popular than the Saturday Morning Cartoon Hour and *The Simpsons* put together, these animated entertainments had their genesis in computer labs, rather than in animation studios. In fact, Russell and Kotok, the designers of the first video game (Spacewar) report that they did not expect or intend for computer gaming to become a new entertainment medium. Rather, Russell describes the appeal as the opportunity to "do interaction and painless education" (quoted in Markoff 2002: D9). However, despite the intentions of its original developers, retail sales of computer games now top Hollywood box-office totals,[9] and computer-based game stations have become familiar living-room fixtures in the form of PlayStation, Sega, or Xbox consoles, while continuing to thrive in arcade settings. All told, gaming is now a primary, if not the foremost, form in which animation is both produced and consumed.

To fully understand the implications of this development for the future of animation, one must first grasp something of the nature of gaming technology. The foundation of current game animation is the class of computer code known as "game engines." In short, this code works to provide the framework in which a game is built and played, describing the types of behaviors that will be allowed, what inputs will be supported to allow for user interaction, the mechanics that provide the stage for the animation to take place (such as the parameters for gravity, collisions, lighting, etc.). In any game, numerous types of engines are at work, including some highly specialized engines such as the "facial damage engine" so lovingly described in the advertising copy for the new Mike Tyson Boxing game for PlayStation.[10] Significantly, these engines do not preprogram any particular narrative structure whatsoever. A robust and flexible game engine, such as the "Quake III: Arena" engine, while designed with a particular game in mind, can be used as a platform on which to build entirely new games, or can be subtly tweaked to create "mods" of the initial game, creating new animated texts within the same gaming framework.

This form of animation is radically different than earlier, analog forms of animation in a number of respects. First, because game-based animation is constructed from code, rather than a series of analog images such as cels, it is flexible and adaptive in a way that no analog animation could be. Rather than being prescribed in advance by the animator, the narrative structure of game-based animation is a collaborative, on-the-fly production which involves the viewer in determining the outcome of the play. While some games are, of course, much more structured than others, the most interesting have no particular predetermined end in mind, only a framework in which a wide array of outcomes are possible. In some of the more sophisticated games, even the animated characters have a flexibility in their behaviors and "decisions" that is not possible with analog animation. In the 2001 release, "Black and White" (from Electronic Arts), the programming of the main characters or "creatures" with which the player interacts provides a form of character-based interactivity and independent motion. Characters thus programmed are known as "intelligent agents," if they are goal oriented, or as "artificial life" (AL, vs. AI), if they are more determined by characteristics that are not goal-specific. What this means in terms of interactivity is that the animated characters on screen can react to your input in a fashion that builds over time, "learning" from events, and helping to shape the narrative in a collaborative way with the human player/s. In Japan, the popularity of animated characters of this form has spawned a new form of super-star – the computer generated "Idoru" (a term loosely based on the English word "idol"). The Idoru, such as the gamine Yuki Terai,[11] are CGI entities who star in music videos, give interviews, have international fan clubs, answer fan-mail, and enjoy the kind of devotion that produces Web sites devoted to their comings and goings, and, generally, function as (even-more) synthetic celebrities.

Clearly, the reception of animation produced in this manner is qualitatively different from the experience of watching a predetermined narrative unfold in animation produced in an analog fashion. In game-based animation, the viewer is also a player, who shapes the narrative in an ad hoc fashion within the relatively open structure provided by the game engine. Rather than watch Bugs Bunny duke it out with Elmer Fudd and win once again, the viewer engages with animated characters in a fashion that is more participatory and, therefore, more engaged – hence the recurring moral panic over gaming "addiction." In South Korea, the capital of online gaming, it is not uncommon for people to spend many hours a day absorbed in the animated world of online games such as "Lineage: The Blood Plague,"[12] which has over four million registered users in Asia. The extent to which online gaming has penetrated the daily life of South Koreans is suggested by the persistence of rumors about players starving to death, so locked into portraying their animated characters online that they forget to feed their real bodies. While these rumors may be unsubstantiated, the cultural shift that supports them is very real, and points to a high level of pene-tration of animated gaming into everyday life. Certainly, animation has become something qualitatively different as it has been integrated with the technologies that make this kind of immersive interaction possible.

An often-noted quality of game animation is the first-person perspective that defines the viewer's relationship to the other characters and the scene. In analog animation, the viewer was almost entirely situated as a viewer of the actions of characters on screen. Elsewhere, I have argued that the first-person perspective of computer gaming can bring about a form of engagement with the screen that resembles a form of ludic psychosis, forming temporary identifications with characters that has the potential to disengage our sense of self from its habitual parameters (Crawford, forthcoming, 2003). While similar effects have been proposed for other forms of spectatorship, such as film, they are certainly more pronounced in gaming and even, I argue, qualitatively different, as the extent of the viewer's interaction in gaming approaches immersion. In this respect, perhaps the most significant development in recent years has been the introduc-tion of new interface technologies, which add a multisensory dimension to the first-person perspective of game-based animation.

Taking animation off the screen: new interface technologies

While earlier forms of animation generally stuck to the screen – either the silver screen of the movie theater or the small screen of the television – digital anima-tion has spread throughout our environment, mediated by an ever-widening variety of devices. Digital animation is now displayed across screens as varied as hand-held Tamagotchi, ATM and information Kiosks, GameBoys, arcade games, cell-phone displays, exercise equipment, Personal Digital Assistants (PDAs), and personal computers, as well as broadcast over television and projected onto movie screens. Furthermore, the uses to which digital animation is put range far beyond entertainment. As animation merges with the computer programming that creates visual interfaces for sophisticated database analysis and the like, animation becomes a central mode of visualizing and interacting with data in fields as varied as space exploration, medicine, industrial chemistry, remote monitoring of factory equipment, military training, teleconferencing, and foren-sics. More than a form of entertainment or art, digital animation has become a widely used mode of interactive information display. As "viewers," then, the contexts in which we encounter animation have proliferated through working and leisure spaces in a way that earlier forms never did. As the computing power to render sophisticated graphics continues to become cheaper and more widely available, digital displays can be embedded in an even broader variety of devices. Further, as digital animation becomes more important to industries with extraordinarily deep pockets, funding for research and development in CGI is poised to outrun even Disney's wildest dreams. This combination of technological development and institutional support can only lead one to speculate that digital animation will become even more pervasive in the coming years, and may take forms that are difficult to conceive of at present.[13]

While onscreen digital animation has become a familiar part of everyday life, an array of new input devices or "interfaces" have also extended the range of interaction with animated scenes and characters beyond the audiovisual realm. Multiple screens may lend themselves to a more immersive form of reception vis-à-vis animation, but it is in the emerging field of "haptics" that immersion becomes something qualitatively different than previous forms of spectatorship. "Haptics" comprises a variety of techniques for engaging the bodily senses of motion and touch, which extend the range of interaction the viewer can have with CGI to a variety of physical forms of interaction. The simplest and most common example of a haptic interface is the joystick, made familiar through its use in arcade and home-computer gaming. The addition of "force feedback"[14] to gaming joysticks and steering wheel-style interfaces is a further step in relating the digital information spun out by the game engine to physical sensations, translating signals to and from the viewer's nervous system in a fashion that previous forms of animation did not directly engage. With a "force-feedback" steering wheel, for example, the player of a driving game can feel the effects of gravitational pull, or the impact of a collision, through increases in tension, jarring, and vibration in the wheel, adding a physical dimension to the interaction.

Further up the scale of sensory immersion are devices such as special chairs designed to deliver sound vibration through the body in response to onscreen events,[15] or recent explorations of the brave new world of "teledildonics," which have proposed sex-toy-like inputs for interaction with animated partners.[16] One of the more exotic forms of haptic interfacing currently being experimented with by an intrepid group of artists/gamers is the new "sensation" known as "PainStation,"[17] which involves the wiring of interface devices to deliver electric shocks to the players of online computer games. As these examples indicate, the reception of digital animation becomes something qualitatively distinct from the reception of earlier animated media as the production of digital animation intersects ever more closely with the development of interactive programming and the creation of new input devices.

In yet another leap "offscreen," the merging of animated interfaces with the field of robotics has allowed for interaction with worlds other than our own. Consider, for example, the "TeleANT" project recently conducted at Carnegie

Mellon University, in which a tiny, robotically controlled camera in an ant colony feeds visual information to a full-screen display on which the ants and their environment are rendered through CGI. The interface allowed people to interact with the ants, pushing grains of sugar around and the like, while real-time animation rendered the interaction in a compelling visual fashion. Through the merging of robotics and animation, the miniature drama of the ant-colony became an interactive experience, something analog animation would not be able to capture. While TeleANT uses digital animation to bring us into intimate contact with a miniature world, projects such as "Eventscope" use similar technologies to allow users to interact with an unfamiliar locale over vast distances, in this case the Martian landscape. Through a complex array of robotics, data collected from NASA missions, and three-dimensional computer-generated animation, Eventscope allows users to travel through a digitally rendered Martian landscape, and to collaboratively guide roving robots through the terrain to explore and collect data (see Figure 6.2 and 6.3).

In a final step away from a strictly onscreen presence for animation, digital technologies have also made possible projects in which the animated characters and objects are on our side of the screen, rather than beyond the glass. In his animation piece, *Movatar*, the influential digital artist Stelarc created an interface in which an animated onscreen character or "avatar" could control the motions of a human actor on stage through the use of exoskeletal robotics (basically, robotic prostheses that enclose the limbs and move the body along with their motion) and electrodes attached to the actor's muscles. In an uncanny inversion of motion-capture animation techniques, the movements of the animated character onscreen could then be translated into electronic data that would animate a human body in the real world in parallel motion. As Stelarc himself describes the process:

Figure 6.2 The TeleANT animated interface (Courtesy of Peter Coppin, Department of Robotics, Carnegie Mellon University)

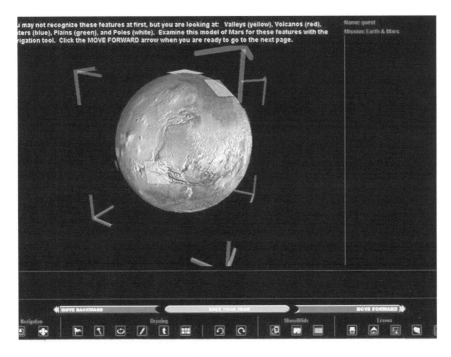

Figure 6.3 Eventscope: interactive Martian data (Courtesy of Remote Experience and Learning Lab, Pittsburgh, PA)

The avatar would become a Movatar. Its repertoire of behaviours could be modulated continuously by Ping signals and might evolve using genetic algorithms. With appropriate feedback loops from the real world it would be able to respond and perform in more complex and compelling ways. The Movatar would be able not only to act, but also to express its emotions by appropriating the facial muscles of its physical body. As a VRML entity it could be logged into from anywhere – to allow a body to be accessed and acted upon. Or, from its perspective, the Movatar could perform anywhere in the real world, at any time, with as many physical bodies in diverse and spatially separated locations....

(Stelarc 2000)

In this admittedly extreme example, one can see the evolution of animation from a form of expression mostly contained on screen, to an integral part of a complex web of technologies which engage the senses in unprecedented ways.

With all of this technological innovation, digital animation in some respects has become a more daunting process than the producers of earlier analog forms of animation might ever have imagined. Take for example, the following description from a computer animation trade magazine, *EFX Art and Design*, in which an animator explains one of the steps he took to create a raised breastplate on his character:

> Step 7 [shows] the splines on the Make Live surface as they have been lofted…I then took the isoparms around the edge on the chest plate and extracted them to make a path for extrusion…I then extruded the spline with a NURBS circle as a profile.
>
> (Meshman vs. Meshman 2002: 44)

Compare that with "Draw bunny. Draw bunny with slightly protruding chest plate," and you have some idea of the level of technical expertise (despite the rumors of "plug and play" animation) that is required to create much of the animated material with which we have become familiar. In some regards, then, the production of animation in its digital form is more clearly an activity of expert culture than most analog forms. Further, to produce feature-length animation in digital media, one still needs an enormous level of computing power, requiring an outlay of millions of dollars which only major studios can afford. In some respects, then, the production of digital animation is a more hier-archical affair than it was in the days of analog.

Democratizing technologies

However, this only tells part of the story. Digital animation technologies, like most technologies, are quite ambivalent in their effects, and it is dangerous to make the claim either that they inevitably culminate in elitism in production, or are inherently democratizing. In fact, both trends are observable in the develop-ment of digital animation. While the most technologically advanced forms of CGI require a high level of computing expertise and enormous expense, there have been other, more accessible applications developed for smaller-scale anima-tion projects. Software programs such as Macromedia's Flash have gained broad popularity with hobbyist and professional animators alike, and require far less technological expertise to work with. While an animator still needs some tech-nical knowledge and, of course, access to a computer, Flash and programs of its type have brought the production of highly polished animated works within the reach of many. Furthermore, a flourishing online community of Flash animators, and other animators working with technologies such as DHTML ("dynamic" HTML) and animated GIFs, are now able to take advantage of the new possibili-ties for distribution that digital animation allows.

While analog video required a physical object (a phenakistoscope, can of film, video tape, etc.) to be reproduced and/or physically transported from one place to another, digital animation is, from its inception, encoded in the highly portable format of zeros and ones. Animation generated from digital data can be uploaded and downloaded on the Web, making the effort of transmission an (almost) physically trivial affair. Digital data can, of course, also be burned onto CDs or DVDs in a fast and increasingly inexpensive process which makes distribution of animated texts a much simpler affair. In some respects, then, digital technologies can be argued to have democratized the processes of producing and distributing animation.

I will close this chapter with a final example of recent developments in animation practice that captures much of what is truly new and interesting about the "digital shift" I have described in this chapter. The practice is called "Machinima" (Ma-sheen-EH-ma), and makes use of game-engine programs such as the "Quake III: Arena" engine in order to create original animated features.[18] In the first stage of production, Machinima uses the modeling software of pre-existing video games such as Quake to create "actors," props, and scenery. In the next phase, the game-engine software is modified to animate an original narrative within the parameters of the engine. As described by Hugh Hancock, the artistic director of Strange Company, a Machinima production house, it is at this stage that all the elements come together, and

> "Scripts" are used to make the characters in the scene walk, talk and fight in cue within the virtual world of the set, and virtual cameras are scripted to follow the action and provide the end viewpoint of the scene.
>
> (Hancock 2002a)

In short, with Machinima, the gaming software supplies all of the building blocks for production, which can then be recombined and modified to create original content. The end result is an animated film that is remarkably polished for an ultra-low-budget production (see Figures 6.4 and 6.5). Hancock describes the appeal for animators as follows: "The greatest thing about Machinima is its democratization of the medium of animation and film – not democratization of access, so much, but democratization of content. This new medium, for the first time, allows hobbyist film-makers to make not only their own wedding video, but their own 'Star Wars'" (Hancock 2002b: 1). All for the price of a copy of a computer game.[19]

The remarkably low cost of producing a Machinima "film" is perhaps its greatest innovation. As Roger Ebert has remarked, "These movies do not require actors, set designers, cinematographers, caterers, best boys, or key grips. They can be made by one person sitting at a computer. This is revolutionary" (Ebert 2000: 68).[20] Furthermore, Machinima exemplifies the radical shifts in the mode of distribution that have accompanied the shift from analog to digital animation. While the distribution of independent animation historically has been an arduous

Figure 6.4 Machinima screenshot from *Barracuda Beach Bar* (Courtesy of Hugh Hancock, Strange Company)

Figure 6.5 Machinima screenshot from *Hardly Working* (Courtesy of Hugh Hancock, Strange Company)

and time-consuming task, Machinima films can be distributed over the Web or burned onto CDs or DVDs. The gaming software used to produce Machinima allows for the film to be broken down into its component parts for transmission, making it small and portable (in terms of kilobytes). Animation comprised of a series of specific images cannot be broken down in this fashion, and so does not lend itself to the same level of portability, even when digitized. The fact that Machinima's graphics are generated from computer algorithms, which are then "run" on a host machine to create a two-dimensional rendering of the film, makes it possible to transmit only the code from which the film is generated, which is then run on the computers it is transmitted to. Once the film's component parts are transferred to the hard drive of another computer containing the gaming software, this same programming works to reassemble and "render" the film on the screen of its new host.

Conclusion

By utilizing the technologies of computer gaming, creators of Machinima, and the more experimental animators working with the digital "medium" of gaming tools,[21] have created a form of animation that exemplifies some of the possibilities for production and distribution that are unique to digital animation. However, Machinima is only a single example among many of the ways in which the shift from analog to digital has affected the practice of animation. Digital technologies have not only reshaped production and distribution practices, but have, perhaps most importantly, created new possibilities for the aesthetics and reception of animated texts.

As this chapter has argued, digital animation has provided an array of tools that were simply not available to animators working in analog media. Consider the cumulative impact of the following: the unprecedented level of realism made possible by computer-assisted modeling and rendering; the uncanny visual language of the hyperreal, "algorithmic" aesthetic; the collaborative/on-the-fly narrative structure of game-technology-based animation; and the integration of immersive, multisensory inputs and interactivity. Together, these digital techniques and practices have transformed the range of possibilities for animators and their audiences, and promise to continue to do so in the years to come.

In this context, it may seem curious that digital animation does not account for a significant portion of animated programming on television. A 1995 episode of *The Simpsons* suggests why this is so. In "Treehouse of Horror VI (Homer)," Homer finds himself suddenly digitized within a three-dimensional, *Tron*-like environment. He takes a few cautious steps around, scratching himself absent-mindedly, and remarks to himself, "Man, this place looks expensive. I feel like

I'm wasting a fortune just standing here" (*The Simpsons Archive* 2002). Homer then proceeds to wander out into the "real world" in three-dimensional form, strolling down Ventura Boulevard. This four-minute sequence took Pacific Data Images four months to complete. Several years after this episode aired, the cost of digital production, while declining, remains high enough that it is still cheaper to produce animation for television through analog methods, especially if this animation, like that in *The Simpsons*, is produced by cheap labor overseas. Will digital animation eventually overtake analog in broadcast animation? In Chapter 3 of this volume, Allen Larson has made the case that market forces, rather than aesthetic considerations, play the decisive role in determining what forms of animation are seen on television. In a few more years, it is likely that the tools for creating digital animation will have become inexpensive enough that the market-based impetus for using analog techniques will become obsolete, and we can expect to see a rapid increase in the proportion of animation for television that is produced digitally.

In another respect, digital animation has already taken over the television screen. If we consider the enormous popularity of console-based gaming, it becomes clear that digital animation is the ascendant form of animation seen on television today. In this regard, we might say that the digital age has already come to television animation via the convergence of television with computing technologies.

Notes

1 See, for example, W. J. T. Mitchell (1994); Sean Cubitt (1998); Kevin Robins (1996); D. N. Rodowick (2001); Jean Baudrillard (1994); and Jay David Bolter and Richard Grusin (2000).

2 Lotte Reiniger, director and animator (1926).

3 This computing power is amusingly quantified as "Megaflops," referring to a rate of one million ("mega") floating point operations ("flop") per second ("s").

4 A telling example of this speedup is the case of home-gaming systems. In 1999, the fastest consoles operated at speeds around 350,000 polygons per second, while in 2002, the Sony PlayStation 2 has a speed of 66 million polygons per second, and the Xbox operates at 116 million per second (St. John 2002: 1+).

5 This is a reference to the famous test for artificial intelligence, proposed by Alan Turing, in which the inability of a human actor to determine whether a computer "agent" is human or not determines whether or not the agent has "intelligence." This test, by the way, is widely disputed as a measure of artificial intelligence.

6 The distinction between real and digitally produced human actors is generally quite clear to any visually literate adult, except, perhaps, for John Ashcroft and members of the US Congress, who in 2002 attempted to pass the Child Pornography Prevention Act, containing a ban on computer-generated child pornography which it designated as virtually indistinguishable from the real thing.

7 This is also known as "performance animation" in some circles.

8 This process can also be done with reflective markings and strobe lighting to record the actor's movement.

9 In 2001, retail sales of computer games totaled $9.4 billion, a 42 percent increase over sales in 2000 (St. John: 1).

10 "Brutal beyond belief!" enthuses the advertising copy.

11 See the official Yuki Terai site (Kutsugi 2002) at http://www.teraiyuki.net/ for "discography," "biography," goods, and more.

12 This game was originally developed in South Korea and was, as of 2001, "the largest subscription-based online game in the world, with over two million active accounts worldwide" (Evans: 2001).

13 One particularly startling intersection of gaming animation and big research monies is the recent development of a virtual "joystick" that a monkey can control with its brainwaves. The monkey in question has been trained to play a version of Pong with its brain and a wire as the only interface (Zacks 2002: 20–1).

14 "Force-feedback" technology incorporates actuators into input devices, which make use of mechanical, hydraulic or electric means to send motion or tactile signals to a user.

15 The Intensor Game Chair is "a chair that will surround you with sound, and rumble your guts," according to gamer reviews (see streettech.com).

16 See for example the prototyped devices at the tellingly named http://www.fu-fme.com site.

17 For further information, see "No Pain, No Game" (McGrath 2002) or http://www.wired.com/news/games/0,2101,50875,00.html (accessed 14 April 2002), or http://www.painstation.de (accessed 21 March 2002).

18 The first Machinima film was *Blahbalicious*, created in 1997. For more information, trailers, and downloads, check online. Some key sites are http://www.machinima.com, http://www.strangecompany.org, and Zarathustra Studios at http://www.z-studios.com.

19 Remember, kids, software piracy is bad, mmkay?

20 It's worth noting here that Ebert doesn't acknowledge (or perhaps realize) that voice actors are in fact needed to create Machinima.

21 See, for example, *Untitled Game* by the artist ensemble "JODI," at http://www.jodi.org, or the collection of artist-created "mods" hosted by the Australian web site, "Select Parks," at http://www.selectparks.net.

Bibliography

Baudrillard, J. (1994) *Simulacra and Simulation*, Ann Arbor: University of Michigan Press.

Bolter, J. D. O. and R. Grusin (2000) *Remediation: Understanding New Media*, Cambridge, MA: MIT Press.

Cohen, P (1994) "StreetTech Hardware Review: Intensor Chair," *StreetTech*. Available at: http://www.streettech.com/archives_Hardware/intensor.html (accessed 15 March 2002).

Crawford, A. (forthcoming, Spring 2003) "Unheimlich Maneuver: Self-Image and Identificatory Practice in Virtual Reality Environments," in M. Hocks and M. Kendrick (eds.), *Eloquent Images*, Cambridge, MA: MIT Press.

Cubitt, S. (1998) *Digital Aesthetics*, London, Sage.

Ebert, R. (2000) "Ghost in the Machinima," *Yahoo: Internet Life*, Volume 61, Number 6: 68.

Evans, D. (2001) "The Future of Online Gaming", *PC Magazine Online*. Available at: http://www.pcmag.com (accessed 12 May 2002).

Final Fantasy: The Spirits Within, DVD, (2001) Chris Lee Productions.

Fox, D. (1984) *Computer Animation Primer*, New York: McGraw Hill.

FUFME (1999) "Fuck you, Fuck me," *FUFME*. Available at: http://www.fu-fme.com (accessed 7 November 2000).

Hancock, H. (2002a) "Introduction to Machinima." Available at: http://www.machinima.com/Whatis/intromach.shtml (accessed 24 March 2002).

—— (2002b) *"Screenshots, Please!"* nomad@strangecompany.org (accessed 24 March 2002).

JODI (2002) *Untitled Game*. Available at: http://www.jodi.org (accessed 12 April 2002).

Kutsugi, K. (2002) "Yuki Terai Official Site." Available at: http://www.teraiyuki.net (accessed 15 April 2002).

Laybourne, K. (1998) *The Animation Book*, New York: Three Rivers Press.

Markoff, J. (2002) "A Long Time Ago, In a Computer Lab Far Away…," *New York Times*, 28 February, Section D: 9.

McGrath, D. (2002) "No Pain, No Game," *Wired News Online*. Available at: http://www.wired.com /news/games/0,2101,50875,00.html (accessed 7 March 2002).

Meshman vs. Meshman (2002) "Inner Conflicts or Pure Madness? Peter Abersten Uses Maya and Photoshop for Award-Winning Image," *EFX: Art and Design*, 33, Autumn: 42–6.

Mitchell, W. J. T. (1994) *The Reconfigured Eye: Visual Truth in the Post-Photographic Era*, Cambridge, MA: MIT Press.

Morawe, V. (2001) "Painstation." Available at: http://www.khm.de/~morawe/painstation /painstation_eng.html (accessed 10 March 2002).

Robins, K. (1996) *Into the Image: Culture and Politics in the Field of Vision*, New York: Routledge.

Rodowick, D. N. (2001) *Reading the Figural, or Philosophy after the New Media*, Durham: Duke University Press.

St. John, Warren (2002) "With Games of Havoc, Men Will be Boys," *New York Times*, 12 May, Section 9: 1.

Select Parks. Available at: http://www.selectparks.net (accessed 27 May 2002).

The Simpson's Archive. Available at: http://www.snpp.com/episodes/3F04.html (accessed 27 May 2002).

Stelarc (2000) "Movatar: Inverse Motion-capture System," Stelarc Web Page. Available at: http://www.stelarc.va.com.au (accessed 15 February 2002).

Strange Company. Available at: http://www.strangecompany.org (accessed 15 March 2002).

Zacks, R. (2002) "Brain Power," *Technology Review*, April: 20–1.

Zarathustra Studios. Available at: http://www.z-studios.com (accessed 15 March 2002).

Part II

READINGS

Chapter 7

BACK TO THE DRAWING BOARD

The family in animated television comedy

Michael V. Tueth

THE YEAR IS 1954, AND IN THE TELEVISION TOWN OF SPRINGFIELD, Mr. Jim Anderson, a reputable agent for the General Insurance Company, enters his comfortable suburban home, greets his attractive and sensible wife, Margaret, changes from his business suit to more casual attire, and spends the evening calmly dealing with the day-to-day concerns of their three growing children. The Anderson family continues this domestic activity week after week for nine years on the popular domestic situation comedy, *Father Knows Best*.

Click the time-travel remote four decades to 1994. Once again in a television town called Springfield, Homer Simpson checks out of his job as safety inspector at the town's nuclear power plant, jumps in his car, throws a radioactive ingot out of the car window, and speeds homeward, almost running over his skate-boarding son, Bart, in the family driveway, finally colliding with his frazzled wife and hyperactive children on the family couch to watch television. It is already the fifth season of *The Simpsons*, an animated television comedy that has become a ratings and merchandising phenomenon. Somewhere, somehow, in those forty intervening years, the television family went crazy.

The subversive view of the American family that started showing up in the 1990s in television's animated comedies came about not only because of the talents of a new breed of animators but also because of a steady development among the viewing population. Viewers had come to expect, even in the familiar format of situation comedy, some presentation of alternative viewpoints and more-or-less direct challenges to the prevailing values and social norms. Darrell Hamamoto has described it well:

> The television situation comedy – the most popular American art form – is a virtual textbook that be can "read" to help lay bare the mores, images, ideals, prejudices, and ideologies shared – whether by fiat or default – by the majority of the American public.
>
> (Hamamoto 1989:10)

This textbook, moreover, is continually revised, and, according to Hamamoto, the lessons get progressively more liberating. In the ideological battles of a liberal democratic society the television sitcom is best understood not as an exercise in mindless reassurance or as a validation of the status quo, but as a step in what Douglas Kellner calls "emancipatory popular culture" (1987: 471–503). Hamamoto claims that, in the midst of canned laughter, situation comedy has offered its own form of social criticism:

> The situation comedy, as an aesthetic form grounded in realism and contemporaneity, has remarked upon almost every major development of postwar American history.... To a greater degree than perhaps any other popular art, the situation comedy has offered oppositional ideas, depicted oppression and struggle, and reflected a critical consciousness that stops just short of political mobilization.
>
> (Hamamoto 1989: 2)

Hamamoto readily admits that the radical social argument in most television comedy is severely restricted by the "altogether different set of premises" of the commercial system that produces and distributes sitcoms. Yet, in one sense, that has worked in favor of the domestic sitcom. While networks are generally reluctant to challenge the prevailing ideology in corporate America, the area that remains more open to examination and criticism is the "private sphere organized around domestic life" (1989: 2). Hence television has continually presented comedies about family life, ranging, as this study hopes to show, from the didactic model of domestic normalcy to numerous comic variations of family arrangements and, eventually, in animated comedies, to a subversive vision of family life.

The medium of television, according to Ella Taylor's study, *Prime-Time Families*, naturally tends to focus on the family. Early in her survey of television families, she observes:

> Few contemporary forms of storytelling offer territory as fertile as American television for uncovering widely received ideas about family...a continuous chronicle of domesticity that has provided a changing commentary on family life – by turns reflective, utopian, dystopian, its mood now euphoric, now anxious, now redemptive.... Television sits in the home, both

part of the furniture and part of the family.... In its own glamorous way, television celebrates the ordinary; and by doing so it suggests that certain versions of family life are normal and others deviant, strange or (by exclusion) nonexistent.

(Taylor 1989: 17, 19)

While Taylor also sees the comic form's "subversive potential of creating divergent meanings," she finds this potential restricted not so much by the commercial system that Hamamoto indicts but by the tendency towards naturalism and realism inherent in live-action programming. The codes of realistic narrative are meant to persuade the viewer that the televised depiction of domestic and work settings reflects the human situation more accurately than "the caricatures of the Disney cartoon" (1989: 38).

The "cartoon" format that eventually arrived on television in the 1990s liberated the domestic sitcom from the straightjacket of visual naturalism that Taylor describes by combining the normative with the deviant aspects of family life in a subversive discourse. But television programming took a long time to reach that point, starting with portrayals of "normal" families, moving quickly to numerous examples of "funny" families, and arriving at the subversive view of family life provided by animation.

Normal families

Two sitcoms of the 1950s have come to represent the high point in the tendency of domestic comedy in its live-action mode to reinforce social consensus and conformity, focusing on the social ideal of the domestic utopia of the nuclear family in comfortable suburbia. The "aesthetic form grounded in realism and contemporaneity" found its most intense expression in *The Adventures of Ozzie and Harriet* (1952–66), which starred a real-life family in a setting that was modeled on their actual Hollywood home. Occasional references were made to Ozzie Nelson's previous real-life career as a bandleader, although the ideal stay-at-home housewife Harriet's earlier life as a singer was not acknowledged. The two sons, David and Ricky, portrayed themselves according to their actual ages, so that in the course of the fourteen years of the show's run, viewers watched them grow into young manhood, get married, and bring their real-life wives into the cast as well. When Ricky developed into a major rock-'n'-roll star in real life, his musical performances became a regular feature of the show. David Halberstam has described the show as "fashioning a mythical family out of a real one" (1993: 516). As Hal Himmelstein succinctly puts it: "the medium of television became our kitchen window as we curiously peeked at the goings-on of our next-door neighbors, the Nelsons" (1994: 128).

The realist aesthetic of the television sitcom progressed easily into a didactic mode; the television families were not simply "the way we live today" but also "the way we ought to live." In its very title, *Father Knows Best* (1954–63) announced its moralistic tone. Gerard Jones describes the year of the show's debut as "a subtle turning point in the national consciousness" (1992: 95). With the end of the Korean conflict, the death of Stalin, the close of the Army–McCarthy hearings, the Supreme Court's ordering of desegregation of public schools, and the "moderate progressivism" of the Eisenhower administration, the US seemed to be settling down into a time of peace, social progress, and considerable prosperity. How was America supposed to behave? Television, in Jones' analysis, functioned as "the centerpiece of every suburban living room," and took center stage in this wave of pop-culture pedagogy. The arrival of *Father Knows Best* on television reshaped the viewers' expectations for the genre:

> *The Goldbergs* and *Mama* had set a precedent for sitcom morality plays but in nostalgic contexts. No sitcom had ever attempted to teach social lessons in a contemporary mass culture setting. *Father Knows Best*, however, flung itself into the task of demonstrating proper family conduct with all the ingenuous confidence of a Sunday school film. The Anderson family was a model social unit for the new suburban society.
>
> (Jones 1992: 97)

The family rules and roles were clear. As Jones describes them, the father was the breadwinner who laid down most of the family rules and refereed disputes. Margaret, the wife and mother, was attractive, witty, sociable, and supportive of her husband's authority, sometimes interceding on the children's behalf. The children, Princess, Bud, and Kitten, were good-natured, if sometimes confused, and always managed to learn that, indeed, "father knew best," even about their own childhood issues.

For a while, this formula worked and changed the expectations of viewers who came to expect not that the families be amusing, but that they be somehow instructive. And, as Jones points out, this new view of situation comedy transformed the genre for some time to come: "Moral lessons became an accepted, even expected part of the form, even when the content didn't seem to justify it. Satire and absurdity became harder to put on the air. The sitcom became mainstream America's candy-coated teacher" (1992: 100). However, as Jones also observes,

> What the Andersons were not – compared with the Ricardos, the Burnses, and even the Goldbergs – was funny…these characters could never be very funny; they were too pure to ridicule. They might be witty in a genteel way, but they were too sweet to be acerbic. Even their laugh-track was restrained.
>
> (1992: 97–8)

In this attempt to use the domestic situation comedy as a "candy-coated teacher," the comedy was disappearing.

The impact of admirable-but-not-funny families such as the Nelsons and the Andersons, therefore, should not be overstated in terms of either their own popularity or their imitators. These two portrayals of an intact nuclear family living in the suburbs were actually not that popular with the wider television audience. They never dominated the Nielsen ratings. In its nine years on the air, *Father Knows Best* managed to make it into the top twenty shows of the season only twice, with rankings of 13 and 6. *The Adventures of Ozzie and Harriet* never made the cut throughout its entire fourteen-season run; its best ratings performance was a 29 ranking in the 1963–64 season (Brooks and Marsh 1999: 1244–8).

The popularity of *Father Knows Best* and *The Adventures of Ozzie and Harriet* was, in fact, something of an anomaly in the history of sitcoms. The success of these presentations might better be explained as the viewers' fascination with what Stephanie Coontz has shown to be a "qualitatively new phenomenon" in American life. Coontz documents the rapid change in family structures after World War II as a departure from the family patterns of the past and the extended family ties necessitated and encouraged by the Great Depression and World War II. Newlyweds were moving into their homes, establishing suburban enclaves of single-family dwellings, separated from the urban neighborhoods of the elder generation. They were also creating a new set of expectations for family life, with an "emphasis on producing a whole world of satisfaction, amusement and inventiveness within the nuclear family" (Coontz 2000: 27). Coontz quotes historian Elaine Tyler May's observation:

> The legendary family of the 1950s…was not, as common wisdom tells us, the last gasp of "traditional" family life with deep roots in the past. Rather, it was the first wholehearted effort to create a home that would fulfill virtually all its members' personal needs through an energized and expressive personal life.
>
> (Coontz 2000: 11)

The young suburban families could look to the Nelsons and the Andersons for instructions in this New Frontier of the American family. Nonetheless, guide-lines for personal and familial satisfaction have limited comic appeal, and the Nelsons and the Andersons found very few imitators in television comedy. Instead, viewers enjoyed shows about widowers, bachelor fathers, divorcees, single parents, adopted children, and even relatives from another planet. These families were just as "nice" as the Nelsons and the Andersons, but they were funnier.

Funny families

The domestic comedies that succeeded in capturing viewers' attention and, in their own ways, continued to serve as "candy-coated teachers" of family morality, were notable for their modified family arrangements. The very popular *My Three Sons* (1960–72) featured a widower who lived with his three sons and his father-in-law. *Family Affair* (1966–71) focused on a single father taking care of a nephew and two nieces who had been orphaned by the death of their parents in an accident. *The Andy Griffith Show* (1960–68) featured Andy as a widower living with his young son, Opie, and Andy's Aunt Bee. The Clampett clan that moved out to California in *The Beverly Hillbillies* (1962–71) was composed of a widower, Jed; his mother-in-law, Granny; his daughter Elly May; and his nephew Jethro. All four of these stories of male-headed, untraditional families did quite well in the ratings during their runs. But nothing could compete with the popularity of the all-male Cartwright clan of *Bonanza* (1959–73). In fact, the most highly rated programs of the 1950s and 1960s, taken as a whole, included only a few sitcoms, domestic or otherwise. The phenomenal ratings success of *I Love Lucy* (1951–57) was not repeated by other sitcoms; only a few of them made it into the top rankings for those two decades. Viewers seemed to prefer a combination of variety shows, quiz shows, rural comedies, and adult Westerns.

In the 1970s, under the influence of Norman Lear, the comedy of many of the domestic sitcoms turned dark, with the argumentative families of *All in the Family*, *The Jeffersons*, *Maude*, and others. Many of the lighter domestic comedies of the decade tended to feature wise-cracking kids, confused parents juggling family and career, and other relatives living in the home.

The hip-but-heartwarming portrayal of family tensions and togetherness on *The Cosby Show* (1984–92) and *Family Ties* (1982–89) certainly appealed to the largest percentage of television viewers in the 1980s. *The Cosby Show* was number one in the ratings for five years in a row, with *Family Ties* not far behind. By the middle of the decade, however, more offbeat domestic comedies such as *Mama's Family* (1983–90), *Roseanne* (1988–97), and *Married with Children* (1987–97) emerged, presenting visions of dysfunctional family life and thriving on the comedy of insult, anger, irresponsibility, and outrageous behavior. Steven Stark offers an appreciative view of the typical humor of family dysfunction:

> There was something refreshing about a loud, studiously sloppy comedy whose lead was a woman 50 pounds overweight…and the characters perambulated in their underwear – insulting each other and belching…. Where *Roseanne* really stood alone in sitcom history…was in her willingness to dump on her children…. *Roseanne* raised verbal child-bashing to an art form…. "They've left for school. Quick – change the locks!" was the cry on

one episode; while on yet another, she jokingly offers to trade one of her offspring for a dishwasher.

(1997: 264–5)

Family comedy on television had evolved from the depiction of normative family life, even with less-than-traditional arrangements, to families that were problematic if not indeed dysfunctional, all of this explored in the codes of realism and naturalism. When animation invaded television, however, the discourse of television comedy was finally free to pursue a more subversive function.

Subversive families

Premiering in December 1989, *The Simpsons* became the first successful animated comedy on prime time television since *The Flintstones* in the 1960s. The typical middle-class family in the archetypal town of Springfield consisted of Homer Simpson, the lazy, overweight, slow-witted father; his well-meaning but often hapless wife, Marge; and, most subversive of all, their son, the underachieving-and-proud-of-it, wise-cracking fourth-grader, Bart. With these characters and Bart's younger sisters, Lisa and Maggie, at the center, the show's creator Matt Groening filled the screen with a large cast of bizarre Springfield residents: the extended Simpson family, the faculty and staff of Bart's school, Homer's boss and co-workers at Springfield's nuclear power plant, next-door neighbors, city offi-cials, merchants, local television personalities, and the strangely frequent celebrity visitors to the town. The technique of animation enabled the scriptwriters to include as many characters as they wanted and to switch scenes as often as possible. Animation increased the opportunity for much more physical comedy, rapid dialogue, and plot twists than live-action comedy could ever manage. It also offered a new view of family life.

This animated picture of dysfunctional-but-happy family life soon found imita-tors on both cable and broadcast networks, and several of them became solid hits. In 1993, MTV offered viewers the adventures of two teenage slackers named Beavis and Butt-Head who spent most of their time watching music videos, abusing each other verbally and physically, and engaging in crude and sometimes dangerous practical jokes. Their parents were nowhere to be found. The show developed a considerable cult following and in 1997 MTV aired a spin-off, *Daria*, an animated comedy aimed at a female audience. The main character, who had been a classmate of Beavis and Butt-Head in grammar school, went on to high school, a teen environment that the brainy, sardonic Daria could only loathe. Her parents were both successful corporate executives who had bequeathed their intelligence to their daughter but could not offer her any attention or quality time. Caught between the emotional sterility of her parents and the brainless frenzy of her peers, Daria had to fend for herself as a brainy nerd doomed to outsider status both at home and away.

Moving from cable to the wider viewership of the FOX network, in 1996 Mike Judge, creator of *Beavis and Butt-Head*, used his own Texas roots as the locale for his new animated comedy, *King of the Hill*, featuring the family of Hank Hill residing in suburban Arlen, Texas. Conservative, middle-aged, lower middle-class Hank sold propane gas and spent a lot of time drinking beer and hanging out with his neighborhood buddies. His wife, Peggy, housewife and substitute teacher, had a mind of her own, clearly influenced by the trickle-down feminism that had made its way into the Texas suburbs. Hank's chubby son, Bobby, was a disappointment to his father, and their live-in niece, Luanne, was too wild and frisky by Peggy's standards.

This was followed in 1999 by a similar comedy on FOX, *The Family Guy*, which in many ways encapsulated all the popular features of the previous animated domestic sitcoms. The father, Peter Griffin, was, like Homer Simpson, overweight, lazy, and irresponsible. Like Beavis and Butt-Head, his favorite pastime was watching television and avoiding work. His wife, Lois, like Marge Simpson and Peggy Hill, was the long-suffering wife and mother of a chaotic household. Their older son Chris was as overweight as Bobby Hill and almost as much of an underachiever as Bart Simpson. Their teenage daughter Meg was as unpopular and nerdy as Daria Morgendorffer and (sometimes) Lisa Simpson, and their one-year-old baby Stewie was precociously destructive enough to rival Beavis and Butt-Head. Thus, in the space of nine years, the innovative had become formulaic.

In 1997, the cable channel Comedy Central introduced, as one of its first attempts at original programming, a daringly transgressive comedy called *South Park*, created by two brash young newcomers, Trey Parker and Matt Stone. The show followed the adventures of four foul-mouthed third-graders in a Colorado mountain town, who constantly heap abuse on one another; utter racist, homo-phobic, and other politically insensitive epithets; and obsess about flatulence, excretion, and other bodily functions. Their parents occasionally appear, and, when they do, are generally presented as ignorant, repressed, frantic, and other-wise unworthy of any child's respect. The mother of one of the characters is regularly referred to as a "crack whore."

Animation seems to have given television comedy the appropriate mode in which a subversive view of family life could be presented even within the nexus of network and commercial demands. This combination of commercial and social sanction and subversive expression finds a close parallel in the long tradition of "carnival," the pre-Lenten revelry with roots in the Dionysian festivities of the Greeks and the Roman Saturnalia. Robert Stam's study of

"Film, Literature, and the Carnivalesque" cites Mikhail Bahktin's description of the function of carnival as an insertion of alternative attitudes in the midst of conventional life:

[Carnival] represented an alternative cosmovision characterized by the ludic undermining of all norms. The carnivalesque principle abolishes hierarchies, levels social classes, and creates another life free from conventional rules and restrictions. In carnival, all that is marginalized and excluded – the mad, the scandalous, the aleatory – takes over the center in a liberating explosion of otherness. The principle of material body – hunger, thirst, defecation, copu-lation – becomes a positively corrosive force, and festive laughter enjoys a symbolic victory over death, over all that is held sacred, over all that oppresses and restricts.

(Stam 1989: 86)

Stam's study applies the Bakhtinian notion of the carnivalesque to the works of Bunuel, Fellini, and Godard, as well as the films of Monty Python, Mel Brooks, the Marx Brothers, and many others (1989: 111). He responds to Eco's contention that such carnival activity is "an authorized transgression deeply dependent on a law that it only apparently violates" by highlighting its function as a "countermodel":

While it is true that official power has at times used carnival to channel energies that might otherwise have funneled popular revolt, it has just as often been the case that carnival itself has been the object of official repression…. Carnival…is the oppositional culture of the oppressed, a countermodel of cultural production and desire…a symbolic, anticipatory overthrow of oppressive social structures…. All carnivals must be seen as complex crisscrosssings of ideological manipulation and utopian desire.

(Stam 1989: 91, 95, 96)

The carnivalesque can be subversive, especially if the countermodel it proposes looks like a lot of fun. Animation thus is television's version of the carnivalesque. *The Simpsons* and other successful animated domestic comedies have been able to explore darker, subversive aspects of family life thanks mainly to the possibilities of the cartoon aesthetic. But, like carnival, they offer their critique in a familiar and ideologically acceptable environment: the traditional sitcom format. It is precisely this mixture of shock and reassurance that distin-guishes the new animated television comedy.

The acceptability of the presentation lies in its inclusion of material which might otherwise disturb a viewer but which is easily incorporated into the cartoon format. Facial features which might seem grotesque are only mildly threatening, as many of the villains, animals, and other characters in Disney films have demonstrated. Violence and destruction are presented in less disturbing forms. The tradition of the resurrection of cartoon characters (Bugs Bunny, Elmer Fudd, Road Runner, Wile E. Coyote, Tom and Jerry) who manage to survive explosions, crashes, long-distance falls, and the crushing effect of heavy objects landing on them or rolling over them is a major expansion of the inherent optimism of most comic plots. Extreme emotional responses are easily expressed in animation. The distorted facial features of most characters lay the ground-work, but the ability to have eyes bug out in terror, faces redden and swell in anger, bodies shrink in fear, tongues hang out with desire for food, drink, or sexual pleasure are all standard techniques of animated comedy. In short, phys-ical action that would be next to impossible to achieve in live-action performance can be demonstrated easily and acceptably in animation. On *The Simpsons*, for example, Homer's guzzling of beer and gorging on food, the acci-dents that occur at home or in the schoolyard, the larger disasters of death and destruction of property, even Homer and Marge's efforts at lovemaking, to name just a few, would tend to offend viewers if presented in graphic realism, but by their very exaggeration in animation they become ludicrous and beyond offense.

Viewers' comfort with animation's presentation of the grotesque, however, also permits the cartoon to offer an alternative view of family life, presenting both parents and children as at least potentially monstrous. The limited range of facial features available in the simpler form of animation chosen by Groening, Judge, Parker, and Stone also tends to present the characters and settings as stereotypical and dangerously close to homogeneous. All the char-acters on *South Park* tend to be portrayed as squat, round-headed and one-dimensional; all the citizens of Springfield have the same bug eyes and overbite as the Simpsons, while all its houses look alike. Animation is capable of conveying both the monstrous and the mundane in family life.

In her thoroughgoing study of animation aesthetics, entitled *Art in Motion*, Maureen Furniss explores the difference between what she calls the "traditional/industrial/hegemonic forms" of commercial cartoons and the "experi-mental/independent/subversive forms" of independent animation, and maintains that a choice of technique reflects an ideological viewpoint. In her catalogue of the contrasts between the two forms, the characteristics of independent animation are as follows: the use of techniques other than traditional ones, the tendency to alter media, the abstract style, the non-linear narrative, the reflection of alternative lifestyles, the challenge to dominant beliefs, and the tendency to be made by artists from marginalized social groups and reflect their concerns (1998: 30).

The Simpsons and the other animated family comedies, while appealing to a wide mainstream audience, also manage to offer a subversive view of family life by use of the techniques of independent animation described by Furniss. They present the familiar television portrait of a comic nuclear family who, with all their eccentricities, continue as a viable social unit. But they also suggest that such domestic stability must now include a subversive view of family life. Furniss' categories, which are readily apparent in the recent crop of animated domestic comedies, especially *The Simpsons* and *South Park*, can be summarized as follows:

The use of techniques other than traditional ones and the tendency towards the abstract and the non-linear

While *The Simpsons* in its present state has become a major industry in terms of both production and merchandising, and its animation is far more complex and detailed than the other four animated comedies under consideration, Groening's art is still rooted in a non-traditional style. The characters on the show resemble the minixmalist/grotesque figures (without the long rabbit-like ears) that populate Groening's comic strip, *Life in Hell*, still in syndication in the alternative press. Perhaps the omnipresence of the Simpson characters in the media has led the public to overlook the fundamental surrealism of Marge Simpson's beehive of blue hair; the absurdity of the perpetual sucking sound of the infant Maggie Simpson; the cartoon-within-the-cartoon personae of Krusty the Clown, Sideshow Bob, and Itchy and Scratchy; the constant smoking of Marge's older sisters, the Bouvier twins; and so on. Even when celebrity guests such as Sting, The Who, and Elton John appear in episodes, using their actual voices, their images are made to conform to the general physiognomy of the Simpsons' universe. There is no attempt to aim for the naturalistic look which, for example, Disney animators sought with the help of live human models for *Snow White*, *Cinderella*, or *Aladdin*, or the animated animals in *Bambi*, *Lady and the Tramp*, and *101 Dalmations*.

The other animated comedies delve even further into the abstract with the simple line-drawing of the facial features of Beavis and Butt-Head and *South Park*'s use of paper cut-out figures as their main characters. The character of Jesus Christ in *South Park* looks like a child's drawing, and some of the minor characters become almost inhuman, with blank-featured heads that resemble eggs. Daria's facial features undergo little change as she stares straight ahead through her horn-rimmed glasses that turn her face into an inscrutable mask. All of the cartoons other than *The Simpsons* tend to display a minimum of movement and of visual setting.

Of the comedies under consideration, *Beavis and Butt-Head* comes closest to non-linearity. *Beavis and Butt-Head* exist in a virtual Beckettian vacuum, with no familial framework, limited range of locale, and usually no sense of time of day or year. The two slackers spend most of their time on the couch watching television with no indication given of what has transpired beforehand or what awaits them.

The plot of each episode often consists of repetitions of the same gag or physical shtick. *The Simpsons* has, over the years, become more linear, as plot-lines have relied on antecedent events from previous episodes. All faithful viewers know that Sideshow Bob has attempted to kill Bart; Barney, the town drunk, has stopped imbibing alcohol; Apu, the manager of the Quickie-Mart, has married and fathered octuplets; and Homer and Marge's youth and high-school years have been recounted. Yet no one has grown older (particularly odd in the family sitcom genre); everyone continues in the same occupation; and practically no one (other than Maude Flanders) has died. The larger narrative engine is stalled.

The tendency to alter media

A subtle change in the experience of the medium of television is accomplished by the self-reflexivity of the new animated comedies. Again *Beavis and Butthead* offers the clearest examples of this, as the inarticulate teenagers devote hours to watching, and often reviling, the music videos on MTV, the very channel that airs the program. Clips from the music videos interact with the cartoon text. *King of the Hill* engages in regular references to media celebrities, current developments in pop culture, and especially the conventions of advertising texts, as, for instance, Hank and his drinking-buddies imagine themselves starring in sexy beer ads. In its broadcast of the 2001 Super Bowl, the FOX Network inserted brief clips of Hank Hill and other characters from the show (which FOX also airs) to comment on the game. This intertextuality of sports-news coverage, entertainment, and advertising further reshapes the viewers' understanding of the medium. The very essence of *The Simpsons* is its connection with and commentary upon previous television comedy. The opening sequence of everyone's trip home honors Fred's commute which opened every episode of *The Flintstones*; *Father Knows Best* lives on in the name of the town; the family gathers each week in front of the family hearth of the television set. Every episode is complete with allusions not only to familiar television texts, but also to films, theater, popular music, literary classics, politics, and history. *The Simpsons* uses the television medium to mine American culture.

A reflection of alternative lifestyles, an expression of marginalized social groups, and a challenge to dominant beliefs

To a certain extent, every one of the animated family comedies gives voice to a marginalized segment of society. In some cases, the main characters themselves personify a certain subculture. Beavis and Butt-Head's monosyllables, grunts, and chuckles speak for those isolated, inarticulate teenagers who are not on the football team, the student council, or the pep squad. Daria Morgendorffer, also living on the margins of her high-school community, offers wry commentary on the popularity of her cheerleader sister, the awkwardness of her male peers, and other features of high-school culture. Hank Hill and his neighbors, while they may now be living in the suburbs of a Texas metropolis, still retain many of the features of their redneck roots and an American "love-it-or-leave-it" mentality.

Even while the Simpson family itself can be classified as middle class, they are surrounded by members of minority groups or other relative outsiders that the Andersons and Nelsons apparently never encountered. Apu, the Hindu owner of the Quickie-Mart and his wife-by-parental-arrangement Manjula; Julius Hebert, the African-American physician who in many ways resembles Bill Cosby's Dr. Huxtable character; Smithers, the assistant to the town tycoon, Montgomery Burns, who may or not be gay, but who is clearly in love with his boss; Ned Flanders, the Simpsons' next-door neighbor who is militantly upbeat and public about his Christianity; and finally the foreign-born groundskeeper Willie all add up to a diverse population for a small town, quite the opposite of the "Whites-only" world of the earlier television Springfield.

South Park positively revels in diversity, usually with politically incorrect glee. One of the children, Kyle, is regularly reviled because he is Jewish. Timmy, a disabled child, uses his disability to serve his own purposes. The portrayal of Chef, the African-American cook who offers the boys the benefit of his vast sexual experience and wisdom in frequently inappropriate remarks and behavior, borders on a racist stereotype. Big Gay Al minces about scantily clad and simpering. Kyle's uncle is a Vietnam-vet guns-rights advocate who spouts right-wing, racist, and homophobic epithets at every opportunity. Almost every episode revolves around a delicate issue in contemporary culture wars, often expressing both sides of the arguments in as tasteless a form as possible.

Most of the comedies likewise tend to challenge authority, mainly by exposing official hypocrisy and, at least, the foibles of those in power. The teenage Beavis and Butt-Head seem to have no contact with their parents, while Daria's mother and father, self-absorbed and obsessed with their professional lives, are clearly deficient in their parenting skills. Beavis and Butt-Head's commentary on the television they watch include cynical comments on the prevailing culture, and their occasional excursions into the mall usually involve a deliberate defiance of rules and regulations. Daria views her teachers and school administrators with thinly disguised contempt.

The Simpsons offers a full display of inept and hypocritical wielders of power: the ruthless tycoon Mr. Burns; the corrupt Mayor Quimby and Chief of Police Wiggums; the emotionally shaky grade-school principal Seymour Skinner, who does not always play by the rule-book, especially if he has a chance to wreak revenge on the rebellious Bart. Bart himself personifies the anti-authoritarian

145

troublemaker; he seems impervious to school discipline, ending up in detention on a daily basis. He never addresses his father as "Dad," but as "Homer." There may be even more defiance of authority in the attitude of Bart's virtuous sister, Lisa. Driven by her concern for the environment, her budding feminism, and her sensitivity to various other social issues, she often ends up confronting the political authorities in her town and even the behavior of her own father. Homer himself defies authority whenever it gets in the way of the life of leisure he seeks, whether it means sneaking out of work at the nuclear power plant or skipping Sunday church services. The boys of *South Park* seem perpetually destined to question the status quo, with their parents and school authorities so intent on controlling their lives and with the occasional visits from interplanetary aliens or other visitors from out of town who present them with alternatives to the prevailing norms of their isolated mountain town.

In its subversive discourse, the cartoon aesthetic allows television viewers to have it both ways. In its display of familial dysfunction and other breakdowns in the social order, animated domestic comedy speaks to viewers who feel marginalized from the dominant culture. Meanwhile, the aesthetic distance of the cartoon allows mainstream viewers to discount the grotesquerie if they so desire. The discourse is liberating for some and reassuring for others. In either case, thanks to animation, the television family is alive and most assuredly kicking.

Bibliography

Brooks, T. and E. Marsh (1999) *The Complete Directory to Prime Time Network and Cable TV Shows, 1946–Present*, twentieth anniversary edition, New York: Ballantine Books.

Coontz, S. (2000) *The Way We Never Were: American Families and the Nostalgia Trap*, New York: Basic Books.

Furniss, M. (1998) *Art in Motion: Animation Aesthetics*, Sydney: John Libbey.

Halberstam, D. (1993) *The Fifties*, New York: Villard Books.

Hamamoto, D. Y. (1989) *Nervous Laughter: Television Situation Comedy and Liberal Democratic Ideology*, New York: Praeger.

Himmelstein, H. (1994) *Television Myths and the American Mind*, second edition, Westport, CT: Praeger.

Jones, G. (1992) *Honey, I'm Home*, New York: St. Martin's Press.

Kellner, D. (1987) "TV, Ideology, and Emancipatory Popular Culture", in H. Newcombe (ed.), *Television: The Critical View*, fourth edition, New York: Oxford University Press.

May, E. T. (1988) *Homeward Bound: American Families in the Cold War Era*, New York: Basic Books.

Stam, R. (1989) *Subversive Pleasures*, Baltimore: Johns Hopkins University Press.

Stark, S. D. (1997) *Glued to the Set*, New York: The Free Press.

Taylor, E. (1989) *Prime Time Families: Television Culture in Postwar America*, Berkeley and Los Angeles: University of California Press.

Chapter 8

FROM FRED AND WILMA TO REN AND STIMPY

What makes a cartoon "prime time"?

Rebecca Farley

Tʜᴇ ᴇᴀʀʟʏ 1990s ᴡᴇʀᴇ ʜᴀɪʟᴇᴅ ʙʏ ᴍᴀɴʏ ᴀs ᴛʜᴇ ɴᴇᴡ ᴀɢᴇ of prime time animation. After the success of *The Simpsons*, new cartoons such as *The Ren & Stimpy Show* (henceforth *Ren & Stimpy*) and *Duckman* seemed to promise that animation had finally conquered prime time. Ultimately many more of these shows perished than thrived, reproducing the short-lived boom that followed the success of *The Flintstones* in the 1960s. "Prime time animation" thus continues to be a problematic category. Moreover, conventional explanations of the success of those few cartoons which did make it in prime time are unsatisfactory, telling us little about the texts themselves or the way they function(ed) within the industrial apparatus.

This chapter, then, asks, "What is 'prime time animation'?" It starts with a look at the industrial context, considering what "prime time" is and what function it serves within the political economy of network television. This in turn reveals the industry's requirement that shows in that slot perform the function of attracting the "family" audience. I then critique the theory of "double-coding," which explains successful "family" texts in terms of their ability to interpellate discrete audience groups. This politically loaded construction imagines audiences as polarized, and explains little about the texts themselves. In the third section, I will perform a close reading of the way two successful prime time animated sitcoms, *The Flintstones* and *Ren & Stimpy*, functioned *as animation*. Considering the whole text – form as well as content – shows that both programs exhibited a high degree of disruptive play. This play, I will argue, is what makes them attractive to viewers and also a risky proposition for broadcasters.

Prime time "family-time"

Animation per se is not a problematic television category, so it is worth investigating the ramifications of the "prime time" label. The simplest definition of prime time – the programming time-slot between 8:00-10:00 p.m. EST – belies its rather more complex implications for broadcasters and producers. The time-slot first gained significance in television's earliest days when, according to industry veteran Cy Schneider, "networks were trying to sell television sets and it was important to demonstrate how television brought the family together and had something for everyone, including the kids" (Schneider 1987: 13). The prime time audience is thus a family audience.[1] In 1975, the National Association of Broadcasters formalized this view, designating 7:00–9:00 p.m. EST as "Family Time" and citing the "general guideline" that such shows should avoid "…anything that could create embarrassment among parents watching with their children" (Barnouw 1990: 480).

Although in 1976 the US Supreme Court ruled that "Family Hour" violated the First Amendment (Johnson 1999: 60), in 1996 and 1997 congressmen and family advocacy groups lobbied broadcasters to re-introduce "family friendly viewing" from 8:00–9:00 p.m. (see, for example, Fleming 1997; Green 1997; Albiniak and McConnell 1999). Their success can be seen as a measure of broadcasters' desperation to retrieve the mass audience that had been leached away during the 1980s by home video recording and cable. As a proportion of all potential viewers, the "family" represents, for broadcasters, the largest coherent audience group or, more accurately, "market" (Freeman 1995: 3).

Walt Disney is generally credited with creating the family market through his early feature films and merchandise campaigns of the late 1930s and early 1940s. The first four Walt Disney features

> were all designed as films for both young and old – clean, non-violent, fantasies with songs and happy endings. They were not targeted at a "family audience" in the modern sense of the term – adults accompanying children as the primary spectators – but over time they helped bring such an audience into being.
>
> (Forgacs 1992: 366)

Later, Disney also created Disneyland as "a place for parents and children to share pleasant times in one another's company" (quoted in Forgacs 1992: 362). Occupying a space between children's afternoon viewing and late-night adult programming, prime time can be seen as a similar "place" in broadcasters' schedules. As WB Network executive Jamie Kellner put it in 1996, "The word family to me is a non-adult concept. There are teens involved, there are kids involved...Family means it's something adults and kids can watch together" (quoted in Rice and McClellan 1997: 20). So although afternoon programming is oriented towards children, and late-night programming is oriented towards adults, prime time is imagined as the time when "families" watch together.

The classic "family" audience suffered a number of blows in the 1990s. First was the fragmenting effect of cable, which targeted niche audiences, accompanied by the growing number of TV sets per home allowing individual rather than family viewing. Second was the unravelling of the notion of the classic nuclear "family" itself. The 1991 showdown between George Bush and *The Simpsons*, followed a year later by Dan Quayle's run-in with *Murphy Brown*, demonstrated the extent to which broadcasters' notion of "the family" was changing.[2] Nonetheless, the "family market" still implies people of different generations watching simultaneously – if no longer "together." The function of prime time, then, is to draw large, mixed-age-group audiences together in front of the television so that broadcasters, who are first and foremost entertainment businesses, can sell that mass demographic to advertisers. Because the mass audience is so lucrative, prime time is also the most acute focus of inter-network rivalry. Shows in that slot must draw strong ratings quickly and consistently; they function primarily to lure people to the network.

Prime time animation in the 1960s

Both *The Flintstones* and *Ren & Stimpy* more than fulfilled this function. Debuting in 1960, *The Flintstones* pilot even beat NBC's established success *Bonanza* (Erikson 1995: 203). It therefore helped latecomer ABC achieve and maintain a secure footing in the ratings competition with rival networks NBC and CBS. *The Flintstones* stayed in prime time for six years – a respectable tenure for any prime time show and a record not matched by another animated series until surpassed by *The Simpsons* in 1997. During that period it was the first animated series Nielsen rated in the top 20 and was, for a time, the fourth-highest-rated program on television (Erikson 1995: 203; Mallory 1999: 80). Leaving aside the vagaries of the rating system, *The Flintstones* clearly satisfied the broadcasters' demographic requirements. When its ratings slipped, *The Flintstones* was sold into syndication where it usually screened as children's fare – a conventional trajectory for defunct prime time shows (Engelhardt 1986: 77). It has been in syndication continuously for forty years, reaching some eighty-seven countries. Its success makes it paradigmatic of Hanna-Barbera's global dominance of the TV animation market, prompting Joe Barbera's boast, "every hour of every day someone, somewhere in the world, is watching *The Flintstones*" (quoted in Mallory 1999: 86).

Prime time animation in the 1990s

In October 1992 *The Flintstones* returned to American prime time on Turner's newly launched cable Cartoon Network (Brown 1992b: 21). From its inception, Cartoon Network was in competition with Nickelodeon, the then-leading cable outlet for cartoons. To strengthen its impact, Cartoon Network scheduled classic prime time animation in the prime time slot, counting on these cartoons to reach the lucrative family market. It worked: 30 percent of their prime time audience were adults (Raiti 2000). " 'We're not positioning The Cartoon Network just as a kids network,' [said] executive vice-president Betty Cohen. 'Toons appeal to people of all ages' " (quoted in Brown 1992b: 21). This presented a significant challenge to Nickelodeon, which had carved a unique niche for itself as a kids' network. Where terrestrial television's Saturday morning cartoons were a "ghetto" of children's programming in a world of adult TV, Nickelodeon shrewdly reversed the arrangement. Adult viewers were explicitly banished to the after-eight Nick-at-Nite block for "nostalgic" reruns of defunct prime time shows such as *I Love Lucy* and *Mister Ed*. For twelve years Nickelodeon targeted an unambiguous demographic of 6–11-year-olds (later extended to include preschoolers), branding itself as a place "where kids can just be kids" and "telling kids to send their parents to their rooms if they watched Nick" (Zoglin 1988: 78).

In August 1991 the network launched Nicktoons, an original animation package consisting of *Rugrats*, *Ren & Stimpy*, and *Doug*. The block screened at 10: a.m. Sunday mornings because, as network president Geraldine Laybourne explained, "it's prime time for our audience" (Greenstein 1991: 16). In this context, Laybourne was not referring to the classic prime time "audience" – a mixed age group might have jeopardized the "pure" demographics Nick presented to sponsors like Mattel (Langer 1999: 157) – but to the stiff competition for child audiences in that time-slot. Nicktoons has been enormously successful. *Rugrats*, pitched at 4–5-year-olds, is now producer Klasky Csupo's flagship show, having been made into two successful movies. *Doug*, pitched at 9–11-year-olds, was sold for US $10 million to Disney in 1995, where it continues to thrive. However, in many ways the story of *Ren & Stimpy* is the most interesting.

The program was, from the start, enormously successful with its target demographic of 6-7-year-olds. However, it also attracted large older audiences.

After sister Viacom network MTV briefly screened *Ren & Stimpy* late on Saturday nights during 1991, Nickelodeon's Sunday 10:00 a.m. ratings doubled to 2.2 million – even though they only had six episodes on repeats (Kanfer 1992: 79). By 1992, a *Wall Street Journal* article estimated that 45 percent of *Ren & Stimpy*'s audience were over 18 (quoted in Brown 1992b: 25). At that point – with the Cartoon Network launch looming – Nickelodeon launched Snick, a prime time package of children's programs, including *Ren & Stimpy* at 9:00 p.m., last in the new block (Brown 1992b: 25). Although Nickelodeon claimed they launched Snick because "the broadcast networks have virtually ignored our audience on Saturday nights" (Langer 1999: 155), the network also needed to consolidate its ratings against any possible incursions by Cartoon Network. Thus the inclusion of *Ren & Stimpy* following the MTV promotion can be seen as a calculated attempt to lure an established, mixed-age audience to prime time on Nick.

Both *The Flintstones* and *Ren & Stimpy*, then, were successful prime time programs. Although there are differences – 1960s broadcast vs. 1990s cable television – the function of "prime time" remained the same. In that slot, both shows were required to serve their network's economic needs by attracting and maintaining large "family" audiences. This they manifestly achieved. Why then does the received wisdom of both broadcasters and TV theory insist that this is all but impossible for television cartoons to do?

What's wrong with double-coding

Theoretical explanations of the ability of cartoons to appeal to mixed age groups were developed – as with so much animation theory – to explain the ability of Walt Disney films to attract family audiences. The theory of double-coding argues that such texts have one "layer" of meaning – usually aligned with the simplistic humor in relatively unsophisticated visuals – which appeals to children, and a second "layer" – usually aligned with the verbal jokes in the soundtrack – which appeals to adults. Though "double-coding" is an academic term, the actual explanation is salient for industry professionals too. For example, describing *Ren & Stimpy*, Nickelodeon executive Karen Flischel said, "[it] follows the 'Looney Tunes' or 'Bullwinkle' model, where there are two levels of appeal – the gross look for kids and the zany humour for the older crowd" (quoted in Langer 1999: 150). It is often assumed that a similar split lies behind the success of *The Simpsons*.

Double-coding is, however, a deeply problematic theory, for several reasons. First, it ignores contextual factors. Adults' disinterest in cartoons is never couched in terms of over-familiarity, scheduling or marketing, while children's willingness to watch is never explained in terms of social influences or the absence of alternatives. Instead double-coding explains the appeal of texts solely in terms of taste; that is, in terms of what people like.[3] Taste in this scenario is causally related to the age of viewers, regardless of influential factors such as race, gender, socioeconomic background, or education. Adults are assumed to enjoy a show intellectually; to appreciate clever cultural references and smart dialogue, but to actively dislike cartoons' rudimentary drawings, slapstick, fantasy, noise and vaudeville elements. Children, on the other hand, are constructed as indiscriminate viewers. Their fondness for noisy, slapstick, simplistic and farcical cartoons is seen not as a legitimate taste but as a deplorable absence of intelligence to be corrected with "educational" programming.

More problematically, double-coding relies on two, false binary oppositions. First, it divides an audience into "adults" and "children," two (apparently) mutually exclusive groups with (seemingly) opposed tastes.[4] This makes it tricky, if not downright impossible, to imagine a single text successfully addressing both – hence the self-fulfilling "problem" of conceiving successful prime time animation. In practice, of course, neither "adults" nor "children" are internally homogenous categories – there are enormous differences between the taste and intellectual capacities of children aged 3 and 11, as indeed there are between 18- and 49-year-olds – and these are enormously complicated by other social factors mentioned earlier. Nor is there a firm line between "childhood" and "adulthood." There is no magical moment when we suddenly "become" adult (and stay that way forever), and there is certainly no guarantee that anyone's taste will ever "mature." A 40-year-old is just as capable of appreciating simplified drawings, farce or slapstick as a 7-year-old.

The second false opposition is set up between a text's form and content. In claiming that "children" and "adults" appreciate different aspects of the text, double-coding theory implies that a cartoon's formal aspects (the silly drawings, wacky sound effects, flat perspective, and lurid colors) have no impact on the way it constructs meaning. Semiotically speaking, this is an untenable position. *All* the elements of a text contribute to its meaning, including the signifier or "vehicle": a cartoon's attractiveness depends not just on its content, but also on the imagination of its visual style, how it sounds, and the comic tension between sound and image. The form is not just a neutral bearer-of-meaning but is itself loaded with culturally and historically specific meaning. Since the "Great Saturday Morning Exile" (see Chapter 2), for example, animation in the West has been historically constructed as a low-quality children's form – it is therefore the *animation* that makes "prime time animation" a problematic category.

What I want to do, then, is to take a close look at *The Flintstones* and *Ren & Stimpy*'s "animatedness" – the way they exploit animation's formal features. The animated form is significant at several textual levels. At the audiovisual level, it allows texts to play around with the most literal aspects of representation (for example, to draw talking pterodactyls). This "playing around" with representation also occurs at the level of content, where an animated text is able (and therefore permitted) to show things not normally acceptable – for example, a living fart – because it isn't "real." Finally, in adapting live-action formats and genres, animated texts manipulate, modify or undermine established conventions, thus stretching the familiar structures of TV representation. Both *The Flintstones* and *Ren & Stimpy* made full use of their animated form at all these levels, and it was this, I shall argue, that made them so successful in prime time.

A modern Stone-Age cartoon

A conventional account of *The Flintstones* might explain the show's trajectory in terms of its content. According to a double-coding approach, *The Flintstones'* success in prime time can be explained because it appropriated an established formula (the sitcom) and its "atomic age" jokes tapped into the *zeitgeist*. When these jokes became less relevant – first through declining standards of writing and later with the passage of time – adults lost interest, ratings slipped, and the show was bumped from prime time. This narrative could explain the success and eventual failure of any prime time show. It does not, however, explain why, out of all the other animation on television then and for the next three decades, *The Flintstones* was not only successful in prime time but inimitably so. This can only be understood in terms of the unique way it deployed its "animatedness."

At the most superficial level, what first catches the eye is a cartoon's audiovisuality. In the case of *The Flintstones* this is worth discussing in some detail, because it was here that Hanna-Barbera refined the technique of limited animation. Though initially an avant-garde cinematic style, Hanna-Barbera's use of limited animation was motivated by – and therefore an "index" of – the pragmatics of television production. All three components of the show's audiovisuality – visual style, the animation itself, and the audiovisual relationship – signify a distinctively made-for-television aesthetic.

The visual style of limited animation – characterized by rudimentary drawings and shallow perspective – was deliberately "roughened" in *The Flintstones*. This had several effects. The practical effect was simply to make the show look good. At the time, TV's black-and-white images were grainy and low-contrast, so *The Flintstones'* crude lines and flat empty spaces looked fresh and clear on the small screen. Hanna-Barbera also had the foresight to work in saturated, unmodulated colors, increasing the show's "sharpness" and adding longevity to its appeal. The unfinished look was also meaningful: it signified television's characteristic immediacy. Joe Barbera described their new mode of production as simply "[taking] away much of the second half of cartoon production, keeping the finished product more like pose reels, closer to roughs…" (Klein 1997: 244). For Hanna-Barbera in 1960, it was more important to be in prime time than to be smoothly "finished."The crude lines and figures were not, therefore, just a suitable style for the "modern stone-age family"; they also signified the experimental nature of the show and drew attention to its status as a pioneering televisual artifact.

Likewise, the style of the animation – the movement of figures – itself indexed both television's characteristic immediacy and *The Flintstones'* experimental status. The "limited" tag describes both the reduced number of drawings per second, as well as the limited number of moving parts (Furniss 1998: 144–51). Practically speaking, the limited animation style was necessitated by the demands of weekly production; it is this sense which has caused limited animation to be known principally as a televisual aesthetic. "Limiting" *The Flintstones'* animation was not just an economic decision, however. In the new context of television technology, limited animation's jerky movements deliberately echoed the rough, jerky style of early cinema animation (Klein 1997: 244). Discarding the prevailing smooth animation aesthetic, *The Flintstones'* rudimentary movements signified that Hanna-Barbera was starting – literally from scratch – a new mode of production.

The third aspect of audivisuality is the relationship between sound and image. The limited animation technique places great emphasis on the soundtrack. The particular importance of dialogue, originally necessitated by the difficulty of moving early TV cameras, has been seen as a distinctively televisual aesthetic (Ellis 1982). In its care and attention to dialogue, then, *The Flintstones* again marked itself as unequivocally "made-for" a medium where the soundtrack dominates the visuals (rather than the other way round, as in cinema).

Overall, *The Flintstones'* audiovisual style drew attention, literally, to the mechanics of television production, exploring *how* this new medium affected representation. *The Flintstones'* content was self-reflexively preoccupied with TV representation. Here, the domestic dinosaur technology functioned as a doubly clever device. First, it supplied endless opportunities for gags, with much of the comedy deriving simply from the silliness of the depictions and the dinosaurs' own ripostes. Secondly, these gags could not have been done in live-action, so they also functioned self-reflexively, that is, to signal a playful willingness to exploit animation's ability to do things that live-action could not. At one level, these gags are about the increasing domestication of post-war American and British society, the "drive to interiority" that was itself centered around the television set.[5] At another level, however, they simply draw attention to *television*, the ascendant crude, modern technology.

This concern with television per se is most explicit at the level of content, in the broad self-reflexive themes which pervade the series. In a cultural context increasingly dominated by entertainment, *The Flintstones* relentlessly references its own production apparatus – the entertainment industries. Characters contest a lawsuit against Perry "Masonry," are caught by "Peek-a-Boo Camera," and rescue "Dripper" the performing seal. They appear on quiz and game shows, win competitions to meet celebrities, perform in beauty competitions, night-clubs, films, TV shows and commercials. Celebrity-obsessed Wilma launches three or four TV careers; Pebbles and Bamm-Bamm are "discovered" by "Eppy Brianstone"; Fred performs as a rock star and in various "movies" as an extra, swamp monster and leading man; Bedrock itself becomes a "location shoot." Foreshadowing *The Simpsons* by a good thirty years, *The Flintstones* guest-starred real-life celebrities, voiced by their flesh-and-blood namesakes, including Ann "Margrock," "Stony" Curtis, and Jimmy "Darrock." This intertextual referencing culminated in a visit to Bedrock by Samantha and Darrin from *Bewitched*. It is important that this self-reflexivity be seen as a function of *The Flintstones'* animatedness. While *The Flintstones* was following a well-established trend set by classic Hollywood shorts, no contemporary live-action TV show could have risked treading such a fine line between spoof and homage, or the irreverent gawking "behind-the-scenes."

A significant proportion of the series' humor therefore derives from its celebration of television. This is no paean of praise, though – it's a comedy, so *The Flintstones* delights in gently undermining the familiar conventions of television representation. The series' format also subverted conventional TV. Just by being an *animated* sitcom, *The Flintstones* drew attention to the construction of this live-action format. The "modern stone-age family" both honors and parodies other two-couple domestic comedies, foregrounding that format's conventions. At the same time, by adapting this format, *The Flintstones* proved that television cartoons could also "do" the half-hour narrative and serial format, and established a precedent for credibly starring "people" instead of anthropomorphized animals. No longer would cartoons necessarily be limited to collections of short clips. *The Flintstones* stretched the paradigms of what cartoons could do on TV.

What made *The Flintstones* attractive, then, was its high degree of self-reflexive play, from the self-consciously "rough" style to the tongue-in-cheek fascination with its own Hollywood origins. This reflexivity works two ways: on the one hand it presented established conventions in a new light, reflecting humorously back on live-action formats. This "spectacularizing" effect – making a spectacle of the limits of the form – renewed the novelty of established live-action formats already beginning to stagnate. At the same time, *The Flintstones* reflexively extended the limits of TV animation. In this sense it can be seen to have functioned as "stretch TV" – it transgressed and broadened the boundaries of what TV animation could do (Turner 1988). These functions must be seen as key to the success of *The Flintstones*. Its ability to surprise and delight, by playfully disrupting conventional expectations of both animation and sitcoms, would have made it heady viewing in the 1960s. If it is difficult, now, to see how *The Flintstones* was once a playful exploration of all aspects of television representation, this is only partly due to the over-exposure of long syndication. It is also because the goal posts have shifted. *The Flintstones* no longer spectacularizes TV, nor stretches its limits. All its major innovations – the refined limited technique, the half-hour format, the "human" characters and "remote" setting – have become the norm for much subsequent television animation.

Immediately following the success of *The Flintstones*, a spate of prime time animation hit the airwaves. None lasted more than a couple of seasons, and then no more emerged for nearly thirty years. The pure economic account of this phenomenon – a "glut" on the market provoking widespread disinterest – is unsatisfactory; after all, the market seems able to sustain any number of live-action sitcoms in prime time and there has never been a fatal glut of crime drama. Instead it must be at least equally true that no follow-up shows fulfilled the "stretching" and "spectacularizing" function sufficiently to draw a prime time audience. Until, that is, the early 1990s brought *The Simpsons* – and *Ren & Stimpy*.

"Happy, happy, joy, joy!"

Like *The Flintstones*, *Ren & Stimpy* was deployed in the prime time slot to secure a large family audience against rival networks. The popularity of the series has prompted several attempts to explain its appeal in both trade and academic journals. However these inevitably fall back on double-coding style constructions of audience tastes. Animation theorist Mark Langer (1999), for instance, argues that the series' design and subtexts made visual and verbal references in a confidential, coded dialogue between the creator, John Kricfalusi, and animation experts Langer calls "animatophiles" – in effect, a third, more sophisticated layer of meaning over the usual two.[6] Similarly, industry writer Martin Goodman (2001) attributes *Ren & Stimpy*'s success to its "elemental, archetypal force," claiming it encapsulated "some of our darkest fears, ones in which the soul and body are powerless against a world out of balance."

Both these accounts fall into the trap of assuming that *Ren & Stimpy*'s older viewers were attracted by the text's intellectual appeal. No doubt there were some smug animation specialists, but an audience constructed around expert knowledge could only have formed a cult core of *Ren & Stimpy*'s larger audience. Nor do any mainstream reviewers refer to *Ren & Stimpy*'s depiction of American "angst" or its "uncomfortable touch of reality" (Goodman 2001). In fact, non-specialist reviews in magazines such as *Esquire* and *Nation's Business* celebrate just the opposite:

> Adults and children alike appreciated the show's complete absence of redeeming social virtue, revelling instead in the characters' pissing, shitting,

sweating, smashing, bashing, greed, thievery, and neuroses – all the things baby boomers adored as tykes before Vietnam-era phobics banished war toys, TV violence, and excessive imagination from the culture.

(Rothenberg 1997: 46)

"Part of the thrill," wrote a reviewer for an online guide to "alternative culture," "was wondering how the Nickelodeon children's network could have sanctioned such a giddily [sic] celebration of flatulence, shaving scum, mucal discharge, and mental cruelty" (Daly and Wice 1998). In short, these reviewers explicitly revel in *Ren & Stimpy*'s disruptive play.

Ren & Stimpy realizes this level of play by fully exploiting its animatedness. For *Ren & Stimpy*, the transgressive part of this function was very important; Nickelodeon needed to draw attention to their commitment to exploring a new, creator-driven mode of production.[7] "At all costs, we wanted to change the face of animation," said Vanessa Coffey, Nickelodeon's vice-president of animation, in 1992. "These episodes are designed to be refreshingly outrageous for at least 15 years" (quoted in Kanfer 1992: 79). To make such an impact, *Ren & Stimpy* played around with and subverted nearly every convention of the cartoon – beginning with the element which first captures the attention: its audiovisuality.

Perhaps the most obvious visual feature of *Ren & Stimpy* is the "grossness and vulgarity" of its design. Ren and Stimpy are spectacularly ugly. The practical function of this visual style was to stand out, glaringly, against the show's smooth, curvy competitors such as *Care Bears* and *Captain Planet*. But this visual style was also meaningful. If, as Forgacs' analysis shows, Disney's "relentless striving for cuteness" helped create and nurture the "family" audience (1992: 363), the look of *Ren & Stimpy* literally signified its active disinterest in such an audience.[8] Like *The Flintstones*, *Ren & Stimpy* strives for a deliberately crude look. Its *mise-en-scène* (the whole of the image) often reveals the mechanics of cartoon construction. Many shots clearly emphasize the contrast between the artistically rendered backgrounds, displaying the texture of paint on paper, and the smooth, "factory-produced" cel layer (the clear sheet on which animated parts are drawn). Such a look was not only startlingly eye-catching – in literally "taking apart" the image this way, *Ren & Stimpy* also flagged its determination to deconstruct and transgress established convention.

The style of the animation enacted the same deconstruction. The limited technique – nothing moves except, say, blinking eyes or moving mouth – frequently erupts into frenzied convulsions of movement. Kricfalusi made full, exuberant use of animation's ability to contort, disfigure, dismantle and otherwise hilariously mistreat his characters. Besides being exhilarating to watch, this exploitation of its animatedness signals the show's determination to literally disrupt other conventions of television animation.

The final component of audiovisuality – the relationship between sound and image – exhibits the same disjointedness. This is mostly realized through offsetting visual events and the corresponding sound effects, which may be incongruous, or incongruously delayed.[9] It is also realized through the soundtrack's own amusing juxtapositions of classical music, original chart-busting songs, and disgusting "organic" sound effects. This goes beyond limited animation's usual emphasis on dialogue, to highlight the soundtrack until it becomes an intrusive gag in its own right.

All the components of *Ren & Stimpy*'s audiovisual style thus shunned the smoothness or coherence that had traditionally characterized TV animation. The effect draws attention to the mechanics of representation and shows how the effort to create a unified text is contrived. Once the mechanical aspects of representation had been opened up as a site of play in this way, *Ren & Stimpy* could also explore the limits of representation – what it could get away with showing. This led to its infamous, seemingly endless displays of bodily effluvia, including brains, blood vessels, nerve endings, hair balls, scabies, spit, "nose goblins," "private moments" in the kitty litter tray, and (years before *South Park*'s Mr. Hanky) a living fart named Stinky. This fantastic gimmick added enormously to the fun of the series (what rude thing will we see today?). It was also neatly metaphoric of the show's broader self-reflexivity. As Mike Barrier put it, "Kricfalusi – like most 10-year-old boys [Kricfalusi was then 42] – never met a bodily function, a rude noise, or a television commercial that wasn't a rich source of comic inspiration" (Barrier 1998: 83). Put another way, *Ren & Stimpy* took equal delight in both bodily and televisual detritus.

This obsession with television permeates the entire series. Unlike *The Flintstones*, however, *Ren & Stimpy* was concerned not with the glamorous, business side of TV but with its trashy, throwaway byproducts – in theme songs, prizes, fandom. An early story line featured Stimpy winning a competition to appear on his favorite cartoon, *The Muddy Mudskipper Show*; both Muddy and theme song reappear, lovingly, throughout the series. In "Stimpy's Fan Club," Stimpy receives so much fan mail that he makes Ren the president of his fan club. Sadly for Ren, many of the fan letters complain about how mean he is to Stimpy – accurately representing the dynamics of *Ren & Stimpy*. Other episodes simply adopt (and twist) the conventions of familiar television genres: the Scooby-esque haunted house ("because it's a good way to kill 12 minutes"); the nature documentary; even, as a couple who occasionally share a bed, the domestic comedy.

Where *Ren & Stimpy* most spectacularly foregrounded television convention, however, is in its reflexive play with the structure of television – what Raymond Williams called the "flow" of American programming; the "interstitial" glue linking "official" segments (Williams 1990). Each episode included *all* the material of classic kids' television – "episodes" of the titular TV series *and* various other "fillers." The fillers took three forms. Most famously, each episode featured in-house "advertisements," with Ren or Stimpy hawking toys just as Fred and Barney had once hawked cigarettes for sponsors of the *The Flintstones* (Erikson 1995: 209). This was an especially daring transgression, mocking the long and heated debate over advertising in children's programming. Next, Ren and Stimpy sometimes appeared in brief interstitials (Nickelodeon calls them "video extras") with titles such as "Breakfast Tips: Let Stimpy show you the way to get your day started right," lampooning the pedagogy of classic children's TV. A third type of self-reflexive filler (dropped as the series progressed) consisted of direct-address closing sequences, with the characters wondering what to do until they "saw" the kids "next week." The "ads," of course, were for non-existent products; the interstitials taught kids to be naughty; the characters, being animated, wouldn't "do" *anything* for a week because they weren't real.[10] It was all an imaginative exercise in form *sans* content.

Together, then, all the segments of *Ren & Stimpy* relentlessly foregrounded its own construction, drawing "viewers attention" to the mechanics, conventions and structures of TV before gleefully transgressing all the rules. It glorified its own status as TV artifact and reveled in its love for all things televisual. This spectacularizing TV – reflexively revealing the usually hidden rules of representation – also transforms the conventions. *Ren & Stimpy* made two key contributions to extending the paradigms of TV animation. First, it flaunted the industrialized mode of production by stripping down limited animation to a highly stylized aesthetic which has since been imitated by (among others) Disney and Hanna-Barbera, in shows such as *Cow and Chicken*, *Angry Beavers* and *Johnny Bravo*. Second, it demonstrated that the "gross look" did not appeal exclusively to children but also attracted adults, a revelation exploited in the degraded aesthetic and content of shows such as *Beavis and Butt-Head*, *South Park*, and *Gogs*.

Intriguingly, *Ren & Stimpy*'s "iconographically trashy" look is cited by John Caldwell in his discussion of prime time's "trash aesthetic" (1995: 97). He notes that "trash television" shows "defy conventional demographics" and suggests that part of their ability to do so is their reveling in superficial pleasures, televisuality, and surface play. Indeed, prime time cartoons – described by even their fans as "bastardized" or "the most banal of genres" – share many characteristics with trash TV, including the "unfinished" look, the noisy soundtrack, the emphasis on physicality and superficiality, and the eclectic audiovisual clutter – they are, as Caldwell puts it, "dominated by informational noise" (1995: 97). So far as it goes, then, the trash aesthetic does describe some of the operations of prime time cartoons. However there are two further elements, critical to the operation of prime time animation, which are largely missing from Caldwell's account. These are the "stretching" function – the transgression of boundaries and exploration of new paradigms – and the prevailing sense of fun.

Prime time, play time

To incorporate both these qualities, with elements of the trash aesthetic and stretch TV, it is helpful to discuss cartoons in terms of play. Play can be thought of as a mode of communication emphasizing disruption, imagination, expressivity and (above all) fun. As a mode, it is a function of the whole text, signaled by an expressive rather than naturalist audiovisual style. Thinking of these texts in terms of their playfulness thus allows a fuller picture to develop, taking into consideration *all* elements of a text including form, genre, sound effects and aesthetic style, as well as content. It specifically recognizes these texts' wilful foregrounding of shallow and superficial pleasures and their determination to use the form for fun, rather than earnest or sophisticated purposes; although they may deal with serious social issues, they do so in an uncompromisingly playful way. A significant clue that a text is invoking the play mode is its depiction of "nonsenses" – for example, the "modern stone-age" technology, talking dinosaurs, and the Great Gazoo in *The Flintstones*; Stinky, Muddy Mudskipper and Log in *Ren & Stimpy* – purely for their surreal comic value. The play tag thereby avoids the double-coding error of attempting to separate form from content.

In refusing to privilege content, approaching cartoons in terms of play also avoids the double-coding tendency to intellectualize the pleasures of the text. In the play mode, the popular entertainment value of a program is located primarily in trivialities. Certainly neither *The Flintstones* nor *Ren & Stimpy* made any grand social statements, wrought any dramatic critique or radical revelations. Rather, what was delightful was the wealth of petty gags – *The Flintstones'* celebrity cameos, bad puns, domestic farce, and sarcastic dinosaurs; *Ren & Stimpy's* spoof products, songs, satire, and extravagant stretch-and-squash. Both shows also featured striking design, wacky sound effects, big noses, hallucinogenic color schemes, good-natured stupidity, and an engagingly self-aware celebration of their own production apparatus.

An emphasis on these pleasures enables discussion of the success (or failure) of these and other shows, garnered without having to attribute audiences' tastes according to their ages – anyone can have a laugh. Enjoying these playful pleasures does not require specialist knowledge or intellectual sophistication. The fun of the expressive visual style, comic animation, disjointed audiovisual relationship, chases, violence and silly songs such as "Happy Happy Joy Joy" are open to anyone. The "appeal to the playful, imaginative, fantasy, irresponsible" is not, after all, "paedocratic" – Hartley's term (1992: 111) – as though it is somehow regressive for adults to have fun, or as though children were never serious, rational or responsible. Indeed, one of the chief qualities of fun is its glee in undermining such power structures (Rutsky and Wyatt 1990), whether through sending up the fan/star relationship, depicting resentful home appliances – or ignoring the rules about what children and adults are supposed to like. The intrinsic leveling quality of fun is what makes play a democratic and inclusive mode. Rather than bisecting the show or imagining a polarized audience – with the inevitable antagonism, hierarchizing and value-loading that follow – it is more useful to see these shows as successful precisely because of their ability to undermine such constructions and provide shared pleasures. Granted, nothing can guarantee a viewer will respond playfully, and certainly age (along with other social factors, including viewing context) may well inflect how individual audience members respond. Nonetheless the play text seeks to interpellate viewers by laying out a feast of trivial pleasures available to everyone regardless of age: irreverence, imagination, silliness, fun – the more the merrier.

If we think of play, then, not as a value but as a quantitative textual quality, we begin to see both what allows a cartoon to succeed in prime time, and also what makes it so risky. The prime time slot, as this essay's opening paragraphs demonstrated, requires texts to attract and retain large numbers of viewers of diverse ages. *The Flintstones* and *Ren & Stimpy* did this by engaging a play mode which spectacularized television, making a novelty of familiar formats, poking fun at convention, transgressing established boundaries. This disruptive play permeated the texts, from their original audiovisual styles to their depiction of imaginary objects, to self-reflexive content and exploration of structure. In this sense, they had a lot going on internally – more, perhaps, than less successful texts. As John Kricfalusi explains, "the kind of cartoons I like to do are the kind the audience naturally likes...'cartoony' cartoons. Where the art, the motion, tells the story...Cartoons that *use* the medium" (quoted in Brophy 1994b: 98, emphasis added). *Ren & Stimpy* did *use* the medium, at all levels, to spectacular effect.

At the same time, this tendency to make fullest use of the medium to show-case disruptive play is what makes cartoons a liability. The fun of exploiting animation's freedom from verisimilitude means texts run the risk of "giving in to entropy" (Miller 1974: 35). The "insertion of the possibility of anarchy" (Turner 1988: 27) brought about by undermining convention, while spectacular to watch, is nevertheless destabilizing. It sets up an often irreconcilable tension between, on the one hand, the need to catch viewers' eyes through a high degree of play and maintain that interest with ever-more creative transgressions, and, on the other hand, an industrialized mode of production which mitigates against such disorderly conduct. From the point of view of the networks, there is always the danger that an unruly show will go too far and alienate the audience. In more than one interview, Kricfalusi blamed this tension for *Ren & Stimpy*'s ultimately fatal production problems: "It wasn't because we were trying to put dirty things in, things you 'can't put on television,' that was causing us problems...It was, 'We don't understand the joke. Your story doesn't make sense. It's illogical.

Change it'" (quoted in Rothenberg 1997: 46). Further, he complained, "Every time we came up with something new, Nick wondered why we didn't stick with what we'd done...They never got it in their heads we were always doing new things. The whole point of a cable station is to give something we can't get on broadcast" (quoted in Granger 1992: 24).

Play, then, is both animation's *raison d'être* and also the aspect which makes it so troublesome for the industry, particularly in the prime time slot where fast results are vital. Where networks want a secure, tried-and-tested formula, a playful text cannot sit still, but has to keep exploring, testing what television can do. A playful text revitalizes familiar formats, giving established conventions a good shaking, and may lead, over time, to new combinations and formats – both *The Flintstones* and *Ren & Stimpy* evolved new aesthetics imitated by subsequent cartoon programming. This is suspenseful to watch, engaging us creatively, irreverently, and with humor. Both *The Flintstones* and *Ren & Stimpy* functioned in this way. It was their high degree of internal playfulness – ever disrupting the conventions of genre, time-slot and content, and testing the limits of visual representation – which made them successful prime time animation. Both series invoked a disorderly, disruptive play in a range of textual elements, ultimately transforming the terrain and, en route, making us laugh. "I don't think the stuff is that weird," said John Kricfalusi in 1992. "We just do what's funny" (quoted in Brophy 1994b: 100). In so doing, prime time animation has the potential to transgress all kinds of boundaries. It's a good reason to keep watching.

Notes

1 For an entertaining dissection of broadcasters' definition of the word "family," see Hartley (1992).
2 See also Price Colman (1999).
3 Here we should bear in mind the networks' notoriously unreliable methods of market-testing (Gitlin 1994).
4 For an extended discussion of this construction, see Seiter (1995), especially Chapter 1: "Children's Desires/Mothers' Dilemmas: The Social Contexts of Consumption."
5 See Moores (1993: 81–6).
6 This "expert register" is sometimes also attributed to *The Simpsons*'s widespread appeal – see for example Rushkoff (1994).
7 This wasn't new at all of course but harked back to the studio system. Indeed, as Langer points out, a great deal of *Ren & Stimpy*'s style and content deliberately invokes the older style of cartoon production.
8 See also Kricfalusi's mentor, Ralph Bakshi, on an "anti-Disney" aesthetic (Brophy 1994a).
9 For a detailed discussion of this tendency in cartoons, see Brophy (1991).
10 It is important to know that, although they may become attached to cartoon characters, children also recognize their unreality from a very early age. See, for example, Hodge and Tripp (1986).

Bibliography

Albiniak, P. and B. McConnell (1999) "Still Pushing for the Family Hour," *Broadcasting & Cable*, 15 November: 24.

Barnouw, E. (1990) *Tube of Plenty: The Evolution of American Television*, second edition, New York and Oxford: Oxford University Press.

Barrier, M. (1998) "Master of the Cult Cartoon," *Nation's Business*, June: 83.

Brophy, P. (1994a) "Interview with Ralph Bakshi," in *Kaboom! Explosive Animation from America and Japan*, Sydney: Museum of Contemporary Art, 88–96.

—— (1994b) "Interview with John Kricfalusi," in *Kaboom! Explosive Animation from America and Japan*, Sydney: Museum of Contemporary Art.

—— (1991) "The Animation of Sound," in A. Cholodenko (ed.), *The Illusion of Life: Essays on Animation*, Sydney: Powerhouse/Australian Film Commission.

Brown, R. (1992a) "Saturday Night's All Right for Nickelodeon," *Broadcasting*, 18 May: 25+.

—— (1992b) "Turner Toons up for Fall Launch," *Broadcasting*, 10 August: 21.

Caldwell, J. (1995) *Televisuality: Style, Crisis and Authority in American Television*, New Brunswick, NJ: Rutgers University Press.

Colman, P. (1999) "Loesch Redefines Family TV," *Broadcasting & Cable*, 1 February: 69.

Daly, S. and N. Wice (eds.) (1998) "*Ren and Stimpy*, alt.culture. an a–z of the '90s," Time Warner. Available at: http://www.altculture.com/ (accessed 15 April 2001).

Ellis, J. (1982) *Visible Fictions*, London: Routledge & Kegan Paul.

Engelhardt, T. (1986) "The Shortcake Strategy," in T. Engelhardt and T. Gitlin (eds.), *Watching Television*, New York: Pantheon.

Erikson, H. (1995) *Television Cartoon Shows: An Illustrated Encyclopedia 1949 through 1993*, Jefferson, NC: McFarland & Co.

Fleming, H. (1997) "Growing Pressure for Family Hour," *Broadcasting & Cable*, 12 May: 9

Forgacs, D. (1992) "Disney Animation and the Business of Childhood," *Screen*, Volume 33, Number 4.

Freeman, M. (1995) "The Sun Sets on PTAR," *Mediaweek* 31 July: 3+.

Furniss, M. (1998) *Art in Motion: Animation Aesthetics*, Sydney: John Libbey.

Gitlin, T. (1994) *Inside Prime time*, London: Routledge.

Goodman, M. (2001) "Cartoons aren't Real! Ren and Stimpy in Review," *Animation World Magazine*, 5.12, March. Available at: http://www.awn.com/mag/issue5.12/5.12pages/goodmanrenstimpy3.php3, (accessed 21 March 2001).

Granger, R. (1992) "'Ren and Stimpy' Creator Talks Back to Nick," *Multichannel News*, 9 November: 24.

Green, M. Y. (1997) "Networks Take Family Friendly Focus," *Broadcasting & Cable*, 29 September: 48+.

Greenstein, J. (1991) "Animated Nickelodeon Seeks to Build Library," *Multichannel News*, 18 March: 16.

Hartley, J. (1992) *Tele-ology: Studies in Television*, London: Routledge.

Hodge, R. and D. Tripp (1986) *Children and Television: A Semiotic Approach*, Cambridge: Polity Press.

Johnson, T. (1999) "The Decline of Television's Family Hour," *USA Today Magazine*, November: 60+.

Klein, N. (1997) *7 Minutes: The Life and Death of the American Animated Cartoon*, London and New York: Verso.

Langer, M. (1999) "Animatophilia, Cultural Production and Corporate Interests: The Case of *Ren & Stimpy*," in J. Pilling (ed.), *A Reader in Animation Studies*, Sydney: John Libbey.

Mallory, M. (1999) *Hanna-Barbera Cartoons*, London: Virgin.

Miller, S. (1974) "The Playful, the Crazy and the Nature of Pretence," *Rice University Studies*, Volume 60, Number 3: 31–51.

Moores, S. (1993) *Interpreting Audiences: The Ethnography of Media Consumption*, London: Sage.

Raiti, G. (2000) "Prime time Animation Fills Growing Niche TV," *Animation World Magazine*, 5.8, November. Available at: http://www.awn.com/issue5.8/5.8pages (accessed 21 March 2001).

Rice, L. and S. McClellan (1997) "Kellner's Latest Surprise: The WB Gets New Legs," *Broadcasting & Cable*, 11 August: 20+.

Rothenberg, R. (1997) "Tooning out TV: 'Ren and Stimpy' Creator John Kricfalusi Returns. Happy, Happy! Joy, Joy!" *Esquire*, February: 46.

Rushkoff, D. (1994) *Media Virus! Hidden Agendas in Popular Culture*, Sydney: Random House.

Rutsky, R. L. and J. Wyatt (1990) "Serious Pleasures: Cinematic Pleasure and the Notion of Fun," *Cinema Journal*, Volume 30, Number 1: 3–19.

Schneider, C. (1987) *Children's Television*, Lincolnwood, IL: NTC Business Books.

Seiter, E. (1995) *Sold Separately: Parents and Children in Consumer Culture*, Brunswick, NJ: Rutgers University Press.

Sinclair, C. (1999) "That's Not All, Folks," *The Standard*, 15 October. Available at: http://www.thestandard.com/article/display/0,1151,6967,00.html (accessed 13 March 2001).

Turner, G. (1988) "Transgressive TV: From *In Melbourne Tonight* to *Perfect Match*," in G. Turner and J. Tulloch (eds.), *Australian Television: Programs, Politics and Pleasures*, Sydney: Allen & Unwin.

Williams, R. (1990) *Television: Technology and Cultural Form*, in E. Williams (ed.), second edition, London: Routledge.

Zoglin, R. (1988) "Letting Kids Just be Kids," *Time*, 26 December: 78.

Chapter 9

"WE HARDLY WATCH THAT RUDE, CRUDE SHOW"

Class and taste in *The Simpsons*

Diane F. Alters

"What is so obnoxious about *The Simpsons*", a friend of mine says, "I don't like the way they look. I don't like the way they sound. I'm not going to watch them!…The humor doesn't appeal to me. A lot of it's slapstick and rude. Violent. I don't find it funny. I don't find it amusing. I don't find it socially uplifting."

(Susan Garcia, 41)

"Occasionally we'll watch Bart Simpson. Occasionally there'll be a really funny show, but when they get crass, I'll turn it off."

(Sharon Hartman, 42)

Introduction

AFTER MORE THAN A DECADE ON THE AIR, *THE SIMPSONS* still represents the worst in television for many parents, despite the appearance of harder-edged animated shows such as *Beavis and Butt-Head* and *South Park*. In a series of open-ended interviews I conducted for a study of media and daily life, some parents, such as Susan Garcia, above, even said that they hated the show.[1] But most of these critical parents eventually also expressed a more positive view, a contradiction that is one of the subjects of this essay. This ambivalent view of *The Simpsons* also worked in other ways: some parents who first described the show as insightful social commentary also worried that it was not suitable for their young children. Even those who said they just thought it was funny watched it with some apprehension. Mixed feelings about *The Simpsons* were frequently voiced: it was one of the most-contested and most-watched shows among the families interviewed.[2] I argue that this ambivalence and anxiety around *The Simpsons* have a great deal to do with class and taste distinctions, as parents sought to distance themselves from a show they defined as lower class, and from television itself, also seen as lower class. Yet they also undermined such distancing attempts by describing their own or their family's viewing in middle-class terms, in a process of legitimation that will be explored below.[3] These conflicting opinions and practices are part of a larger, dynamic social process, as I view cultural practices and cultural production as major, constitutive elements of a social order (Williams 1981: 12).

A similar process of legitimation also occurs in other places in American culture: middle-class periodicals such as the *New York Times* and the *New Yorker* have also sought to elevate *The Simpsons*, animation, and television against a wider tendency to view them as lower class. In what follows, I discuss these efforts in terms of what Pierre Bourdieu calls "competing principles of legitimacy," in which the order of cultural importance of various genres in the field of cultural production changes as a result of internal and external processes (Bourdieu 1993: 50–5). In addition, Bourdieu's conception of *field* offers an instructive model for studying social relations, as a *field* is made up of both subjective and objective positions, both of which respond to synchronic and diachronic changes (Bourdieu 1993: 29–73). The concept of field is Bourdieu's attempt to study culture in terms of both individual experience and social structure, and it is especially relevant in terms of my research because I talk with audience members about individual experiences but also examine this talk in terms of social conditions and relations. This approach allows me simultaneously to look at the ambivalence of viewers as contradictions held in a kind of tension as I seek to explore the social relations of cultural consumption that underlie that ambivalence.

In the two families presented here, the process of distinction seemed strongly connected to their tenuous class position, as both had a somewhat precarious relationship with middle-class status. Their cultural capital (education and related tastes) marked them as middle class, but their low economic capital was a marker of their proximity to a lower-class position. The stakes involved in policing the boundaries of taste in these families were particularly high, as they needed to maintain or increase their cultural capital to guard against the effects of any loss of economic capital – a loss that could plunge them definitively into the lower class, with material and symbolic consequences. As a result, they struggled to secure more highly regarded middle-class positions by laying claim to more cultural capital. This analysis emphasizes the symbolic dimensions of class relations as well as their economic dimensions; class identity is seen as a matter of perception and also as materially constructed (Bourdieu 1984: 482–4).

In addition, the interviews suggest a link between class/taste and gender, as it was mothers who seemed to worry most about taste. It was mothers who most often expressed their reservations about *The Simpsons*, described attempts to control their children's viewing, and thus took on certain aspects of a woman's traditional, historically constructed role as moral guardian. However, in both families the parents' home roles were linked in some way to their roles outside the home, and there were indications that power was shared in connection with television. This link between class/taste and gender underscores the complexity of social relations involved in understanding the role of popular culture in modern life.

To explore this complex process of distinction, this essay examines the two case-study families in some detail. I do not intend to universalize these families but to explore them as "particular case[s] of the possible," a way of emphasizing particularities in a social context (Bourdieu 1984: xi).[4] Family members are treated here as historical subjects whose engagement in mediated popular culture offers a way to elucidate their positions in relation to the society around them.[5] In this essay, I focus on the social conditions of the two families and how they regarded *The Simpsons* and its central characters, members of a working-class nuclear family who struggle with and sometimes triumph over the chaos wrought by social change.[6]

Class and taste

In my first interview with the Hartman family, the mother, Sharon, 42, brought up *The Simpsons* as a way of emphasizing that her family was *not* the Simpsons.[7] She said the show was unsuitable for her children, Glen, 14, Laura, 9, and Amy, 8, because the bad words and unruly behavior – Bart's in particular – were inappropriate models for well-behaved children.[8] Indeed, in an individual interview Laura remarked that her mother sometimes denied her request to watch *The Simpsons* with this exclamation: "No! I don't want my kids growing up to be brats!"[9] Still, the Hartmans watched *The Simpsons* often enough for the children to be able to enthusiastically describe plot details – something that Sharon cheerfully acknowledged when her daughters caught her in a contradiction in her concern to distance her family from that of the Simpsons:

> Some of the shows, just because of their attitude towards things – we don't watch *The Simpsons*, hardly at all, and it's mostly because, I'm sorry, I'm not going to raise a spoiled, rotten brat! [*Her daughters, 9 and 8, have been giggling while she speaks. She pauses and laughs.*] Yeah, occasionally, yes, they will watch that, and occasionally, it's okay. But it's not a steady-diet kind of thing.

This characterization of the Simpsons as ill-behaved was one of several declarations by Sharon that sought to distinguish her children as well-mannered, a supposed middle-class quality. In this instance, she interpreted her children's giggles as a check on her initial implication that the family seldom watched the show, and she sought to clarify her words by insisting that although they did see the show, their viewing was limited.

Sharon Hartman's critique of *The Simpsons* – she also said it was "rude" and "crude" – is based on stereotypes of working-class culture. Like Archie Bunker, the Simpsons bear many markers of working-class stereotypes: Homer's beer belly, his low-level security job at the nuclear power plant, his marriage to Marge while they were still at high school. Even their diet is mock working class, pure fantasy Elvis: pork chops, mashed potatoes, and Homer's stay-home-from-church breakfast of a caramel-filled waffle wrapped around a stick of butter on a toothpick ("Homer the Heretic," 8 October 1992). The writers sometimes flirt with the Simpsons' class status, occasionally making them so crude as to be "white trash," as Homer's breakfast suggests. More often, however, their supposed working-class attributes are emphasized, as when they are contrasted with "white trash" carnival workers who take over their house ("Bart Carny," 1 January 1998), or wealthy socialites ("Scenes From the Class Struggle in Springfield," 4 February 1996).[10] Although they have at least one marker of being middle class – their house – their low economic position and their stereotypical working-class tastes are otherwise fairly constant in the show. George Meyer, a writer and executive producer for the show, describes the house as middle class, although "their finances are kind of glossed over" in relation to the house because they would not have been able to afford it on Homer's income (Owen 1999: 64+). The Simpsons are a nuclear family (Homer is the wage-earner, Marge stays home and is largely responsible for the three children), a form associated with the white middle classes in the 1950s and subsequently naturalized as "traditional" in American society as a whole (Coontz 1992; Mintz and Kellogg 1988). The depiction of a nuclear family is intentional – the show's creators wanted to keep a "traditional" core to the series as a setup to the "quirky" jokes, according to Meyer (Owen 1999).

Often, the jokes play off the Simpsons' stereotypical working-class attributes, with much humor derived from Homer's ignorance, his drinking buddies' travails, or Marge's taste in household decorations. Barbara Ehrenreich, writing before *The Simpsons* was a half-hour show on television, sees other white working-class stereotypes on television as largely manufactured by middle-class writers who would have been more inhibited about caricaturing other groups, including racial groups. She describes these stereotypes of the white working class: "Its tastes are 'tacky'; its habits unhealthful; and its views are hopelessly bigoted and parochial" (Ehrenreich 1989: 7). In fact, she argues, the American working class is much more complex and diverse. She notes that Archie Bunker was an "ambiguous" character, having lovable qualities (like Homer) as well as his stereotypical working-class ignorance. In some ways, Homer is an extension of Archie, an example of television's exploitation of what Ehrenreich calls the "humorous possibilities" of a class that had begun to be defined in the 1970s as "reactionary, bigoted, and male" (Ehrenreich 1989: 114). This representation has mellowed somewhat: although Homer is sometimes reactionary and bigoted, he is a more complex and sympathetic character than Archie Bunker.[11]

More importantly, *The Simpsons* is not about Homer in the way that *All in the Family* was about Archie Bunker – and indeed the parents discussed here sometimes talked about watching "*Bart* Simpson," the character that loomed largest for them because they were so concerned with their own children's behavior and its class-based implications. *The Simpsons* offers standards of family and behavior through stories about characters struggling with basic and changing issues in American family life. When the behaviors of the family were coded as working-class, this worried Sharon Hartman – for her, the Simpsons were somewhere near the bottom of a hierarchy of families. As a cultural product the show itself was at rock-bottom, one of the worst shows her children watched, mainly because of its general "crudeness," in Sharon's view, and its depiction of children as "brats," a quality she cited several times in the interviews. In addition, Sharon, like other parents interviewed, considered television itself to have little cultural value. Ellen Seiter also observed this widespread opinion in her own audience research and described television as "the least legitimate of media forms" (Seiter 1999: 4).

In Bourdieu's view, cultural consumption fulfills the social function of legitimating social differences (Bourdieu 1984: 7, 257–317). In Sharon's case, denying the "rude, crude show" implied that she embraced more polite, middle-class cultural products. Since cultural practices are closely linked to one's education (a form of cultural capital) and one's social origin, experience, and ways of thinking (the "habitus"), Sharon distanced herself from *The Simpsons* in an effort to situate herself in the middle class. Like the French working classes that Bourdieu analyzes, the Simpson family served as a negative reference point for the Hartmans: "As for the working classes, perhaps their sole function in the system of aesthetic positions is to serve as a foil, a negative reference point, in relation to which all aesthetics define themselves, by successive negations" (Bourdieu 1984: 57). Making distinctions is an effort to signify class status, and to slip in class is to lose power in both a material and symbolic sense. In an American context, class slippage is all too possible, as misfortune easily leads to a "downward slide" for all but the "most securely wealthy," as Ehrenreich notes (1989: 15; 2001).

Indeed, like many families in the US, the Hartmans faced the possibility of such a downward slide. For example, they rented their small house, a situation particularly precarious for those earning near minimum wage. Rent is "exquisitely sensitive" to market forces that have significantly pushed up the price of housing in recent years (Ehrenreich 2001: 199–201). In the city in which the Hartmans lived the rental vacancy rate was in the low single digits, making rental housing scarce and expensive. John Hartman, the 43-year-old father, held two part-time, low-paying blue-collar jobs while Sharon worked part-time as a clerk. They had spent the last decade or so following their religion and had lived frugally while John founded two ultimately unsuccessful churches in other cities. In terms of cultural capital, they had many middle-class attributes. Both John and Sharon had undergraduate degrees, and both grew up in families that were at least middle class, with John's perhaps more well-off in terms of economic and social capital, his father being a medical doctor. The Hartmans sought to retain this foothold in the middle class, although their own low income made that foothold precarious.

Sharon also made a point of describing habits that added cultural capital to the family's stock: family members read many "classic" books, frequently used their library cards, and encouraged the children to excel in highly academic programs.[12] Perhaps in part to demonstrate their cultural capital, John and 9-year-old Laura were playing a game of chess when I arrived one evening. The Hartman children clearly were "readers," as Sharon termed it – they summarized favorite book plots as deftly as they did story lines from *The Simpsons* and other TV shows. In describing herself and her children as "readers," Sharon was drawing on a sense of "reading" as a cultured pursuit, a definition which has developed from the Renaissance to today and which eventually came to connect reading literature with social class. Reading, as understood by Sharon, functions as "polite learning" in the domain of "taste" and "sensibility" (Williams 1977: 51). More complexly, Sharon, like the mother in my other case-study, compared reading books with watching television, an evaluation that broadens this definition of reading to include reading television shows – or at least *The Simpsons* – as literature, a point explored in the next section of this essay.

Sharon's attempts to distinguish her family from that of *The Simpsons* and to downplay their viewing of the show also seemed aimed at me as an academic. It is possible that she saw me as a representative of high culture (and thus dismissive of popular culture, although I stated otherwise) because I was studying for a doctorate and taught at a university. In any case, she wanted to make sure I did not confuse her family with the Simpsons. It is a "class privilege" of audience researchers that they have access both to the high culture represented by academia and the low culture of television (Seiter 1999: 27). Sharon also claimed this "class privilege" as she emphasized the family's interest in reading and education and her critique of television and *The Simpsons*. In addition, Sharon's distancing from *The Simpsons* and television was perhaps also an attempt to turn back another stereotype, one that connects evangelicals such as herself with the working class. As a group, evangelicals have less education and less cultural capital than non-evangelicals, although those attributes have begun to change in recent years (Roof 1999: 99–104; Wuthnow 1988: 132–72). Indeed Sharon and John, who both converted during college, were part of a more educated neo-evangelical movement. Sharon may have wanted to distance her family from class-based stereotypes about her religion in case I held such views of evangelicals.

It is significant that it was Sharon, not John, who most consistently and firmly described standards for behavior and distanced herself and her family from what she saw as a low-culture product. In doing so, Sharon took on a woman's role as moral guardian of the domestic sphere. This ideology has roots in the nineteenth-century distinction between public (husband as breadwinner) and private (wife as homemaker, child-rearer) realms, but is complicated by Sharon's own role as one of the family's wage-earners and John's position as a former pastor. Sharon's attempts to distinguish the Hartmans from the Simpsons were supported by her husband, although unlike Sharon he did not initiate discussion of these distinctions or elaborate on them. Instead, he leveled his sharpest critique at themes connected with his former career as a pastor: he identified as "unacceptable" story lines that "mock Christianity and might be mocking something that someone has done being a Christian, trying to be a Christian." Sharon indicated support for this position, but left such assessments to John to make and act upon. As a result, he had turned off an episode in which Homer concocts his own religion to get out of attending church, prompting some friendly visits from God ("Homer the Heretic"). Despite John's reservations, one child, Laura, knew the plot of "Homer the Heretic" and had thought about it because her best friends agreed with Homer's complaint that church is boring. Still, to all the Hartmans, some shows were just funny. For example, John liked *Simpsons* episodes about aliens, a theme more distant from his religion. The overall point is that the Hartmans held their ambivalence in a kind of tension: the father objected to a particular episode because he believed it mocked Christianity and the mother abhorred the Simpsons' conduct and voiced her concerns about her children's behavior in relation to the show, but they still found episodes they all could watch and enjoy.

Distinctions and gender in a transitional space

Susan and Bob Garcia had many disagreements about the value of television in general and *The Simpsons* in particular, but they had achieved a kind of ragged harmony about both in their actions and their assessments of them. What they achieved at home with television is not unlike what they constructed outside the

171

home, where they tried to share responsibility. Over time, their attempts at power-sharing outside the home helped structure how they lived inside – and perhaps vice versa. Although they were very different in their approaches, they ended up sharing power in regard to television, due to complex mental and material accommodations they made to one another's approaches.

Susan and Bob's differences regarding *The Simpsons* and television were expressed in their use of space in their house.[13] *The Simpsons* was a major reason Bob Garcia, 44, had enclosed the porch of their house, creating a special room for the television set so that he and the children, Peter, 10, and Janie, 8, could watch without disturbing Susan, who hated the show. *The Simpsons*, which aired in rerun every weekday evening, took up one-third of the daily hour-and-a-half of television Susan allowed the children to watch during the school year. (The other shows they chose, eclectically enough, were *Wishbone* and *Fresh Prince*, and on weekends the limit was eased so that they could watch sports.) In explaining this arrangement, Bob and Susan made some gender distinctions but it also seemed that in some ways they tried to share power over television much as they tried to share work inside and outside the home. Usually only one parent at a time worked at a low-paying job so that the other could be at home to help with the children's schooling, and they frequently switched places to do so, a situation that will be elaborated below. By focusing on this household, I describe how one family dealt with many social divisions that challenged the parents' efforts to construct a life that positioned their children in the middle class both symbolically and economically. With their work arrangements, Bob and Susan Garcia in effect challenged gendered roles in the American economy, while at the same time they also reproduced and challenged gendered practices at home in relation to television and work. Their practices and opinions open up a space to examine how certain ways of thinking are reproduced and challenged in one family – a particular case of the possible.

Bob described the television room with some irony as a "family value" because it maintained harmony in the family by separating Bob's and the children's *Simpsons* viewing from Susan's dislike of the show. Thus the room is a kind of borderland or transition space where differentiation can best be examined because contradictions operate most clearly. In fact, a complex array of contradictory sensibilities made up the television room. When Bob showed me the coal-burning stove he had installed in the TV room, he used the Spanish word for coal, *carbón*. This was a reference to his Mexican-American background – he had installed the stove because the aroma of coal reminded him of his childhood. Bob described both good and bad experiences emerging from his background; good in what he called his "mixed" marriage (Susan was of Anglo-American background) and in his college involvement in the Chicano movement, and occasionally, bad in his conservative city.[14]

Enclosing the porch marked the third time the television had shifted location in the Garcia home, and the story of where it was placed highlights some of the tradeoffs the Garcias made to keep harmony. Shortly after Bob and Susan married, they bought the three-bedroom house and arranged it to accommodate their separate interests: one bedroom was theirs, one was his for the television set and one was hers for her sewing machine. When Peter was born, the sewing room became the nursery and the sewing machine went to the living room, eventually coming to serve as a table for the family computer. The television remained in a room of its own. A few years after Janie was born, the children moved to separate bedrooms and Bob enclosed the porch for the television set. Susan explained why:

> I hated going into houses and seeing the *whole house* built around a television. I just wanted a place where I could get away from it. And, we like company and sometimes someone comes over to watch television, and we have a place where we can have a conversation or a game without a television. And so that was my insistence, and that was how we accomplished it, by enclosing the porch so that we could have a TV room and still have a whole living room.

The history of the Garcia family's television space highlights the contradictions in the social relations represented in the family.

The Garcias had negotiated a set of work roles that implicitly challenged more traditional divisions of labor in a household. Early in the marriage, Bob and Susan had agreed on a kind of serial employment: one would work full time for pay for a year or so while the other stayed home with the children. Sometimes the "home parent," as they called the non-waged person, also worked part-time for pay outside the home but only if that parent could still devote a great deal of time to the children's schooling, to be an advocate for them. This included carefully choosing schools, studying curricula, and working on library, fundraising and other school-support activities as well as helping with homework. Both had wanted to be deeply involved in their children's daily lives and to encourage their academic success, something that would have been much harder for Bob to do if he had always held the primary paying job. On the surface, it seemed that Bob had taken on a women's notion of "success" as more home-centered and economically weaker than male success – a socially constructed standard analyzed by Maria Markus (1987: 102–3). More complexly, both Bob and Susan challenged those gendered standards of achievement, and in the process had to sort out related problems associated with these divisions.

When the children were younger, the home parent worked few or no waged hours, but those had increased as the children grew older. At the time of the interviews, Susan was the home parent and worked almost twenty hours a week as a secretary – more than usual for the home parent – while Bob worked full-time as a custodian. A few months after the initial interviews, they "traded off," with Bob working part-time for wages and Susan full-time as a secretary. As home parent, Susan cooked and had more domestic duties than Bob. After the switch, he took on most but not all of her domestic tasks. The Garcias' economic arrangements were aimed at helping the children excel at book-based learning in order to secure a claim to the middle class. Like Sharon Hartman, Susan was adamant that she wanted her children to be educated "readers" rather than television viewers.

The Garcias' arrangement committed them to low-wage jobs, although both had college degrees and at least theoretical access to better-paying but less-flexible middle-class professional jobs. They had opted out of the long period of almost thirty years that is required to establish oneself securely in the middle class in order to maintain professional jobs (Ehrenreich 1989: 76). This period is a time to obtain graduate degrees, devote long hours to work, and pay others to care for the children – things that the Garcias did not want to do. Indeed, Bob had recently left a job in which he had faced a promotion after five months. "They wanted me to work *a lot*," he said, laughing. "Family is our priority. I wasn't going to spend sixty hours a week working somewhere, not getting to eat dinner with my family too often." In return for working at low-wage jobs, which were plentiful in their city in the 1990s, they got flexibility – but not cultural capital or much economic capital. (Unlike the Hartmans, the Garcias' economic situation was not connected with religion – Bob was an atheist and Susan an agnostic.) The Garcias had paid off the mortgage on their small house, a purchase that would help cushion them in a recession, but they still worried about stretching their paychecks. They always tried to find jobs with health insurance, for example. They sometimes joked about being poor, but their somewhat precarious economic status was no joke.

How the Garcias constructed their lives was to some extent played out in the television room and around *The Simpsons*. The show was an important symbol of Susan and Bob's differing opinions of television, and it had prompted changes in their daily lives to accommodate those differences. For example, when Peter was small, Susan had objected to his watching *The Simpsons* with Bob, but made an accommodation that seems to speak to gender distinctions. She related her story:

> Bob likes to sit and watch *The Simpsons* after dinner. You could ask him why. God knows. [*laughs*] And because it was a cartoon show, Peter [10 at the time of the interview] liked it. He was kindergarten age. He would sit down and watch it with him.

I thought at the time, "This is not a child's show. This is not a five-year-old's show. I don't care if it's funny-looking cartoon characters who do the kinds of things that Bugs Bunny did. It's not a children's show."

Now, I voiced that opinion to Bob, and he didn't care. He liked to watch the show and he liked to have his boy tucked under his arm. So I thought, "Well, okay." That wasn't a battle I was going to win.

And, frankly, I used it. It gave me half an hour to sit down and do something I wished to do. And be off duty.

So, they – and that's been going on for years, and obviously, Janie [8 at the time of the interview] grew up into that, too. I think they like to sit and watch it together now that they're older, it's less totally inappropriate. The language is still really – they'll say, "Bart just said a rude word." Cost a quarter to say those words in my house!

Susan's comment about being "off duty" during *The Simpsons* in some ways expresses the historical role of women as domestic laborers in American households. *The Simpsons* signaled a welcome break from domestic tasks, as Susan did somewhat more domestic work, such as cooking, even when she worked for wages. But her sense of being "off duty" also involved being excused from her role as the moral guardian who pointed out bad words and bad behavior. And in any case, Bob also had taken on the role of moral guardian, as he warned about language and behavior when he watched *The Simpsons* with his children – an example of a kind of power-sharing about television that is related to their attempts to share wage-earning and child-rearing roles.

Gender was also involved in the distinct ways in which men and women watched television in David Morley's classic study of working-class London families. Morley observed that women tended to watch television with distraction because they were usually engaged in some domestic duty at the same time, while men could view without disruption (Morley 1986: 147). The differences Morley saw between men and women stemmed from the social roles they occupied within their homes, not from their biological characteristics (1995: 175). This applies to Susan and Bob, but in a somewhat different way. In the London study, Morley observed that the home was defined primarily as a site of leisure for men, away from their employment outside the home, while for women the home was seen as a place of work, whether or not they also held jobs outside the home. In the Garcia home, labor roles were not so starkly divided, as Susan and Bob shared work outside the home and tried to do the same inside, although Susan sometimes did more domestic tasks than Bob, for example cooking. Neither, however, considered the home to be a leisure site for the man and a work site only for the woman, as they carefully switched home roles when they switched paid-work roles.

Both parents assigned gender to the acts of "reading" and "watching television," a situation also evident in many ways in American society. Susan was the reader of books, while Bob was the television watcher with considerable knowledge of early television. In fact, Susan described television viewing as a "guy thing." Bob had become engaged with television as a pre-teen when he watched *The Monkees* on Saturday mornings, and eventually amassed a vast collection of videotapes of other favorite TV series. He read magazines, but few books. Historically, book-reading has been gendered in American society. As Janice Radway notes, most book-reading and book-buying in the US is done by women, and middle-class women have been assumed to be book-readers because they have the money and time (Radway 1984: 44–5). Interestingly, both Garcia parents described the children as "readers," although they also watched television regularly with their father. This contradiction may have something to do with the sense in which the parents regarded reading as a mark of learning (thus representing high cultural capital), while television-watching (low in cultural capital) could be shunted off to the television room and at any given moment ignored. In any case, both parents shared the notion that reading has great value, and although Bob did not read as many books as Susan, he certainly worked to encourage book-reading among his children, who each had stories about the time spent reading with him.

A distracted mode of viewing may have also played a role in Susan's dislike of *The Simpsons*. It is possible that because she watched with distraction, she did not become engaged in the show and did not get the rewards it offered to more engaged viewers. The show's "textual density," one writer observes, "gives rise to innumerable small touches that reward attentive viewing" (Owen 1999). In contrast, Susan seldom made it through an entire episode, although she tried to find something she liked in the program. She voiced a critique that emphasized her strong reaction to the look and feel of the show rather than particulars such as plot or language, which she had criticized earlier, also in general terms.

Diane: So *The Simpsons*. How did you figure out it was not one of those shows that you thought was great for kids?

Susan: Oh, I'd sit down and watch it a few times. Bob was enjoying it, so I'd sit down. It's something we could do together. After a long day of work, you sit down, want to be together. I hated it.

Diane: Do you remember the episode that got to you? Or is it cumulative?

Susan: Cumulative, I would assume. I don't know, it's just not appropriate.

Diane: So, bad words. Plot?

Susan: Yeah, sure. [*We were interrupted briefly by a telephone call.*] "What is so obnoxious about *The Simpsons*," a friend of mine says, "I don't like the way they look. I don't like the way they sound. I'm not going to watch them!" That's a start.

Diane:	That's a start.
Susan:	Yeah. The humor doesn't appeal to me. A lot of it's slapstick and rude. Violent. I don't find it funny. I don't find it amusing. I don't find it socially uplifting. [*Both laugh.*]
Diane:	Do the kids talk to you about it, or do they know it's something you don't like?
Susan:	They know it's something I don't like. And every now and then, I'll go and watch it with them. I don't hold my nose up that much. Sometimes I just want to sit down. Sometimes I just want to be with the kids. Sometimes that's the warm room. The fire's been going, and it feels good to sit down. And I want to see what they're doing. Usually, I can't sit through the whole thing. Had enough, and I get up and walk out.
Diane:	So even when you volunteer to watch it, it doesn't work for you.
Susan:	Right.

It was important to Susan that a show have some social value, and the fact that she did not find *The Simpsons* to be "socially uplifting" counted against it in her eyes. It was not like the Public Broadcasting Service shows she said she sometimes watched, nor was it "quality television" in the way that critics described *Hill Street Blues*, the last show in which Susan had become absorbed. In fact, she described watching that show, intensely, without disruption, in a way that corresponds to Morley's description of male viewing described above. She had regularly watched the detail-heavy police drama when she was single and living alone, with no husband, children or other family-based distractions. She had found the show's "upscale" commercials fascinating, especially because they contrasted greatly with the working-class characters depicted on the show. In fact, Susan said she *read* about television – in newspaper and magazine stories about new programs, the industry itself, actors – more often than she watched it. She said she did so because she believed that TV was important in American society and to her family, a comment that indicated she, like Sharon Hartman, claimed access to my "class privilege" of studying television. In this, Susan demonstrated the complexity of social relations around *The Simpsons*. However, social roles were only one aspect of the Garcias' approach to the show.

Although Susan and Bob's television habits were different, their notions of taste were similar, and this may speak to their attempts to share power at home. Bob criticized *The Simpsons* in terms similar to Susan's. When I brought up *The Simpsons* in an individual interview, Bob made a face. He clearly had mixed feelings about his children watching, as the following passage indicates:

Bob:	*The Simpsons* is an animated cartoon that is not a children's cartoon.
Diane:	Oh, you seriously don't think it's for children?

177

Bob: No. It was never for children. Fox produced it not as — *The Flintstones* was the first prime time, animated children's cartoon. *The Simpsons* is not an animated children's cartoon. It's a sophisticated adult animation. And I think it's cute, the story lines and the comedy is cute. It's adolescent humor on a scale of too many dirty words and the representation of behavior that you might not want to let your children participate in! [*He laughs.*]

Diane: Yeah, what about that?

Bob :   [still laughing] Now, unfortunately, my kids sit here and watch it with me, and enjoy it. I often have to say, "Don't ever do that!" and "These are bad words!" They owe us a quarter. We charge a quarter in here, in the house....

        It's the one that [*he slaps his hand, hard*] that I shouldn't let them watch. And there's no other program that they watch is worse than that one.

While Bob continued to watch and enjoy *The Simpsons*, he also criticized language and behavior depicted on the show and expressed uneasiness that his children watched it with him. In this, he seemed to share with Susan a role as the moral arbitrator of the family's tastes and her efforts to distance herself and her family from working-class attributes, while at the same time he and the children continued to watch a show that both felt represented the worst on television. In a similarly mixed assessment, Susan described her family as a "TV family" because, thanks to Bob, they had always had a cable connection and Bob's watching was "non-negotiable," although she and Bob worked to emphasize the family's readerly attributes as well. These contradictions indicate that the Garcias had accommodated *The Simpsons* and television spatially, intellectually, and emotionally, keeping their contradictory evaluations in a kind of tension, in Bourdieu's terms, between mental and social structures. One particular consequence was that Susan and Bob had opened a door to considering *The Simpsons* as more important in the hierarchy of cultural goods than they had originally described, indicating a process of legitimation that will be considered in the next section.

Legitimating *The Simpsons*

While Susan disdained television, with Bob sharing her critique and at the same time watching guiltily, Susan also found some good things in television-watching. She noted that her children watched television for the stories, just as they read books (and indeed, the children recounted plots of books and of television shows in similar, detailed, and enthusiastic fashion). She said they were reader-like in their focus on television stories because she had limited their watching to an hour-and-a-half a day, forcing them to actively choose what to watch and thus to watch more carefully. The children's treating *The Simpsons* as stories also led Susan to a conclusion that conflicted with her declarations of dislike for the show: if *The Simpsons* could be read like a book, then it might not be so bad. Likewise, in a separate interview, Bob said he saw television programming in general in American culture "as an extension of story time," and in his family in particular, as books and stories:

> I think that my kids have the ability to understand TV as limited, at-arms-length kind of stories, just like they enjoy the books that they read. They're just books and stories. So to a large extent, yeah, that's the way I see it as well, they're just books and stories.

This view is in keeping with the Garcias' emphasis on book-based learning. But it also suggests a larger move to redefine television as literature, with *The Simpsons* as a prime example. There is an important contradiction in what the Garcias had to say about television. They used a naturalized, contemporary definition of books: that books represent "real" learning, a mark of the educated (and middle-class) person, as does criticism, as in the children's recounting of plots and ideas. As Williams notes, "literature" and "criticism," in the perspective of historical development, are "forms of class specialization and control of a general social practice" (Williams 1977: 49–51). The Garcias struggled to expand those notions by contemplating *The Simpsons* as part of what was once the exclusive province of "literature": as stories, with the children's skill in relating them an example of book-reading competence. In addition, defining television and *The Simpsons* as literature would legitimate the children's watching, as it would Bob's extensive knowledge of television and the time spent accumulating this knowledge.

Another indication that the Garcias saw *The Simpsons* as literature was in the respect Bob and Susan accorded their children's commentary on the show. The commentary was treated as acceptable behavior, with neither parent interrupting their children when they recounted and evaluated plots, often loudly and excitedly, with one prodding on the other.[15] The parents were quiet and sometimes smiled while the children did this, encouraging them to continue. In contrast, in another family I interviewed, the mother tried to change the subject when her 13-year-old daughter began to recount a *Simpsons* plot, and the father objected outright when the girl brought up another *Simpsons* story later on. But even these parents tried to legitimate the show, although in an evaluation geared more to adult competence than to that of children: they said the show was good social satire.

This move to legitimate *The Simpsons* by assigning it high-culture attributes is not unique to the Garcias and the Hartmans. The *New York Times* has also sought to reveal "quality" attributes of *The Simpsons* and other television shows, as it did in a story that identified many of the show's writers as Harvard graduates, a fact that the reporter clearly felt would be a surprise to *Times* readers. The story also noted the high economic and cultural capital of television writers and producers: they are "frequently better-paid and at times better-educated" than those in the more glamorous movie business:

> Prime-time television may be reviled in intellectual circles for its supposedly lowbrow sensibilities, but many people in the medium regard this as a second golden era, both in terms of money and the quality of writing. Few things demonstrate the growing attractiveness of the field more than the presence of dozens of Harvard graduates (as well as many other Ivy Leaguers), particularly in the realm of comedy. Writing staffs of shows like *The Simpsons*, *King of the Hill*, *Saturday Night Live* and *Late Show with Dave Letterman* have come to look like Harvard alumni clubs.
>
> (Sterngold 1997: C11)

Further, these writers thought television allowed for more creativity than movies or novels, indicating a superior position in the field of cultural production. As further indications that a process of legitimation is taking place for *The Simpsons*, George Meyer, a top writer (and Harvard graduate), was profiled in the *New Yorker*, and the former poet laureate Robert Pinsky praised *The Simpsons* in a long essay for the *New York Times* (Owen 1999; Pinsky 2000).

This critical praise for *The Simpsons* is to some extent informed by the fact that its creator, Matt Groening, a political cartoonist, is vocal and articulate in his own analysis of American society, in contrast to Matt Stone and Trey Parker, the creators of *South Park*. For example, in an interview with *Mother Jones*, Groening is reflexive and critical as he sums up his work:

> I grew up completely overwhelmed by TV, and part of the reason why I have gone into television is as a way to justify to myself all those wasted hours of watching TV as a kid. I can now look back and say, Oh, that was research. For me, it's not enough to be aware that most television is bad and stupid and pernicious. I think, "What can I do about it?" Is it the nature of the medium, the structure of the networks these days, or some failure of the creators that keeps television so lousy? I feel a little bit like a fish trying to analyze its own aquarium water, but what I want to do is point out the way TV is unconsciously structured to keep us all distracted. With *The Simpsons* and *Futurama*, what I'm try to do – in the guise of light entertainment, if that's possible – is nudge people, jostle them a little, wake them up to some of the ways in which we're being manipulated and exploited. And in my amusing little way I try to hit on some of the unspoken rules of our culture.
>
> (Doherty 1999)

This analysis would also resonate with Bob Garcia and other parents who invested a lifetime in watching television and the past decade enjoying *The Simpsons'* commentary on contemporary life.

Conclusion

I have examined the ambivalence of some parents' analyses of *The Simpsons* in a framework suggested by Bourdieu. This has enabled me to look at parental objections to the show as class distinctions based upon perceived working-class attributes of its characters and the show itself, and the negative status of television within the wider field of cultural production. Once examined in domestic spaces, furthermore, the social relations around the show can be seen to include inevitable and complex gender divisions for which I have attempted to account. Different attempts to legitimate the show are also apparent in the two families discussed here and in middle-class periodicals that seek to attribute middle-class characteristics to *The Simpsons* in terms of production and quality. In this analysis, I have suggested that a process of distinction is at work around *The Simpsons*. This process deserves further study, as my interviews indicate some rich possibilities for describing and understanding the social relations and structures in which this process operates.

Bourdieu reminds us of the importance of studying the cultural product itself, the production of the value of the product, and the social conditions and relations in which it is embedded, all understood as manifestations of the field of cultural production as a whole (Bourdieu 1993: 37). By discussing the tensions and contradictions around *The Simpsons* in two families, I have attempted to illustrate how complex and fruitful this study can be. Further investigation of family life and cultural sensibilities could tell us much about how these divisions and processes operate in contemporary life.

Notes

1 All names of interviewees are pseudonyms. Although this analysis is my own, my interviews were also part of the "Symbolism, Media and the Lifecourse" project funded by the Lilly Endowment, Inc. at the University of Colorado's Center for Mass Media Research. The study was directed by Dr. Stewart M. Hoover, and Dr. Lynn Schofield Clark, Associate Director. The field researchers included Joseph G. Champ, Lee Hood, and myself. A total of 249 people in 62 families were interviewed in their homes in this interpretive study. The families were of a variety of socioeconomic and racial/ethnic backgrounds and included parents who were single, divorced, remarried, unmarried or same sex. The families were not selected randomly and were not intended to be representative of the US population, or to be average or typical cases. The fact that interviews were carried out in the context of the family is important: media use, especially television, is seen as a social activity occurring within the context of the family as a set of social relations (following Morley 1986: 2). The methodology of the

"Symbolism, Media and the Lifecourse" project is discussed at length in Hoover (1996) and Clark (1999).

2 These comments from parents and children in my qualitative interviews were similar to opinions expressed in a series of national surveys carried out by the Annenberg Public Policy Center of the University of Pennsylvania. In 1998 and 1999, children aged 10 to 17 said *The Simpsons* was the third show the parents were most likely to prohibit their children from watching, after *The Jerry Springer Show* and *South Park*. In 1997, the same age group said *The Simpsons* was the second most prohibited, behind *Beavis and Butt-Head*. In contrast, in 1998 and 1999, children aged 10 to 17 also told pollsters that *The Simpsons* was their favorite program, up from the fourth-place position that age group awarded it in 1997 (after *Seinfeld*, *Home Improvement* and *Family Matters*). It is no surprise that *The Simpsons* was not on the list of shows parents most encouraged their children to see in those years, nor was it among the best shows for kids as rated by parents in those years. However, in 1998, children aged 10 to 17 rated *The Simpsons* top of programs they perceived to be best for their age group, although it slipped to second place, behind *Seventh Heaven*, in 1999 (Stanger and Gridina 1999).

3 Animation itself is often defined as less valuable in general. Television animation writers, for example, are less well-regarded and lower-paid than live-action writers (Argy 1998). However, the parents I talked with did not see much difference in cultural capital between animated and live-action sitcoms, both of which they discounted in seemingly equal measure. Still, the fact that *The Simpsons* is animated was a mark against the show for some parents who regarded animation as a children's medium but *The Simpsons* as an adult story – the show was questionable in part because its stories did not fit their notion of animation.

4 Bourdieu uses this term to describe his focus on French society and his intent "to avoid unjustifiably universalizing the particular case" (Bourdieu 1984: xi).

5 The historian George Lipsitz discusses the notion that people are historical subjects who make meaning in part through popular culture (Lipsitz 1988: 147–61).

6 I argue elsewhere (Alters 2002) that interviewees' unsettled feelings about the show were prompted in part by the unsettling stories *The Simpsons* tells. Its characters engage with the dislocations provoked by three important, ongoing changes in American society during the past half-century: in family structure, in religious practice, and those changes prompted by the arrival of television in American homes. For more than a decade *The Simpsons* has observed, satirized, exaggerated and otherwise aired many fears provoked by these changes, with stories of family squabbles, attitudes towards gays, religious diversity, God, television violence and effects of television on children, among many others ("Hurricane Neddy," 29 December 1996; "Itchy and Scratchy and Marge," 20 December 1990; "The Joy of Sect," 8 February 1998; "There's No Disgrace Like Home," 28 January 1990; "Treehouse of Horror IX," 25 October 1998). In this essay, the stories are treated as context for parental critiques of the show.

7 I interviewed the Hartmans over the winter of 1997–98.

8 What constituted bad language in *The Simpsons* varied from family to family in this study. I did not ask children to repeat bad words for me. However, several parents said they objected to such words as *hell*, *damn* and *butt*.

9 With this, Sharon discussed characters in *The Simpsons* as people, just as she talked about live-action family sitcom characters as people. Like other interviewees, she merged animated shows and live-action ones: both are sitcoms and both are about families. This does not mean that interviewees saw *The Simpsons* as live action, but rather that the show has an air of reality that can absorb, entertain and, conversely, offend. This may have had to do with the success of *The Simpsons*, which has led to the proliferation of animated family sitcoms, naturalizing it as a television form (Hontz 1999). Robert Pinsky makes a related point when he describes television as a "literal medium" that makes people feel they are watching something happen, even in cartoons and in "cartoonlike" sitcoms such as *Gilligan's Island* or *The Beverly Hillbillies* (Pinsky 2000). Pinsky says *The Simpsons*, which he regards as one of the best shows on television, plays with this literal quality.

10 The academic use of the term "white trash" represents a way of indicating differences within whiteness. Wray and Newitz (1997) use the term to examine various constructions of white-

ness across class, gender, and sexual lines as well as how the constructions vary according to region and place.

11 See, in particular, "Saturdays of Thunder" (14 November 1991), for an illustration of this point.

12 "Classic" books for the Hartman girls included *The Chronicles of Narnia*, a series by C. S. Lewis; *Where the Red Fern Grows* by Wilson Rawls; and *Little House on the Prairie* by Laura Ingalls Wilder.

13 I interviewed the Garcias over the fall and winter of 1997 and maintained contact with them for the next three years.

14 Elsewhere, I call this room a domestic "*transfrontera* contact zone," a reference to a term used by José David Saldívar (1997: 14) to describe attempts "to invoke the heterotopic forms of everyday life whose trajectories cross over and interact." This point deserves far more attention, and I develop it elsewhere (Alters 2002). For the more limited purposes of this essay, Bob Garcia's Latino background contributes to the contradictions within the broader field of cultural production considered here.

15 For example, they offered a detailed discussion of "Bart the Daredevil" (6 December 1990) and "Treehouse of Horror VI" (30 October 1995), in particular a segment about Homer entering a third dimension.

Bibliography

Alters, D. F. (2002) "The Family Audience: Class and Taste and Cultural Production in Late Modernity," unpublished Ph.D. dissertation, University of Colorado, Boulder.

Argy, S. (1998) "'Toon Time!" *Written By: The Magazine of the Writers Guild Of America, West* (November). Available at: http://www.wga.org/WrittenBy/1998/1198/ToonTime.html (accessed 26 December 2001).

Bourdieu, P. (1993) *The Field of Cultural Production: Essays on Art and Literature*, New York: Columbia University Press.

—— (1984) *Distinction: A Social Critique of the Judgment of Taste*, trans. R. Nice, Cambridge, MA: Harvard University Press.

—— (1977) *Outline of a Theory of Practice*, trans. R. Nice, Cambridge, UK: Cambridge University Press.

Bourdieu, P. and Wacquant, L. J. D. (1992) *An Invitation to Reflexive Sociology*, Chicago: University of Chicago Press.

Clark, L. S. (1999) "Learning from the Field: The Journey from Post-Positivist to Constructivist Methods," a paper presented to the Popular Communication Division, International Communication Association (May).

Coontz, S. (1992) *The Way We Never Were: American Families and the Nostalgia Trap*, New York: Basic Books.

Coontz, S. with M. Parson and G. Raley (eds.) (1999) *American Families: A Multicultural Reader*, New York: Routledge.

Doherty, B. (1999) "Matt Groening," *Mother Jones*, March/April. Available at: http://www.mother-jones.com/groening (accessed 26 December 2002).

Ehrenreich, B. (2001) *Nickel and Dimed: On (Not) Getting By in America*, New York: Metropolitan Books/Henry Holt.

—— (1989) *Fear of Falling: The Inner Life of the Middle Class*, New York: HarperCollins.

Gray, C. E. (1999) "Myths of the Bourgeois Woman: Rethinking Race, Class and Gender," in A. Lugo and B. Maurer (eds.), *Gender Matters: Rethinking Michelle Z. Rosaldo*, Ann Arbor: University of Michigan Press.

Groening, M., (creator) and S. M. Gimple (ed.) (1999) *The Simpsons Forever! A Complete Guide to Our Favorite Family, Continued*, New York: Harper Perennial.

Groening, M., (creator), R. Richmond and A. Coffman (eds.) (1997) *The Simpsons: A Complete Guide to Our Favorite Family*, New York: Harper Perennial.

Hontz, J. (1999) "Tide of Toons Tips Sitcoms: Nets' Animated Orders Invigorate Aging Comedy Format," *Variety*, Volume 374, Number 2, March 1–7: 65.

Hoover, S. M. (1996) "Social Flow in Media Households: Notes on Method," a paper presented to the 20th Scientific Conference, The International Association for Mass Communication Research and the Network for Qualitative Television Audience Research, Sydney, Australia, 29 August.

Krais, B. (1993) "Gender and Symbolic Violence: Female Oppression in the Light of Pierre Bourdieu's Theory of Social Practice," in C. Calhoun, E. LiPuma, and M. Postone (eds.), *Bourdieu: Critical Perspectives*, Chicago: University of Chicago Press.

Lipsitz, G. (1990) *Time Passages: Collective Memory and American Popular Culture*, Minneapolis: University of Minnesota Press.

—— (1988) "'This Ain't No Sideshow': Historians and Media Studies," *Critical Studies in Mass Communication*, Volume 5: 147–61.

Markus, M. (1987) "Women, Success and Civil Society: Submission to, or Subversion of, the Achievement Principle," in S. Benhabib and D. Cornell (eds.), *Feminism As Critique: On the Politics of Gender*, Minneapolis: University of Minnesota Press.

Mintz, S. and S. Kellogg (1988) *Domestic Revolutions: A Social History of American Family Life*, New York: The Free Press.

Morley, D. (2000) *Home Territories: Media, Mobility and Identity*, London and New York: Routledge.

—— (1995) "The Gendered Framework of Family Viewing," in S. Jackson and S. Moores (eds.), *The Politics of Domestic Consumption: Critical Readings*, London and New York: Prentice-Hall, 173–85.

—— (1986) *Family Television: Cultural Power and Domestic Leisure*, London: Routledge.

Owen, D. (1999) "Taking Humor Seriously: George Meyer, the Funniest Man Behind the Funniest Show on TV," *New Yorker*, 13 March: 64+.

Pinsky, R. (2000) "Creating the 'Real,' in Bright Yellow and Blue," *New York Times*, Section 2, 5 November: 12+.

Radway, J. (1984) *Reading the Romance: Women, Patriarchy, and Popular Literature*, Chapel Hill: University of North Carolina Press.

Roof, W. C. (1999) *Spiritual Marketplace: Baby Boomers and the Remaking of American Religion*, Princeton: Princeton University Press.

Saldívar, J. D. (1997) *Border Matters: Remapping American Cultural Studies*, Berkeley: University of California Press.

Seiter, E. (1999) *Television and New Media Audiences*, Oxford: Oxford University Press.

Stanger, J. D. and Gridina, N. (1999) *Media in the Home 1999: The Fourth Annual Survey of Parents and Children*, conducted by Roper Starch Worldwide, Philadelphia: The Annenberg Public Policy Center of the University of Pennsylvania.

Sterngold, J. (1997) "Looking for Laughs? Call a Harvard Grad; As Writers and Producers, Young Alumni Find They Can Make a Lot of Money Fast," *New York Times*, 26 August: C11.

Williams, R. (1981) *The Sociology of Culture*, Chicago: University of Chicago Press.

—— (1977) *Marxism and Literature*, Oxford: Oxford University Press.

Wray, M. and A. Newitz (eds.) (1997) *White Trash: Race and Class in America*, New York: Routledge.

Wuthnow, R. (1988) *The Restructuring of American Religion: Society and Faith Since World War II*, Princeton: Princeton University Press.

Chapter 10

"MISERY CHICK"

Irony, alienation and animation in MTV's Daria

Kathy M. Newman

DARIA MORGENDORFFER, WHO STARRED IN HER OWN MTV animated show, *Daria*, was a smart-mouthed, misanthropic 16-year-old, perpetually dressed in a mustard-yellow shirt, a green jacket with wide lapels, a charcoal-colored skirt, big round glasses and knee-high combat boots. With her sharp tongue and wicked sense of humor, Daria made being a brainy misfit look cool. In the first episode which aired in the spring of 1997, Daria was found by psychologists at her new school, Lawndale High, to be suffering from "low self-esteem." She explained to her lawyer-mother, Helen, that she did not have low self-esteem, she simply had "low esteem for others." And thus began the five-year run of one of MTV's most successful animated features.

For five years Daria stood out as a sage among fools. Her family included her impossibly perky younger sister, Quinn, her workaholic mother, Helen, her dopey, stressed-out dad, Jake, and her mother's sister, Aunt Amy – a cool and attractive thirty-something. Her best friend was the artsy Jane Lane, whose savage bob, skinny legs, dark jacket, and combat boots made her a perfect gothic gal-pal for Daria – especially when Daria's own sister refused to acknowledge they were related. Jane's older brother, Trent, a post-high-school rock-'n'-roll wannabe, was an occasional crush-object for Daria, but her only real "relation-ship" was with the dashing, wealthy Tom (who was Jane's boyfriend first). Back at Lawndale High, where most of *Daria* took place, Jane and Daria were surrounded by the vacant cheerleader/quarterback combo of Brittany and

Kevin, Quinn's fashion club, the overachieving African-American student-body president, Jodie and her boyfriend "Mack," the pimple-faced Upchuck, and a variety of angry-to-incompetent teachers. Finally, there was the school's principle Ms. Li, who was anything but principled when it came to raising money for Lawndale High.

While not a huge hit by network standards, netting a ratings share of between 1 and 2 percent (one to two million viewers), *Daria* became a signature show for MTV during its five-year run from 1997 to 2002. A spin-off from *Beavis and Butt-Head*, on which Daria first appeared as the geeky girl Beavis and Butt-Head taunted with "Diarrhea, cha cha cha," *Daria* scored better among television critics and female viewers than the raunchy, dumb-ass duo which brought her to life. In 1998, Van Toffler, then general manager of MTV, suggested that Daria had become a "poster child" for the music network: "She has an attitude about parents, school, siblings that is common to the experiences of our audience. She is a good spokesperson for MTV…intelligent but subversive" (Kuczynski 1998: 8E).

Daria was intelligent and subversive – an unusual combination for prime time television. When *Daria* first debuted in 1997, *The Nation* called Daria Morgendorffer "a 10th grade Dorothy Parker" (in Span 1997: G01), and the TV critic for the *New York Times*, John J. O'Connor, declared, "she is every glorious misfit I ever knew…I think I'm in love" (1997: C16). For the cerebral, writerly types who liked television Daria was the outcast she-hero who dared to say things they were too scared to say in their own teenage years. As Walter Belcher remarked, "this ultimate outsider says things I wish I had said in school. She says things I wish I had thought of today. She's like a 50-year-old deadpan Jewish comic in the body of a 16-year-old" (2000: 4).

At the same time, others have argued that Daria's "deadpan" sense of humor was too morbid for teenagers. Josh Ozersky complained that Daria represented a kind of "living death" – a teenager who used her "omnivorous deadpan contempt" as a weapon against the world. He called her a "grim reaper in a dress," and argued that she was more dangerous than Marilyn Manson: "*Daria* is particularly insidious, I think, because of the corrupt role model it offers teenagers…Irony, for adolescents, is infinitely more appealing than sex or violence" (Ozersky 1997: 47). Some viewers have concurred, arguing that the teen nihilism reflected in programs like *Daria* was at the heart of school tragedies such as the Columbine shooting in 1999.

Perhaps the real irony, however, was that the theme of death in *Daria* contradicted the spirit of animation – the art of "giving life" to inanimate forms. As Alan Cholodenko has argued, "[A]nimation has to do with endowing with life and with motion" (2000: 9). And, while Daria was not suicidal, nor did she seriously wish death on those around her, she was not terribly lifelike. She was a form of "living death": animated, from a technical point of view, but not "animated" in her voice variation, expressions, or physical gestures. When Daria was embarrassed she turned a pale shade of pink; otherwise, her perpetually half-closed eyes and monotone voice betrayed little emotion. Moreover, when she was not complaining about the meaninglessness of life she could be found reading books such as *Being and Nothingness* by Sartre.

Daria, therefore, represented an important milestone in the evolution of animation: *Daria* worked as a metacommentary on the problems inherent in animation itself. Through *Daria*, MTV animators raised a series of questions about animation and ontology: What does it mean to endow inanimate drawings with life? How do we reconcile the illusion of life with life itself? How can we use animation to make sense of death? At a less metaphysical level, Daria herself represented a new kind of animated heroine. A far cry from the Disney nymphets, Daria was a teenage girl who hardly ever thought about boys in a romantic way. And, while animation has been used to endow female characters with seductive assets (as Jessica Rabbit says: "I'm not bad, I'm just drawn that way"), through *Daria* animators used their artistic powers to create a young woman whose brain was more important than her bust. Daria was not only a proto-feminist, she also had her moments as an anti-corporate activist. She was verbally disdainful of the corruption, consumerism, and commercialism that surrounded her, but she also tried to do something about it. She was the epitome of an ironic heroine.

Irony is a concept that has branded much of the cultural discourse surrounding "Generation X." In the Gen-X tribute film *Reality Bites*, the character Lelaina (played by Winona Rider), after a devastating job interview, asks Troy (played by Ethan Hawke), to define irony. Troy explains: "It's when the actual meaning is the complete opposite from the literal meaning." And, according to the *Oxford English Dictionary*, irony usually takes the form of "sarcasm or ridicule in which laudatory expressions are used to imply condemnation or contempt." This was precisely the logic behind *Daria*, in which Jane and Daria frequently used sarcasm and ridicule to maintain their own sense of sanity and community. Irony, far from being a "corrupt role model" for teenagers, functioned in *Daria* as a means to bring the important characters together. *Daria* made it clear that irony is about community, not sociopathic behavior. Moreover, *Daria* has helped to bring "actual" teenagers together under the rubric of the fan world created by the show. As one fan put it: "If (*Daria*) represents anything, it's the upbeat, fun, pro-active side of teen nihilism" (Pal 1997:T4).

Daria fans themselves are definitely more pro-active than nihilistic. On more than 100 *Daria* fan sites devoted viewers have posted their own "fan-fiction": fan-authored *Daria* episodes which have been created for communal enjoyment and constructive criticism. Fans also use these sites to talk about their health, their families, their own depressing childhoods, and their meaningless jobs. *Daria*, for these fans, is what Kenneth Burke has called "equipment for living" – a story through which fans have been able to make sense of the world (Burke 1941: 293–304). Far from contributing to the teen nihilism represented by the Columbine shootings, *Daria* has served as a forum through which such tragedies could be debated. Fans used *Daria*, ironically perhaps, to deal with their own feelings of alienation. In the process they have created a genuine Internet community.

A brief history of *Daria*

Daria first appeared on *Beavis and Butt-Head* in 1996. Her character was created by one of the *Beavis and Butt-Head* story editors, Glenn Eichler. In the beginning her outfit was a bit disheveled: her glasses looked like they were falling off her nose, and she wore a brown sweater with buttons and blue leggings. And, even in her protean existence on *Beavis and Butt-Head* Daria possessed a special relationship to irony. In the final *Beavis and Butt-Head* episode, "Beavis and Butt-Head are Dead," Daria offered her mono-feeling assessment of the duo's demise: "I guess it's kind of sad that they're dead and all…But it's not like they had great futures ahead of them." Daria, on the other hand, did have a great future. As Beavis and Butt-Head were staging their own mock-deaths, *Daria* co-creators Glenn Eichler and Susie Lynn Lewis were producing the first episodes of Daria's very own show.[1]

Daria and the Morgendorffer family moved from the suburb of "Highland" on *Beavis and Butt-Head* to the suburb of "Lawndale" for the first episode of *Daria*. Daria's mother, Helen, asked Daria if her new high school would be like her old high school. Daria replied: "Not much chance of that happening. Unless there's uranium in the drinking water here, too." Lawndale High, where much of the action on *Daria* took place, was a sly send-up of the suburban high school (see Figure 10.1). The principle, Ms. Li, was always finding new ways for corporations to contribute to the school's coffers, whether she was letting modeling agencies search for talent on campus, starting a cyber-cafe, or signing an exclusivity contract with a soft-drink company. But unlike most suburban high schools, at Lawndale High the outcasts had the best lines. When Brittany, the buxom cheerleader, complained that she hated it when the lunch trays were wet, Daria concurred: "That which doesn't kill us makes us stronger" (Episode 101, "The Esteemers").

Much of the drama of the show centered on the bond between outcasts, and, especially, the bond between Daria and Jane. They became friends in the first episode when Daria failed a psychological test and was sent to the self-esteem class, which was taught by the hapless Mr. O'Neill. Here Daria met Jane, who was

Figure 10.1 Another excruciating day at Lawndale High for Daria and Jane (Courtesy of MTV)

taking the class for the third time because she had nothing else to do after school. Jane helped Daria pass the self-esteem test in record time, and they escaped to Daria's bedroom, which looked like a padded cell. Jane told Daria that she had the coolest room: "I wish there had been a schizophrenic shut-in living in our house before we moved in." In Daria's room Jane and Daria watched countless episodes of "The Sick, Sad World," which seemed to be the only television show broadcast in the hamlet of Lawndale. In the early episodes of *Daria*, Daria and Jane were fast allies, with only the smallest of incidents – like the time Jane joined the track team and temporarily became popular – threatening their friendship.

In later episodes, however, the friendship between Daria and Jane was tested through a series of love triangles. In the first triangle, Daria had a crush on Jane's brother, Trent, who had Jane's punk sensibility, but not her sense of humor. He took himself very seriously, and told Daria she was the "coolest high school girl" he knew. Though their crush was never consummated, the Trent/Daria story line led many in the *Daria* fan community to demand resolution. These "shippers," Internet fan-slang for fans who want central characters to have a relationship ("shippers" is short for "relationshippers"), carried on fan-site wars with the "anti-shippers," fans who thought Daria had more integrity as a single girl. There were also fans who speculated that the real sexual tension was between Daria and Jane, not Daria and Trent.

Much to the dismay of the "anti-shippers," in the third season Jane herself landed a boyfriend. She started dating a rich and handsome young man named Tom, and, predictably, Daria resented Tom because he interfered with her friendship with Jane. Gradually, Daria began to accept their relationship, and Daria and Tom became friends. But when Jane's relationship with Tom started to falter, and Tom and Daria were caught in an impulsive embrace, Jane banished them both; as a result, Daria and Tom started a relationship. In an unlikely resolution, Jane forgave them both, and they were all able to go out on a double-date in the fourth season.

On the whole, however, it was misery, and not romance, that defined the typical *Daria* plot line. In one of the signature episodes of the series, "Misery Chick," Daria became the center of attention when tragedy befell Lawndale High. A high-school football alumnus named Tommy Sherman returned to Lawndale to be honored with the dedication of a new set of goal posts. Sherman made an ass of himself, and Daria and Jane joked about how funny it would be if something terrible happened to him. In the next scene Sherman was killed by the very goal posts designed for his commemoration. Everyone at Lawndale – even the teachers – turned to Daria for guidance in their time of mourning. The square-jawed, pigskin-for-brains Kevin asked Daria for some "words of wisdom or whatever." "Like what?" Daria replied. Kevin explained, "I don't know. I figure you think about depressing stuff a lot. You're that type. You know?" The self-esteem teacher, Mr. O'Neill, also turned to Daria: "You probably think about the dark side all the time....The thoughts other people try not to have. That's your thing, right? Facing the void? Yes, I'm sure you're dealing with it. I'm not dealing with it! (*Mr. O'Neill starts to cry*)" (Episode 113, "Misery Chick").

But Daria was not as miserable as she seemed. As she explained to Jane, "I'm not miserable. I'm just not like them." In this episode Jane was upset too. She felt badly because she and Daria had joked about Sherman dying, and then he died. As Jane told Daria, "I don't like it when I say people should die and then they do. I don't want that kind of responsibility. At least not until I've got a job in middle management." Daria assured Jane they had nothing to do with Sherman's death, and Jane convinced Daria that she should take advantage of her new-found popularity as the "misery chick." In the final scene Daria wised up and charged the president of the fashion club, Sandi, $10 for advice about her sick cat. If she was going to be the misery chick she might as well make a profit:

Jane:	You just made ten bucks off of that poor girl's suffering.
Daria:	Yeah, that was wrong.
Jane:	Really. Next time…
Daria:	Twenty.

(Episode 113, "Misery Chick")

In this episode Daria used her ironic position as the "misery chick" to get ahead. When she realized that she could not shed her image as the most depressing girl at Lawndale, she simply decided to make money from the misery of others. And, in true ironic fashion, her perceived misery brought her closer to the community in its time of need.

"Misery Chick" reflected the themes and rhythm of a typical *Daria* episode. Each episode began with a crisis, whether it was a crisis at school (for example, the Sherman death), a crisis at home (for example, Quinn and Daria getting grounded), a journey of some kind (a field trip to the mall, or to the paint-ball arena), a school project (a lab experiment, or decorating the gym), or a crisis around Daria's appearance. The heart of each episode usually involved Daria and Jane doing something they did not want to do, or getting punished for something they should not have done.

At the same time, while each episode usually involved an annoying popularity achievement on the part of Daria's sister Quinn, an unsuccessful advice session with Daria's parents, the unprofessional behavior of one or more of Daria's teachers, and some extreme display of stupidity by Brittany and/or Kevin, Daria and Jane usually wound up on top. Daria often profited, literally, as she did in "Misery Chick" with the $10 she received from Sandi; in "College Bored" Daria charged college students for writing their term papers, and in "Malled" Daria was the ten-thousandth customer at the doo-dad shop, and won a ton of doo-dads. In this episode the employees at the doo-dad shop showered her with balloons, confetti, and doo-dads. Daria said: "Winner?" and Jane had to explain it in terms Daria would understand: "You know, it's not a word for loser." Daria and Jane, who thought of themselves as losers when it came to the social pecking order, often found themselves "winning" at the close of each episode – in however ironic a fashion.

The irony of *Daria* can be further understood by thinking about the role that *Daria* and animation have played within MTV as a network. Lauren Rabinovitz has argued that animation has been crucial to MTV's emergence as a "postmodern" cable channel. As the channel evolved from an eclectic "new music" forum into an outlet for pop and heavy metal music in the late 1980s, according to Rabinovitz, MTV turned to animated logos as a way to have both consistency and change in the look of the channel (1989: 99–100). Executive producer of animation at MTV, Abby Terkuhle, explained that "from the first day we started as a network with the ten-second animated IDs, we have always invited animators to 'throw paint at our logo.' I believe that animation has actually played a significant role in the creation of our network's image and its popularity" (Klein-Häss 2002). As a result, according to Rabinovitz, animation became part of the signature style of the channel. No matter what style of animation was used – clay-mation, puppets, drawings, black-and-white, color, etc. – what defined MTV was animation as a form. Ironically, as MTV began to develop a corporate identity the MTV trademark became the possibility of change itself.

Animation was not only used to signify the MTV logo; animation increasingly became incorporated into the music video format. Peter Gabriel's award-winning video, "Sledgehammer," done in the style of clay-mation, was one of the early animation projects by Nick Park (*Wallace and Gromit*, *Chicken Run*). Other musical artists, including Dire Straits ("Money for Nothing"), A-ha ("Take on Me"), and Michael Jackson ("Leave me Alone"), produced successful animated videos. Ironically, perhaps, the animated music video was a logical evolution of the form; as Paul Wells has argued, early cartoons themselves were a kind of "music video": "The early Fleischer Brothers shorts and the initial output of the Warner Brothers Studio are essentially early forms of the music video in the sense that the cartoon events often directly accompany, and take their narrative imperatives from, a song" (Wells 1998: 98; see also Chapter 1 of this volume). And thus animation, both at the level of the MTV logo, and the MTV music video, has been central to the identity of music television.

In the late 1980s MTV created a division of animation to monitor the creation of the MTV animated logos. In 1991, under the direction of Abby Terkhule, MTV launched an animation anthology show called *Liquid Television*. Two years later MTV created *Beavis and Butt-Head*, and began a tradition of creating adult-oriented, animated features. Other animated series included *AEon Flux* in 1995 and *MTV Oddities*, which featured *The Head* and *The Maxx*. In 1997 *Daria* was created as a spin-off from *Beavis and Butt-Head* and MTV also launched the popular clay-mation celebrity spoof, *Celebrity Death Match*, in which clay-mation mega-stars fight each other to a gruesome and humorous bitter end.

Like *Daria*, *Celebrity Death Match* uses animation as a form to explore themes of death and destruction. The outrageous death scenes, resulting in smooshed body parts and flying bits of clay, recall the more violent of the Warner Brother cartoons, such as *Road Runner*, in which Wile E. Coyote is foiled in a different and more spectacular way in every episode. Perhaps, then, animation has never been exclusively about the creation of life; perhaps animation is really about the contingency of life, and our imaginative manipulation of the terms of life and death. As the animator creates life, so, too, does the animator take it away. And thus the dour, deadpan antics of Daria and company in fact may be part of a long-standing tradition of irony within animation itself.

To animate or not to animate

Daria was not only an ironic character, she was also ironically drawn. As reviewers have noted, the animation style of *Daria* was relatively static. If animation is generally associated with elements such as surrealism, visual play, transformation, and metamorphosis (think of the spinning of the Tasmanian devil, the elasticity of Bugs Bunny when he pops out of his rabbit hole, the explosions which transform characters into charcoal, only to have them bounce back to life), the animation style of *Daria* was marked by its flat, unchanging nature. As *Daria* nay-sayer Josh Ozersky pointed out, disdainfully, the characters always looked exactly the same, down to their outfits and their hairstyles.

> The result is a weird lifelessness. The show's drawing style also seems lifeless, polished and flat. There are no stray lines, no evidence of a draftsman's loose hand. Every character is aseptically bordered with thick black lines: Even their hairstyles look like icons.
>
> (Ozersky 1997: 47)

And thus the categories which are usually used to divide animated narrative into its component parts – categories such as "metamorphosis," or "penetration" (an animation technique which allows the viewer to see the inside of a machine, or a character's internal organs), rarely apply to the animation technique used by *Daria* animators. While fans have described this style as "realistic," in some ways the static quality of the animation used in *Daria* was actually "unrealistic": the characters showed little movement and were visually unchanging in a way that transformed them into iconic figures.[2]

And thus *Daria*, with its static, life-defying animation technique, seemed to violate one of the fundamental principles of animation. Animation, by its very nature, has allowed animators to "give life" to inanimate objects: drawings, clay, puppets. The Czech surrealist animator, Jan Švankmajer, has argued that animation allows him to "give magical powers to things" (quoted in Wells 1998: 11). Likewise, media theorist Alan Cholodenko argues that animation "has to do with endowing with life and with motion." He argues that animation's special relationship to creation, or, the "beginning" should force us to pay special attention to ontology – theories of being – when we think about animation. At stake in thinking about animation is the creation of life itself (Cholodenko 2000: 9).

In a similar way Sergei Eisenstein, writing about Disney in the 1940s, noticed the exact moment at which the outline of a drawing began to "take on an independent life."[3] He argued that even when we know that animated figures are not real, we sense that they are alive:

> We *know* that they are…drawings, and not living beings. We *know* that they are projections of drawings on a screen. We know that they are…"miracles" and tricks of technology, that such beings don't really exist. But at the same time: We *sense* them as alive. We *sense* them as moving. We *sense* them as existing and even thinking.
>
> (Eisenstein 1986: 59)

One technical reason for this illusion of life is the way in which animation hides the physical aspect of its construction. As Edward Small and Eugene Levinson have argued, animation is characterized by the "self-effacement of the production process" whereby the number of frames-per-second "automatically erases their 'brushstrokes.'" Unlike standard cinematography, where cuts and angles have to be matched in the editing process in order to create a realistic flow of action, in animation any form can be transformed into any other form with surprising fluidity. And thus animation appears "natural" at the very moment that it offers surrealistic movements and metamorphoses which cannot be performed "in real life" (Small and Levison 1989: 69).

In contrast, however, other theorists have argued that animation actually calls attention to the techniques by which it is made. As Michael O'Pray has argued, animation allows us to witness the "omnipotence of thought." The satisfaction of animation, he argues, lies in the animator's ability to represent impossible worlds, but also the "skill and virtuosity" involved in creating those impossible words. We "thrill to the means of representation," he argues, and not just to the representation itself (O'Pray 1997: 200). Animation pioneer Norman McLaren had a similar way of thinking about animation. As Small and Levinson (1989: 68) tell us, tacked to his animation gear in the 1960s was the following definition of the form:

- Animation is not the art of DRAWINGS-that-move but the art of MOVE-MENTS-that-are-drawn.
- What happens *between* each frame is much more important than what exists *on* each frame.
- Animation is therefore the art of manipulating the invisible interstices that lie between the frames.

In other words, animation, by its very form, calls attention to the way in which it is made. It does this by calling attention to the "space" between the individual cels, which in turn creates the effect of movement for the viewer. And, if animation is a process which takes place between frames, rather than within the frames, then it might be useful to think of animation itself as a dialectical process: a process which mediates between individual images to create the illusion of life.

So why then would the creators of *Daria* use the dialectical possibilities of animation to create such deadpan, lifeless characters? Why use a form that is about the creation of life to create the illusion of non-life? The creators of *Daria* made a self-conscious critique of the principles at stake in animation as a form. They used *Daria* to show that animation could be about death, as well as life. Moreover, they chose irony as their mode of address. Daria was an animated girl without a bust line; a negative person who often helped make life better for her friends; an adolescent who was usually the smartest person in the room; and an animated cartoon character who reveled in her complete lack of animation. At the same time, we were never meant to believe that she was as depressed, or as depressing, as she seemed. *Daria* took the raw material of adolescence – the humiliation, pressure, bitterness, and self-loathing – and turned it into something positive.

And thus the power and the appeal of *Daria*'s other messages – messages about feminism and consumerism – were strengthened by the ironic tension that structured the show. *Daria* called attention to itself by frustrating the life-affirming conventions of animation with which we have become familiar. *Daria*'s creators invented a new form of animation, a kind of "anti-animation." Although the drawings were cold, flat, and lifeless, even nihilistic in their aesthetic, the plots of the individual episodes were life-affirming: the characters still were able to create and maintain relationships with each other. They even had room to grow and change: Daria got a boyfriend, Quinn got tired of being stupid, Jake realized he was too stressed out by his job, and Helen admitted that she worked too hard. *Daria* creators drew a cold and alienating world, but through humor they maintained a sense of life.

Feminism in combat boots

Ironically perhaps, animation is an artistic form in which the role of "creator of life" has belonged almost exclusively to men. At the same time, however, women have been central to the labor-intensive process of creating the finished product. From the beginning, studios such as the Disney studio used women workers to mix paint, trace images, and paint the cels. According to Elizabeth Bell, women painted an average of 250,000 paintings for each feature film. Women were also employed as stenographers and typists who transcribed conversations about the production process in "sweatbox" sessions. As Bell explains it, "the hands of women, painting and transcribing the creative efforts of men, performed the tedious, repetitive labor-intensive housework of the Disney enterprise" (1995: 107).

Sex role differentiation has been at issue not only in the production process, but also in the finished product. As Irene Kotlarz has argued, female creatures such as Minnie Mouse "were often just a visual counterpart of the male with added eyelashes, bow and high heels" (1992: 27). In contrast, the human character Betty Boop was a grotesque combination of female body parts, making her part sex goddess, part little girl. In a similar way Olive Oyl was elongated in a disturbing way, merging the form of a little girl with an elderly spinster. In the

Disney tradition women have retained a childlike quality (early Disney characters were often modeled on the bodies of young dancers), but with womanly figures. Even modern Disney heroines, such as Ariel in *The Little Mermaid* and Belle in *Beauty and the Beast*, are represented as teenage girls with impossibly Barbie-esque proportions.

Daria offered an explicit critique of this tradition. Daria was neither a "little girl" nor a buxom babe. She was first and foremost an intellectual, as signified in part by the frequent references to her as "a brain." At the same time, Daria did have a body. There were several episodes devoted to her struggles with her appearance, including an episode in which she had her navel pierced to impress a guy (Trent, Jane's brother), and another episode in which she thought about getting contact lenses. Although she was not physically expressive, during her five-year run she kissed a boy, held hands, blushed, sat on a peanut butter sandwich, and was stung by a bee.

And while Daria came across as a geeky intellectual, her best friend Jane was a genuine tough chick. They both wore combat boots, but Jane had black hair, bluntly cut, with multiple piercings, rolled-up shorts, and lipstick. While some of the earliest drawings for Jane cast her as an eighties-style punk, her character evolved into an edgy, artsy, attractive, and, ultimately more emotional female role model, especially when compared to Daria. Jane and Daria were both creative, although Daria was the "writer" and Jane was the "artist." Together they used their creativity to make fun of the girls at school who seemed to care only about appearances.

In one of the more memorable episodes from the first season, "Arts 'N Crass," Daria and Jane plotted to undermine a school art contest called "Student Life at the Dawn of the Millennium." They decided to represent life, "student life," as it really was, to "tell the truth about how much it can suck," and "to blow away the story-book fantasy about how great it is to be young." Jane painted a poster showing a beautiful girl looking in the mirror, while Daria wrote the verse to go along with the picture: "She knows she's a winner, she couldn't be thinner. Now she goes in the bathroom and vomits up dinner." Their art teacher, Mrs. Defoe, liked the poster, but the hard-edged principle, Ms. Li, gave the girls twenty-four hours to change the poem or withdraw the poster. When they refused, the poster was changed against their will, and entered in the contest. Daria and Jane defaced their poster, and Ms. Li threatened them with expulsion. When Daria's mom, the lawyer, heard about this, she threatened to sue the school for altering Daria's poster to begin with. In fitting ironic fashion, the bubbleheaded Brittany won the contest with her "Just Say No to Drugs" poster (Episode 201, "Arts 'N Crass").

Throughout *Daria*, Daria and Jane, while neither of them was overweight, represented alternatives to the body-conscious teens who were their peers. The more traditionally "feminine" characters, the big-breasted Brittany, with her shrill little girl's voice, and the perfectly proportioned Quinn, with her tiny nasally voice, were the persistent targets of the sardonic humor of Daria and Jane. In the frequent episodes which featured the "Fashion Club," the fashionable girls were made to seem ridiculous. Quinn's obsession with her looks became something even Quinn was willing to reconsider as the show evolved. By season five she was tired of being stupid and started to study more (even though it was with a cute tutor). With these plots Daria reversed the normal order of the universe; Daria and Jane, who were technically "losers," became winners in the animated world. Or, at the very least, they always had the last laugh.

In the last twenty years animated television has been a good place for the de-Disneyfication of the female form. *Daria* has been in good company with animated adolescent role models such as *The Powerpuff Girls*, Lisa Simpson from *The Simpsons*, and Velma from *Scooby-Doo*. In fact, aside from avant-garde animation, the most progressive, interesting, and least stereotypical animated women are on television, rather than in films.[4] Perhaps this is because television is recognized as a more "feminized" medium, with women playing an important role as the target audience of television commercials. Moreover, with the demographic impact of the "Echo-boomers," the children of the baby boomers, programmers have begun to create more television programs for young women (Tobenkin 1994: 25–6).

In another nod to the theme of feminism, in the episode "Speedtrapped," Daria and Quinn, while driving to help Jane, Trent and the band get out of jail, pick up a cute hitchhiking cowboy named Travis (à la Brad Pitt in *Thelma and Louise*). Travis, using sweet talk, wrangled the bail money from Quinn, while Jane and the band managed to get out of jail by playing a concert for the sheriff. In the final scene Daria proved she was not a timid driver by nearly running over the "cute cowboy" who stole their money. It was not the same kind of statement as driving off a cliff, but the *Thelma and Louise* reference was clear. And, if anything, the ending to "Speedtrapped" proved how efficacious Daria could be: she chose attempted revenge over certain suicide.

The "malling" of America

The ironic mode that characterized *Daria* was also used to critique American mass culture. *Daria*, like other prime time animated shows, made frequent references to other media, especially film and television. Many of the show's titles were variations on film titles from classic Hollywood ("It Happened One Nut"; "Dye, Dye, My Darling," etc.). Occasionally *Daria* made direct reference to other television shows, as in the episode "The Lawndale File," which spoofed the popular FOX series, *The X-Files*. In this episode Mr. O'Neill tried to explain to his students that in the 1950s movies about aliens were really movies about communists. His lecture failed, however, when his students became confused and began to think that Daria and Jane were alien communists sent to infiltrate Lawndale. Quinn started dressing in a black turtleneck sweater, Trent wrote a happy song, and even Daria's father Jake became afraid that his daughter was an "atomic communist." She finally convinced him that she was not a member of an anti-capitalist cabal:

Jane: So you finally convinced your dad that you're not a communist?
Daria: Yeah, I'm showing him how much I love money by hitting him up for it every chance I get.

In this episode Daria and Jane were imagined to be communists, even alien subversives, for the simple reason that they were the only students in the class who understood Mr. O'Neill's lecture about the 1950s. At another level, however, this episode marked one of those rare moments in the popular culture of the post-Cold War era when communism was referenced – in however ironic a context. This reference to communism, and another episode in which Daria started an *anti-Communist rally*, provokes the question: was *Daria* a politically subversive show?

Animation can be a subversive form. As Jan Švankmajer has argued, it subverts reality by making ordinary, inanimate objects move: "Suddenly, everyday contact with things which people are used to acquires a new dimension and in this way casts a doubt over reality. In other words, I use animation as a means of subversion" (quoted in Wells 1998: 11). Likewise, Paul Wells has argued that animators can violate gender boundaries with ambiguously animated forms: "Animation has the capability of rendering the body in a way which blurs traditional notions of gender, species and indigenous identity….It is in this sense that animation as a *form* is acknowledged as having a potentially radical vocabulary" (1998: 11). Animation, by releasing its subjects from the laws of photographic representation, has the potential of allowing us to imagine new worlds and new forms of being.

At the same time, however, animation is an essentializing form. As Jeanette Winterson has argued, animation is literally, and figuratively, "flat"; it is not a good medium for exploring depth of character and complex plot. She sees it as "closer to dance in terms of human delineation" (1992: 27). This explanation helps us to understand why, given the utopian possibilities of animation, animated characters are often representational clichés – why stereotypes of women, racial minorities and sexual minorities are so exaggerated and crude when they appear in animated form. Animation, in theory, can remold conventions of representation. Yet at the same time caricature is dependent on the artist's ability to deploy the very same conventions that might otherwise be over-turned.

Daria, while it failed to remold convention at the level of animation, did attempt to expose the collusion of capitalism and public education. Principle Li, who was one of the only ethnic characters on the show (Asian-American), was an unsubtle parody of a school administrator who kept her eye on little but the bottom line. In one of the first season's episodes, "This Year's Model," Ms. Li accepted a fee from the Amazon modeling company in return for allowing them to recruit on campus. When her students challenged her about the ethics of this decision, Ms. Li was quick to defend it: "The school is receiving a fee for its cooperation, but every cent is going to capital improvements! We're finally going to get those bulletproof skylights for the swimming pool" (Episode 106, "This Year's Model"). And, while the models succeeded in recruiting one of the Lawndale students (the football star, Kevin), Daria exacted her revenge by sending a letter in Ms. Li's name inviting an outfit of "soldiers-for-hire" to recruit on campus. In the final scene a school assembly was interrupted by a unit of renegade soldiers. As usual, Daria had the last laugh.

Although *Daria* often raised controversial political issues, the show treated the idea of collective action with some ironic distance. In the episode "Lucky Strike," Daria was asked to become a substitute teacher when one of the strike replacement teachers was discovered to be a pedophile. Daria agreed, and, in essence, became a scab. The show constructed this decision as a dilemma (a good angel urged her not to take the job, while a bad angel urged her to see this as an opportunity to take revenge on her teachers and her sister, Quinn):

Devil Daria:	Not so fast. You'll get out of gym class.
Angel Daria:	You? A scab?
Devil Daria:	Oh, great. Touched by an angel.
Angel Daria:	You'd be betraying your teachers.
Devil Daria:	Hey, yeah! You'd be betraying your teachers!
Angel Daria:	You'd just be falling into the same trap that management always uses to keep wages low and workers weak.
Devil Daria:	Oh, go dance on the head of a pin. You could make Quinn's life really miserable.
Angel Daria:	Huh. That's a good point.
Devil Daria:	Hey, you hungry?
Angel Daria:	Yeah, we can pick this up later.

When the dialectical struggle between the angels collapsed over a snack break, it became clear that at the very moment at which the serious issues were being addressed (low wages and weak workers), they were simultaneously being dismissed. In an unusually happy ending Daria survived her experience as a scab, turning it into a rare opportunity to bond with Quinn. In addition, the teachers ultimately won their demands.

These episodes cannot be decoded as simply "subversive": they did not show the students or the teachers making an effective collective effort towards the dismantling of the power structure. But these episodes did suggest that teenagers were capable of having a commonsense understanding of what was wrong with what Daria called "our hollow, consumer-driven society." And, although Daria ultimately agreed to be a scab in "Lucky Strike," it was remarkable to see that she even understood what a scab was, and why it was wrong to be one. It is rare to see strikes referenced in any way within televisual culture. Daria was smart about the problems facing schools and teenagers under capitalism, and it might be wrong to blame her (and the show's creators) for not yet having a solution to these problems. Irony does not equal revolution, but it might represent the first step towards mounting a critique of the system.

The social world of fan-fiction

Another way to assess the potentially subversive political effect of *Daria* is to examine the essays and the "fan-fiction" produced by *Daria*-philes. There are over 100 Web sites created and maintained by *Daria* fans, offering episode summaries, show transcripts, character descriptions, news about the show, as well as "fan-fiction": *Daria* episodes written by fans, for fans. Many of these Web sites also contain essays which perform a kind of "cultural criticism" of the fan-fiction, and address the community about what it means to be a fan of the show.

In considering the fans' view of *Daria* it is helpful to consider Kenneth Burke's proposition that stories become our "equipment for living." Burke argues that, like proverbs, fictional narratives are "strategies for dealing with situations." Burke considers works of art to be "strategies for selecting enemies and allies, for socializing losses, for warding off the evil eye, for purification, propitiation, and desanctification, consolation and vengeance, admonition and exhortation, implicit commands or instructions of one sort or another" (Burke 1941: 304). And thus in the context of the *Daria* fan world, it becomes clear that *Daria* has become a strategy for dealing with the process of alienation itself. Since Daria is an outcast in the world she inhabits, and yet simultaneously the star of her own show, fans are drawn to her because of the tensions she embodies. As for naming enemies and allies, Daria names smart kids, ugly kids, punk kids, and artists as "allies," and fashion-mongers, superficial people, corrupt authority figures, and, occasionally, parents, as "enemies." *Daria* offers both consolation (for outcasts) and vengeance (for virtually everyone else).

One of the most poignant of the *Daria* fan-essays addresses one of those "situations" for which *Daria* has served as "equipment" for comprehending: the Columbine high-school shootings of April 1999. In the essay "Columbine's Most Wanted," *Daria* fan Peter Guerin took direct aim at *Daria* critics, such as Peggy Charrens and Donald Wildmons, who attacked the program for corrupting their children. Guerin eloquently struck back, arguing that *Daria* might have been able to help outcasts such as Klebold and Harris to deal with the difficulties of being branded a "loser":

> I am not saying that perhaps Klebold and Harris would not have gone on their bloody rampage if they had watched "Daria," but I would challenge the Peggy Charrens and Donald Wildmons of this world to take a very close look at the show before they condemn what they do not know or understand. Perhaps they will see themselves or even their own children in the program. Perhaps they will see that not all the outcasts in school are the duster-clad, gun-toting type. Perhaps then they will not be so quick to judge.
>
> (Guerin 1999)

In other words, Guerin argued that *Daria* was about preventing the kind of alienation that might lead to mass-murder. Rather than seeing Daria as a "grim reaper in a dress," Guerin saw Daria as a mature, level-headed role model, who forgave the popular people for their prejudices, had friends of her own, and, most importantly, had a sense of humor.

For fans such as Guerin, the "consolation" offered by *Daria* was real. In his essay about Columbine, Guerin talked about the alienation he himself suffered when he was in school. He described being sent to "special education" classes because of a behavioral problem. He described himself as among the "Untouchables" in his school, "due to something that was an accident of birth, something that I could not control." He explained that time, and *Daria*, helped him to see that violence was not the answer:

> I must admit there were times I wanted to "pay back" my tormentors, but at least I had the moral decency not to act them out....It's been twelve years since I graduated from high school, and over the years I have tried to contact some of the people I knew. To these people I have over the years expressed my forgiveness for what had happened to me. Perhaps my watching "Daria" has helped in some way as well.
>
> (Guerin 1999)

For Guerin, *Daria* has indeed been a kind of "equipment for living." The show has helped him to come to terms with abuses he suffered in his youth, and to advocate a safe and sane solution to teen harassment. *Daria* was not the problem, he argued, rather, *Daria* was part of the solution.

In some cases the appeal to the fan-fiction community is deeply personal, suggesting that the attachments that are formed through the production of fan-fiction go far beyond *Daria*. Peter Guerin, for example, in his essay about the announced cancellation of *Daria* as a series, asked members of the fan community to pray for his ailing mother: "I hope all of you keep my mother in your thoughts and prayers; she is facing surgery for an intestinal problem and by the time this essay is posted she'll have a long recovery in front of her" (Guerin 2001). Guerin was willing to accept the end of the production of *Daria*, but he still wanted to use the occasion as an opportunity to appeal to the community at large.

Conclusion

In January of 2002 MTV debuted *Daria*'s final feature, a made-for-TV movie called "Is It College Yet?" in which the *Daria*-gang graduated from high school. And thus ended a five-year run of a show that redefined irony for a combined audience of Gen-Xers and their younger siblings. *Daria* launched repeated critiques of the banality of the suburban world, critiquing capitalism, public education, consumer culture, the obsession with weight and beauty, and the pressure on teenagers to achieve. At the same time, the mode of Daria's critique was frequently ironic, denying the value of the very world she was trying to transform. She was persistently sarcastic, morose, inexpressive, and yet at the same time a frequent "winner" in a world in which she had been assigned the position of "loser."

However, the fan community produced by *Daria* has been, in contrast, refreshingly sincere. They are still writing essays and fan-fiction episodes, posting responses to these stories and essays, and meeting each other outside of the Internet. Whatever Daria's personal philosophy, and enduring negativity, she has produced a surprisingly optimistic fan culture: TV viewers who believe in the value of artistic production and the possibility of change. For them, *Daria* does not propagate nihilism; rather, the show has become a way of dealing with nihilism itself. *Daria* has become a strategy for naming a situation (alienation), and fan Web sites have become a site for genuine artistic production, critique, and community. As Daria says when she is interviewed by the media about her plans for the future: "Don't worry, it'll get better. It has to." This is the message *Daria* fans take from the show, regardless of the ironic endings of many of the episodes. Their optimism comes, in part, from their refusal to be alienated from each other.

Notes

1   "Beavis and Butt-head (heh, heh) are Dead – Sort of" (*CNN Interactive* 1997).
2   See Wells' *Understanding Animation* (1998). In Chapter 3, "Narrative Strategies," Wells outlines the various visual techniques important to the understanding of animated narrative (68–126).
3   Sergei Eisenstein (1986: 59).
4   The major collection of avant-garde animation by women was produced by the British Film Institute: *Wayward Girls and Wicked Women* (1992).

Bibliography

"Beavis and Butt-head (heh, heh) are Dead – Sort of" (1997) *CNN Interactive*. Available at: http://gabrielmedia.org/news/beavis-dead.html (accessed 8 May 2002).

Belcher, W. (2000) "It's Time to Fall for 'Daria' and Gang," *Tampa Tribune*, 27 August: 4.

Bell, E. (1995) "Somatexts at the Disney Shop: Constructing the Pentimentos of Women's Animated Bodies," in E. Bell, L. Haas, and L. Sells (eds.), *From Mouse to Mermaid: The Politics of Film, Gender, and Culture*, Bloomington: Indiana University Press.

British Film Institute/Connoisseur Video (1992) *Wayward Girls and Wicked Women*.

Burke, K. (1941) *The Philosophy of Literary Form: Studies in Symbolic Action*, Berkeley: University of California Press.

Cholodenko, A. (2000) "The Illusion of the Beginning: A Theory of Drawing and Animation," *Afterimage*, Volume 28, July: 9–12.

Eisenstein, S. (1986) *Eisenstein on Disney*, in J. Leyda (ed.), Calcutta: Seagull Books.

Gitlin, T. (1993) "Flat and Happy," *Wilson Quarterly*, Volume 17, Number 4, Autumn: 48.

Guerin, Peter (2001) "The Beginning of the End." Available at: http//www.outpost-daria.com/essay/pg_the_beginning_of_the_end.txt (accessed 30 May 2002).

—— (1999) "Columbine's Most Wanted." Available at: http://www.outpost-daria.com/essay/pg_columbines_most_wanted.txt (accessed 30 May 2002).

Klein-Häss, M. (2002) "ATV: The Edgy World of MTV Animation." Available at: http://anp.awn.com/MTVmain.html, (accessed 8 May 2002).

Kotlarz, I. (1992) "Imagery of Desire," *Sight and Sound*, Volume 2, Number 6, October: 27.

Kuczynski, A. (1998) "Daria Morgendorffer Brings Actual Sentences to MTV," *The Star Tribune*, 25 May: 8E.

O'Connor, J. J. "Teen-Ager's Scornful Look at Cuteness," *New York Times*, 3 March: C16.

O'Pray, M. (1997) "Eisenstein and Stokes on Disney: Film Animation and Omnipotence," in J. Pilling (ed.), *A Reader in Animation Studies*, London: John Libbey.

Ozersky, J. (1997) "A Woman of Her Times: What's the Danger in 'Daria'? The Ultimate Teen Weapon: Irony Without Vulnerability," *St. Louis Post-Dispatch*, 6 June: 47.

Pal, S. (1997) "Dear Daria: MTV Character is the Acidic Animated Darling of many Viewers," *Times-Picayune*, 21 July: T4.

Quinn, M. (2002) "Daria Episode Summaries." Available at: http://www.outpost-daria.com/ep103.html, (accessed 8 May 2002).

Rabinovitz, L. (1989) "Animation, Postmodernism, and MTV," *The Velvet Light Trap*, Number 24, Fall: 99–100.

Rich (2001) "Why Bother." Available at: http://paperpusher.simplenet.com/why_bother_.html, (accessed 10 October 2001).

Small, E. and E. Levinson (1989) "Toward a Theory of Animation," *The Velvet Light Trap*, Number 23, Fall: 66–74.

Span, P. (1997) "Wither Daria: Meet the Teen Terminator; MTV's Hot New Toon is Sharp, Funny – and Female," *Washington Post*, 1 June: G01.

Tobenkin, D. (1994) "Syndicators Programming to Girls; At Least Four New Kids Shows Feature Female Leads," *Broadcasting & Cable*, Volume 124, Number 48, 28 November: 25–6.

Wells, P. (1998) *Understanding Animation*, London: Routledge.

Winterson, J. (1992) "Outrageous Proportions," *Sight and Sound*, Volume 2, Number 6, October: 26–7.

Chapter 11

"WHAT ARE THOSE LITTLE GIRLS MADE OF?"

The Powerpuff Girls and consumer culture

Joy Van Fuqua

Pictures that move! Drawings that speak! Impossible things! They are constituted to make you happy, these cartoon kindergartners, even while they are knocking the teeth from a villain's mouth.... From the bills in the mail, the boss at your shoulder, the mean kid on the corner, the aphids on the roses, the clog in the sink, and all the various grown-up voices of sensibility nattering in your head. Relief is only a cartoon away.

(Lloyd 2001)

DURING AN **ESPN** CABLECAST OF A **WNBA** (Women's National Basketball Association) game between the New York Liberty and the Detroit Shock, my attention shifted from the pleasing spectacle of the women's athletic competition unfolding on the basketball court to the area that is, in the parlance of sports marketing, referred to as "courtside signage." Against a backdrop of advertisements for L'Oréal Cosmetics, female athletes such as New York Liberty's Teresa Weatherspoon amazed spectators and viewers in the bleachers and at home with her, as usual, unsurpassed athletic prowess. The WNBA game foregrounded the ways in which female power (in this case, athleticism), at the level of signification and spatial arrangement, is literally surrounded by a dominant, corporate discourse of conventional feminine beauty.[1] However, the traditional feminine beauty imperative was constantly challenged not only by the athletes themselves but also by the spectators. The crowd-scanning camera showed a variety of spectators who had somehow managed to eschew eyeliner and lipstick in favor of tattoos and piercings (with rocker Joan Jett sitting in front of Hillary and Bill

Clinton). In fact, one could surely argue that a significant portion of the strategic pleasures for lesbians and other fans of the WNBA comes not only from watching the game on the court, but in making a game out of watching the spectators, of scanning the crowd for queer faces, styles, and signifiers. While the corporate perspective insists on framing female power and athleticism through the lens of conventionalized femininity, the players and fans – and even some of the commercials – acknowledge the limitations of this perspective. Like the Maybelline commercials – "Maybe she's born with it, maybe it's Maybelline" – featuring Sarah Michelle Gellar that punctuate *Buffy The Vampire Slayer*'s femme heroics, the intertextual relationship forged between advertising texts and women's televised sporting events emphasize the friction of the power/puff relation.

In addition to WNBA games on Lifetime or ESPN, children's cartoons have also begun to attract their share of female fans starved for images of women and girls that represent the multidimensional aspects of female culture. Produced by Cartoon Network (and AOL Time Warner, its mega-media parent company) as an original children's animated series, *The Powerpuff Girls* engage a series of relationships between power and puff, the home and the laboratory, science and nature, text and context. Moreover, while Ellen Seiter has described the stronghold of "toy-based programs" as founded in children's cartoons, *The Powerpuff Girls* is one of the few such television texts that was not originally conceived in relation to its merchandising possibilities (Seiter 1995: 169). Given the merchandising cross-promotion imperative of today's media conglomerates, Cartoon Network reproduces *The Powerpuff Girls* as a multitude of intertextual commodities. Cartoon Network may boast of the gender-bending attributes of its pint-sized super-heroines in terms of viewing audience, but when it comes to consuming the commodity intertexts, this activity is explicitly gendered as female; the merchandise intertexts unequivocally construct young girls as the ideal consumers. In this way, the intertexts re-frame the girl-power message of the primary text in such a way as to equate consumerism with empowerment. It is significant that an executive at Warner Brothers Consumer Products, vice-president of apparel Patti Buckner, has pointed out that while boys comprise 50 percent of the viewing audience for *The Powerpuff Girls*, "no product line for boys has been developed" (*KidScreen* 1999: 42).

This essay places *The Powerpuff Girls* within two interrelated contexts: the apparent *generic* boom in the cultural products featuring "girl-power" and the construction of 'tween girl markets for those cultural products. Toward that end, this essay attends to the gender-bending characteristics of *The Powerpuff Girls* through close textual analysis and the structure and gendered address of the commercial intertexts. While *The Powerpuff Girls* program calls into question various forms of gender essentialism, it has also been successful in constructing a vision of girlhood that even XYs can enjoy. Although the relationship of girl viewers to the main program text extends to consumption of *Powerpuff Girls* "intertexts" (merchandise), the relationship of boy viewers with the program does not necessarily include consumption of accompanying commodities. In other words, boys may be encouraged to watch, but they are not encouraged to consume the commodity intertexts – all that shopping stuff is strictly for girls (or so the merchandising suggests). That is, the program text may indeed have cross-gender (and generational) appeal,[2] but, the commercial intertexts almost uniformly represent girls and young women as the ideal consumers of puff stuff. This phenomenon, in itself, is neither positive nor negative, neither progressive nor reactionary. What it does highlight is the way that conventional notions about femininity and masculinity may work to reframe primary cultural texts that appear to question the very definition of girlhood.

Butt-kickin' babes

Part of the parade of "butt-kickin' babes" represented by films such as *Charlie's Angels* and *Lara Croft: Tomb Raider* (based on the computer game) and prime time television series such as *Buffy The Vampire Slayer*, *Dark Angel*, *Xena: Warrior Princess* and *Witchblade*, Cartoon Network's prime time and daytime series *The Powerpuff Girls* features prepubescent heroines with curfew rather than cleavage. Similar to Max (Jessica Alba) in James Cameron's *Dark Angel* and Jaime Sommers (Lindsay Wagner) in *The Bionic Woman*, the three Powerpuffs, Blossom, Buttercup, and Bubbles, have been physically enhanced through scientific experimentation. However, unlike Max and the other enhanced full-grown heroines circulating through current popular culture, the genetically enhanced Powerpuffs do not sport outfits with plunging necklines or form-fitting tights. Figure 11.1 shows PpG fan art representing Blossom as Lara Croft, the transformation from Powerpuff to Tomb Raider accomplished without resort to bust lines.[3] Although I would not want to argue that the Powerpuff Girls are beyond or free from sexualization, the context and specificity of the program text seem to mitigate against this in ways that post-pubescent girl-power films and television texts do not.

In fact, its origin story – that it was produced by a 20-year-old animation student at California Institute of the Arts in Valencia, California – has been incorporated into the narrative world of the program as a means of distinguishing it from its mass-marketed counterparts. A children's prime time cartoon with both child and adult, male and female fans, *The Powerpuff Girls* provides a rich example of the transformation of an "art-school" project into a mass-media *product*. The story of the "conception" of "The Whoopass Girls" and the three-minute film called *Whoopass Stew* emphasizes its non-commercial, artistic origins. The origin

Figure 11.1 Blossom as Lara Croft

story may function as a type of "anti-economism" in which the subversive aspects of *The Powerpuff Girls* depends upon its continued erasure of things commercial.[4] This tension between the artistic and economic has been emphasized by *The Powerpuff Girls'* creator Craig McCracken in various interviews.[5] Another way to read the repetition, in different media forms and sources, of the McCracken origin story is to say that it serves as a way to distinguish *The Powerpuff Girls* from other commercial texts.

The result of a laboratory experiment gone awry, Buttercup, Blossom, and Bubbles owe their power to a variety of factors, not the least of which include the 1990s rise of "grrrl culture" (Kearney 1998b: 285–311). Although *The Powerpuff Girls* is popular with both male and female viewers of various generations and genders, their creators are men.[6] As the progeny of Professor Utonium's laboratory and McCracken's student film project, the Powerpuffs are not your average little girls. Apart from the fact that they have two "dads" instead of a mom and a dad, these three superheroes brandish brawn, brilliance, and cuteness in place of the current filmic and televisual fascination with lips, tits, and ass.

Another way to account for the popularity of *The Powerpuff Girls*, both text and intertexts, is to say that they typify a certain configuration of girl-power both inside and outside of media institutions. In her analysis of mass-media representations of teenage girls, Mary Kearney has suggested that the proliferation of girl superheroes in film and television has as much to do with wider cultural shifts in our ways of conceptualizing gender as it does with an increase in the number of women in decision-making positions within media institutions:

> The emergence of girl power shows are the result not only of changes to dominant notions of femininity and masculinity (which are now being reconfigured in relation to generational identity), but also transformations in the television industry, specifically the increase in female executives, producers, directors, and writers, as well as the introduction of new networks such as UPN, WB, and FOX and the greater expansion of television channels through cable and satellite transmission. In turn, the emergence of these girl-power shows can also be related to the proliferation of discourses about girl empowerment and the proliferation of assertive teenage girls through other cultural media such as magazines, film, and music.
>
> (Kearney 1998a: 480)

Engaging in various interpretations of martial arts and cartoon-specific defenses, the Girls slug it out with the cleverest of mutant "evil" guys (and, with the exception of "Princess Morbucks," "Sedusa," and "Him" – a kind of *Yellow Submarine*-inspired devil-as-drag queen – all of the evildoers are gendered male). Reminiscent of the mutant "Penguin" from Tim Burton's *Batman Returns*, most of the foes in the "city of Townsville" and its surrounding areas have been altered through either environmental and/or scientific events, or some combination of the two. As "freaks" themselves – not of nature, but of science – the heroines of Townsville are unequivocally embraced by the citizenry and its leadership, represented by the bumbling miniature Mayor, while its villains are punished again and again and never seem to learn from their "misdeeds." In fact, the continued existence of the community is dependent upon the maintenance of the strange and "unnatural" characteristics of these three, wee 5-year-olds.

Kearney attributes the linkage of power and puff in the representation of female action-adventure heroines to the "necessity for contemporary females to embody simultaneously both genders if they want to succeed in patriarchal society and male-dominated activities" (1998a: 479). According to this Spice Girl articulation of feminism, "ideologies of female empowerment have merged with conventional feminine practices (the use of cosmetics, body-revealing clothing, high-heeled shoes), to allow for a greater spectrum of female appearance and behavior" (Kearney 1998a: 479). However, this vision of female possibility can also have the effect of further recuperating and accommodating certain feminine ideologies – ones that continue to be oppressive for many women and girls who do not wear a size 4 and a 36D bra.

Cartoon Network executive Linda Simensky has credited the character of Lisa Simpson of *The Simpsons* with paving the way for "the world's cutest superheroes" (Loos 2000: 25). Whereas ten years earlier, it was "unheard of to have a female lead in an animation show," Simensky notes that, along with an increase in the numbers of women in positions of power at networks comes a proliferation of female characters. While this relationship is not guaranteed, Simensky's remarks do underscore the material aspects of getting female lead characters on television in animated or non-animated programs.

The marketing frenzy that consumers witness today in terms of the promotion of mass media, film and television texts, is a further result of many factors, not the least of which have to do with product merchandising and licensing. Simensky points out that the proliferation of character and franchise-centered intertexts is a result of, among other things, the mutually reinforcing relationship between the rise of Warner Brothers' Studio Stores in shopping malls in the early 1990s and the revitalization of Warner Brothers' animation through such original animated series as *The Powerpuff Girls*. In 1988, just one year before Warner Communications merged with Time Inc., Warner Brothers studio began a "new animation division to produce daily and later weekly television series" (Simensky 1998: 176). Steven Spielberg was a moving force behind such original animation series as *Steven Spielberg Presents Tiny Toon Adventures*, which became syndicated in 1991 and, according to Simensky, was soon followed by *Taz-Mania*, *Batman: The Animated Series*, *Steven Spielberg Presents Freakazoid!*, *Steven Spielberg Presents Animaniacs*, and others. Indeed, this branding of the WB as, specifically, "WB Kids" began with its first broadcast in 1995. It is not as if broadcasters had never before recognized youth as a market: Nickelodeon has also promoted itself as the "kids-only network." According to Henry Jenkins (1998: 29), one way of understanding the branding and structuring of television networks as specifically for kid consumption is to see this as an effort to "erect a sharp line between the realms of children and adults." While earlier television programming from the 1950s, for example, has been described by Lynn Spigel as offering "a dissolution of age categories" (1998: 110), today's emphasis on ever-younger consumers (with *Teletubbies* probably being the youngest in terms of audience address) tends to define childhood as, first and foremost, a consumer category.[7]

Usually reserved for Hollywood-produced blockbusters – the ur-texts within mass media – franchises can also refer to specific mass-media products that can be reproduced, in varying forms, across a variety of media sources (Schatz 1997: 75). In this sense, Cartoon Network's most recent hot property, *The Powerpuff Girls*, can be understood as a case-study in the process of, as Eileen Meehan has described it, the production of the "commercial text and the product line that constitutes its commercial intertext" (1991: 61). *The Powerpuff Girls'* popularity and commercial profitability needs to be placed within the context of Cartoon Network's attempts to carve out and expand its ideal audience as well as a wider cultural framework within which particular genders are commodified in many ways. The commercial text and product lines work to construct a seamless loop of reception and consumption.

Figure 11.2 Powerpuff-inspired Rave Wear (Courtesy of The Cartoon Network)

From children's magazines such as *Kid Power* to Cartoon Network's *The Powerpuff Girls Powerzine*, girls are shown in Figures 11.2 and 11.3 consuming candy, carrying Powerpuff backpacks, dancing with Powerpuff Girl-inspired rave clothing. The cartoon's creator, Craig McCracken, is photgraphed surrounded by Powerpuff stuff – various plushies (stuffed dolls), T-shirts, a thermos, pillows, watches, hats. McCracken's wallet, full of dollar bills, signifies the financial rewards of such ubiquitous, intertextual commodification.

Although *The Powerpuff Girls Powerzine* (the official magazine of the Powerpuff Girls) uniformly depicts young girls as the preferred consumers of the commercial intertexts, Cartoon Network's Linda Simensky has remarked that the official breakdown of the *Powerpuff* audience is "two-thirds kids, one-third adults" (Lloyd 2001: 4). Moreover, *Powerzine* appropriates both the non-commercial style of "DIY" 'zine culture through the simulation of "diary" writing and the commercial style of teen beauty/fashion magazines.

Powerzine is divided into two clearly designated sections: one for the Powerpuffs and one for their arch rivals. Like the official fan magazines of boy bands such as The Backstreet Boys, *Powerzine* includes "big pictures of the Girls!"

211

Figure 11.3 Consuming the *Powerpuff Girls* (Courtesy of Cartoon Network)

that fans are encouraged to rip out and hang up. This audience connection between popular boy bands and the Powerpuffs, however, is not only obliquely incorporated: the trio appear as a band even as they deny "tenacious rumors to the contrary." An additional musical reference includes an article discussing Bis, the "techno-punk" Scottish trio which performs "The Powerpuff Girls (End Theme)" on a compact disc collection of Powerpuff Girls tunes.[8]

A survey of Powerpuff Girl commodities shows an emphasis on manufacturing utilitarian, yet inexpensive items such as hair clips or lunch-boxes that can be displayed. In addition to various kinds of Powerpuff Girl dolls, consumers can buy backpacks, handbags, metal boxes, T-shirts, jeans, socks, underwear, pajamas, talking key chains, PEZ dispensers, luggage tags, mouse pads, beanbag chairs, pencil boxes, animated watches, picture frames, foaming bath crystals, diaries, chalk and chalk boards, posters, stickers, coloring books, videos and DVDs. Almost all of these commodities are – at least in their representations in magazines – gendered feminine. Other products such as skateboards that are advertised in the magazine *Kid Power*, are gendered masculine with images of Bart Simpson from *The Simpsons*, male characters from *Dragonball Z*, *Digimon*, *Gundam Wing*, *X-Men*, and stars from the *WWF* (*World Wrestling Federation*).

Powerzine includes advertisements (although there are stylistic similarities between advertisements and editorial content), episode guides for fans, features that encourage active participation by readers and test the knowledge of viewers about the show (through a variety of games). They further facilitate distinct identities for each character, and address readers as devoted fans. The 'zine may invoke some of the trappings of 'zine publishing, but it also has many similarities in form as well as content to other girl magazines such as *YM*. These similarities include features such as "Powerscopes" (horoscopes), "Ask the Professor" and "What's Your Power Pulse?", that encourage readers to participate in official Powerpuff Girl consumer culture. Readers get to decide, among other things, which Girl they are closer to in terms of personality. Moreover, the 'zine is full of posters that readers may cut out and place on walls, etc. Among the females that have made it into the Powerpuff Girl pantheon are a mixture of real-life and fictional heroes including Eileen Collins (the first woman to command a space shuttle mission), Ms. Keane (the Girls' kinder-garten teacher at Pokey Oaks), Tasha Schwikert (an up-and-coming young gymnast), Joan of Arc, Ms. Sara Bellum (the pun on "cerebellum" nicely emphasizing the intelligence of the Townsville mayor's female assistant in *The Powerpuff Girls*), Sylvia Earle (an underwater explorer and environmental activist), Binti Jua (an 8-year old gorilla who protected a 3-year-old human boy when he fell into pen in the zoo), and Princess Leia. The 'zine also includes a classified section that is full of fake classified advertisements and personals asking for dates for the Professor.

Even though the advertised Puff stuff and *Powerzine* tend to assume that girl-children between "diapers and driver's permits" are the ideal consumers of these products – and, by extension, the ideal *fans* – the program text displays a knowing sense of gender play through its story lines, characters, and audience address. Some of this gender irony also marks the consumerism of the intertexts, but it is important to see how the texts and intertexts engage viewers and consumers in different ways. While many of the episodes focus on dislodging assumptions about gender and girl-childhood, others thematize the processes of cross-promotion and (inter)textual commodification.[9] For example, in "Super Zeroes" (20 October 2000), "Powerpuff Professor"(9 February 2001), and "Film Flam" (20 April 2001). McCracken both distances himself from and legitimates the production and consumption of the various texts of *The Powerpuff Girls*.

At the center of the magazine is a "Special Product Preview!" section that introduces the female readers to new Puff stuff. On the first page, the preview includes a description of the intertextual merchandise that encourages viewers to extend the reach of the program through commodity consumption:

> Electronica music? Vertigo graphics? Folders and pens? Cartoons have come a
> long way since a hefty side of ribs toppled Fred Flintstone's car – and riding
> the edgy, fast and often loud cartoon revolution is *The Powerpuff Girls*, a blend

of whimsical girlishness, crime-fighting and graphic design, dedicated to saving the world before bedtime. (Which is, given the abundance of nighttime crimes on the show, pretty loosely enforced.) But the Powerpuff revolution hasn't stopped with a TV program. There's goodies, too. The superhero super-group have unleashed a whole line of Powerpuff stuff, from key chains to clothing, on kids nestled somewhere in between diapers and driver's permits. Products you'll find in this section can be purchased at your local retailer.

(*The Powerpuff Girls Powerzine* 2001: 49)

The items included in the "Special Product Preview!" section are gendered not only in terms of product specificity (hair clasps, cosmetic mirrors, etc.); they are also color-coded pink.[10] While their specificity in terms of nature of product and color-code does certainly not limit their consumption to females, it is worth noting that the descriptive text attached to each item of Puff stuff explains how to use the item and who should use it. For example, the card "It's Good to be a Girl" includes the instructions: "Send a salutation to friends and family with a Powerpuff card or two. So slap on a stamp and write on." While I would not want to quibble about the extent to which it is "good to be a girl" and think that everyone should have the opportunity to enjoy being a girl (no matter what one's particular gender), the commercial intertexts tend to collapse – rather than open up – consumerism and girlishness. This questioning of the nature of girlhood seems to be central to the primary text, with specific episodes thematizing this issue (for example, "The Rowdyruff Boys," "Slumbering with the Enemy," and "Bubblevicious").

Moreover, one of the defining characteristics of *The Powerpuff Girls* is the way that it references contemporary popular culture. Hardly the only animated program to engage in such referencing practices, it nonetheless displays a highly self-conscious understanding of its own status as a cultural text. Perhaps only superseded by *The Simpsons*, in terms of generic reflexivity *The Powerpuff Girls* can be understood as providing a running commentary upon the nature of textual commodification and consumption. In "Powerpuff Professor," Professor Utonium worries about the extent to which he spends enough time with "his girls." One morning he tells the Girls that he wants to take them to see *The TV Puppet Pals Movie*. Remembering that *The TV Puppet Pals* is "the Girls' favorite show" and that "they watched it every night before they went to bed," the Professor takes them to see the movie version of the television program. However, their viewing experience is interrupted by a "slimy monster" that tears through the movie screen. Fortunately, the Girls switch from spectators to superheroes and defend the rest of the movie audience from the attacking creature. Professor Utonium decides that the only way he will be able to spend quality time with the Girls is if he becomes a superhero too.

In "Film Flam," however, the issue of textual cross-promotion is made even more explicit when a "big time Hollywood producer/director/agent" named Bernie Bernstein comes to Townsville to make a movie about the Girls. Reading about their superhero feats in a newspaper, Mr. Bernstein develops an elaborate caper in which he only pretends to be making a movie in Townsville. Along with a host of accomplices, Mr. Bernstein convinces the Mayor, the Girls, and Professor Utonium to let him film a portion of the movie in a bank supplied with real money. The episode presents the media industry as a collection of scam artists out to take advantage of the Girls, the Professor, and, at least potentially, the program's creator, Craig McCracken. The Professor is the one who "saves the day" by dressing as a woman. Disguised as a woman, he gains access to "the set" (the bank) where the robbery sequence is being filmed. Looking a lot like Dustin Hoffman dressed as "Tootsie" (from *Tootsie*), the Professor interrupts the pending robbery and tells the Girls about the scam. They respond that it wasn't really a good idea to make a Powerpuff movie anyway. However, in a display of uncharacteristic glee, the Professor replies that the "Powerpuff Girl movie about the making of a Powerpuff movie" would however be a really great idea. Given that an actual Powerpuff movie was released in the summer of 2002, this episode may be seen as a commentary on the marketing of this franchise and, perhaps, McCracken's role in the marketing imperative.[11]

"Weak, helpless, and scared": (un)doing gender in *The Powerpuff Girls*

While gender-bending seems to be thematized, to greater or lesser extents, in each episode of *The Powerpuff Girls*, there are a few episodes that stand out as particularly interesting in their treatment of the power/puff relationship. In "Slumbering with the Enemy," for example, a slumber party, one of the social activities most closely and readily identified as part of girl culture and girl friendships, is represented as providing a space in which the Girls and their "normal little girl" friends can have fun. If it is the case, as Simon Frith (1981) and Angela McRobbie (1991) have argued, that the home and, in particular, girls' bedrooms, have been a center for various kinds of girl subcultural activities (focused on feminine forms of consumption: beauty products, heterosexual romance, and pop music), then "Slumbering with the Enemy" acknowledges this site as especially significant for the formation and negotiation of girls' subjectivity. Further, this episode features a context within which the commodities featured in *Powerzine* might be consumed. The episode thematizes the bedroom as not only the ideal space for one of the enactments of girl friendship but also for commodity consumption.

In both "The Rowdyruff Boys" and "Slumbering with the Enemy," the villain Mojo Jojo tries to defeat the Powerpuff Girls through forms of gender trickery. While serving time in prison for his latest attacks on Townsville, Mojo Jojo figures out how to concoct a boy version of the Powerpuff Girls. He combines "snips and snails and puppy dog tails" and a bit of Chemical X (that he finds in the toilet in his prison cell) and – voila! – the Rowdyruff Boys are born! Appearing in the bold color version of the Powerpuff Girls' pastels and donning backwards baseball caps, the Rowdyruffs proceed to try to "kick the butts" of the heroines. Ms. Sara Bellum intervenes with some gender commonsense and assists the Powerpuffs in their battle. She tells the Girls to "try being nice" rather than fight the Rowdyruffs. Indeed, by going against their nature (by acting in stereotypically girlish ways), the Powerpuffs defeat the Rowdyruffs.

This tension between "normal" girlish behavior and Powerpuff characteristics is highlighted in "Slumbering with the Enemy." In yet another attempt to foil the Powerpuff Girls, Mojo Jojo dresses up as a little girl (with blond wig and pigtails) and joins the slumber party. Renamed "Mojeesha" (a reference to the sitcom *Moesha*, featuring an African-American teenage girl as the lead character), the villain arrives at the party just in time to partake of the girlish festivities. Only the Powerpuff Girls figure out that "Mojeesha" is really the evil simian genius, Mojo Jojo. In a montage sequence set to music, all the "girls" (normal and otherwise) play games, pose as fashion models, look through *Dreamboat* magazine and then go to sleep.[12] Mojeesha seizes this moment of slumber to throw Antidote X on the Powerpuff Girls. Antidote X counteracts Chemical X (the element that makes the girls into superheroes), giving Mojeesha/Mojo Jojo a short-lived victory. Yet, as Mojo Jojo reveals his true identity to the girls, he says that Antidote X has made the Powerpuff Girls "just like your friends, you are the same as they are: weak, helpless, and scared!" Mojo Jojo continues to berate the Powerpuff Girls by saying that they are now "normal little girls – useless normal little girls who can't do anything because they are normal." However, the "normal little girls" respond with menacing stares and arms akimbo. They grab Mojo Jojo and save the day as the announcer yells, "Go! Normal Girls! Go!" While the episode focuses on some of the more traditional elements of girl consumerism, it nonetheless provides an alternative way of understanding contemporary girl culture by contesting the normative assumptions regarding girls and power. It is telling, then, that the contest between the normal little girls and Mojo Jojo occurs in the girls' bedroom, the apparent domestic center of girl subcultural consumption and production (Kearney 1998b: 286). Indeed, the kinds of girlish pleasures that brought the Powerpuffs and their friends together enable them to save the day (again). In spite of the program's content, which represents girlhood as power-*ful* rather than power-*less*, the commercial intertexts tend to reframe this power in terms of consumerism.

While it is the case that *The Powerpuff Girls* is enjoyed by fans of all genders, and across the child–adult generational divide, the commercial intertexts depict the consumption of *Powerpuff Girl* items as a distinctly female thing. This disjuncture need not mitigate the power of *The Powerpuff Girls* and I do not want to suggest that watching the television show is somehow liberating while consuming *Powerpuff Girl* items is not. Rather, what an analysis of the texts and intertexts makes possible is a richer way of accounting for the sense that viewers make of this commercial product. However, as television texts overflow their designated positions in the program schedule and circulate in different, consumer-friendly incarnations, how does this process redefine the engagement of viewers with the program? Attending to texts and intertexts enables – whether in the form of television programming and commercial or television programming and tie-in merchandise – the opening up of the ways that specific media products are produced, circulated, and consumed. Consideration of both kinds of texts may illuminate not only the marketing imperatives of media conglomerates, but the various ways in which consumption occurs.

The texts of *The Powerpuff Girls* represent a contradictory view of girl-power. On the one hand, the primary program text calls into question structuring assumptions regarding the nature of girlhood. On the other hand, the commercial intertexts relocate certain activities, namely shopping and consumerism, as uniquely feminine pursuits. While Blossom, Bubbles, and Buttercup eschew the apparent pleasures of shopping malls in favor of reaping the rewards of "saving the world before bedtime," the commercial intertexts still emphasize that the thing girls do best is buy.

Notes

1 The emphasis on power surrounded, if not contained, by signifiers of conventional, feminine beauty is made explicit in ESPN's 2001 promotional campaign for the WNBA. Shot in black-and-white, a WNBA player shoots baskets on a court. At the close of the commercial, in the bottom left-hand corner, the text reads: "Basketball is Beautiful" followed by a cablecast game schedule. Given that many of the WNBA players are African-American, this seems a particularly interesting slogan with its re-articulation of a key phrase ("Black is Beautiful") from Black liberation struggles of the late 1960s and 1970s.

2 In an interesting acknowledgment of the cross-generational appeal of *The Powerpuff Girls*, the 20 January 2002 issue of the *New York Times Magazine* published an advertisement for the program. Appearing amongst advertisements for such posh products as the 240-HP Nissan Pathfinder, the Acura RL, and financial consultants Solomon Smith Barney, Cartoon Network promises "the best fights on TV" with *The Powerpuff Girls*.

3 Fan artist "Marcos" uploaded the image "Blossom as Lara Croft" on 30 July 2001. As a "crossover" scanned pencil art drawing, this image offers Blossom equipped with hiking boots, over-the-shoulder holsters, and water-gun weapons. See: http://fanstuffs.ppginstitute.com for more PpG original fan art.

4 My thanks to Carol Stabile for making this point.

5 See Robert Lloyd, "Beyond Good and Evil," *LA Weekly*, and Jen Fried, "Puff Daddy" (2001: 46–50).

6 Some of the most popular girl-centered television programs have been produced and written by men (*My So-Called Life* by Marshall Herskovitz and Edward Zwick; *Buffy The Vampire Slayer* by Joss Whedon; *The Powerpuff Girls* by Craig McCracken) demonstrating that primary textual authorship is not necessarily a determinant of a given program's meaningfulness for female viewers.

7 For differing views of the implications of this phenomenon, see Kline (1995) and Seiter (1995).

8 *The Powerpuff Girls: Heroes and Villains* compact disc was produced by Devo's Mark Mothersbaugh and includes songs from artists such as Frank Black, Shonen Knife, Apples in Stereo, and David Byrne.

9 In addition to the proliferation of networks, programs, and stores specifically addressing children as a preferred market, industry-specific publications such as *KidScreen* document the ways that mass-media conglomerates construct and shape genres and audiences. A brief survey of the magazine's Web site indicates the degree to which children's markets are integral to mass-media conglomerates' profits. Identified as an "international trade magazine serving the information needs and interests of all those involved in reaching children through entertainment," *KidScreen* functions as a database of the most recent trends in the corporate construction of children's markets. In relation to *The Powerpuff Girls*, articles detail how, as early as 1998, Cartoon Network used various promotional vehicles – including sponsorship of the "Wacky Racing NASCAR" at the Winston Cup races in Rockingham, North Carolina and Atlanta, Georgia. Painted "shocking pink complete with shimmering stars and decals depicting the Powerpuff Girls," the NASCAR was included in the first part of Cartoon Network's marketing campaign. Fully aware of, and indeed playing on, the apparently ironic juxtaposition between the "paint job and the gritty high-testosterone racing world," this embodies the central conceit of the cartoon: the power is in the puff! Hoping that the ideal viewers would identify the program as "not a girls' show" but a "super-hero show that happens to feature girls," senior vice-president of marketing for Cartoon Network, Craig McAnsh, says that what he really wants to "*drive* is the fact that the episodes are full of action sequences and power" (emphasis added). The success of the race car as promotional *vehicle*, then, depends upon the audience (watching live at the race track and on television) reading against type or the turning of cultural signifiers of passivity and weakness into activity and strength.

10 For an analysis of the history of product design and color, see Sparke (1995).

11 Although interviews with McCracken have emphasized his positive response to the film project, it is significant that Cartoon Network has allowed him to maintain most of the creative control and rights over the production.

12 Nestled in the pages of *Dreamboat* magazine is a drawing of Craig McCracken wearing an E-Bay T-shirt.

Bibliography

Fried, Jen (2002) "Puff Daddy," *Bust*, Spring: 46–50.

Frith, S. (1981) *Sound Effects: Youth, Leisure, and the Politics of Rock and Roll*, New York: Pantheon.

Jenkins, H. (1998) "Introduction: Childhood Innocence and Other Modern Myths," in H. Jenkins (ed.), *The Children's Culture Reader*, New York: New York University Press.

Kapur, J. (1999) "Out of Control: Television and the Transformation of Childhood in Late Capitalism," in M. Kinder (ed.), *Kids' Media Culture*, Durham: Duke University Press, 122–39.

Kearney, M. (1998a) "Girls, Girls, Girls: Gender and Generation in Contemporary Discourses of Female Adolescence and Youth Culture," unpublished Ph.D. dissertation, University of Southern California, Los Angeles.

—— (1998b) "Producing Girls: Rethinking the Study of Female Youth Culture," in S. Inness (ed.), *Delinquents and Debutantes: Twentieth-Century American Girls' Cultures*, New York: New York University Press, 285–311.

KidScreen (1999) "WB Powers into Junior Apparel," Available at: http://216.191.209.135/articles/magazine/19990901/26550.html?word=Powerpuff (accessed 25 May 2002).

Kline, Stephen (1995) *Out of the Garden: Toys, TV, and Children's Culture in the Age of Marketing*, New York: Verso.

Lloyd, R. (2001) "Beyond Good and Evil," *LA Weekly*. Available at: http://www.laweekly.com/ink/01/01/cover~lloyd.shtml (accessed 2 January 2002).

Loos, T. (2000) "Breaking Through Animation's Boy Barrier," *New York Times*, 17 September.

McRobbie, A. (1991) *Feminism and Female Youth Culture*, Boston: Unwin Hyman.

Meehan, E. (1991) "'Holy Commodity Fetish, Batman!': The Political Economy of a Commercial Intertext," in R. Pearson and W. Urrichio (eds.), *The Many Lives of Batman: Critical Approaches to a Superhero and His Media*, New York: Routledge.

The Powerpuff Girls Powerzine (2001) Cartoon Network, H & S Media, Inc. Publishers.

Schatz, T. (1997) "The Return of the Hollywood Studio System," in E. Barnouw, et al. (eds.), *Conglomerates and the Media*, New York: New Press.

Seiter, E. (1995) "Toy-Based Video for Girls," in C. Bazalgette and D. Buckingham (eds.), *In Front of the Children: Screen Entertainment and Young Audiences*, London: BFI, 166–88.

Simensky, L. (1998) "Selling Bugs Bunny: Warner Brothers and Character Merchandising," in K. S. Sandler (ed.), *Reading the Rabbit: Explorations in Warner Bros. Animation,* New Brunswick: Rutgers University Press, 172–93.

Sparke, P. (1995) *As Long as It's Pink: The Sexual Politics of Taste*, London: Pandora Press.

Spigel, L. (1998) "Seducing the Innocent: Childhood Television in Postwar America," in H. Jenkins (ed.), *The Children's Culture Reader*, New York: New York University Press, 110–36.

219

Chapter 12

"OH MY GOD, THEY DIGITIZED KENNY!"

Travels in the *South Park* Cybercommunity V4.0[1]

Brian L. Ott

D URING ITS FIRST SIX YEARS, COMEDY CENTRAL – which was created in 1991 by the merger of two other comedy channels – was barely a blip on the televisual landscape and, in fact, many cable systems did not even carry the channel. But that all changed drastically in 1997 when Comedy Central launched *South Park* – a crudely animated series about the lives of four 8-year-old boys (Stan Marsh, Eric Cartman, Kenny McCormick, and Kyle Broslowski) and their small Colorado town. Almost immediately the new series generated both success and controversy. Success came in the form of high ratings.[2] Within a year of its debut, *South Park* was "the top rated series on cable, seen by some five million people every week" (Collins 1998: 76), and with nearly 60 percent of its audience between the ages of 18 and 34 (Marin 1998: 60), the show was, according to one advertising executive, a marketing "gold mine" (Ross 1998: 38).

The controversy stemmed from the show's content, which privileges violence, profanity, and scatological humor, as well as racial and ethnic slurs. Indeed, when *South Park* premiered, "[it was] the only television series not on pay-TV to get a running TV-MA (for mature audiences) rating" (Kloer 1998: L3), and Comedy Central aggressively promoted it with the slogan, "Alien abductions, anal probes and flaming farts. *South Park*. Why they created the V-chip!" Adding to the controversy was the fact that despite its "mature" rating, 28 percent of the audience was under the age of 17 (Harris 1998: C2) and 5 percent under the age of 11 (Collins 1998: 76). Though public outrage over the show's content no doubt aided in its rise to popularity and fueled the multi-million dollar-a-year merchandising industry of clothing, toys, and videos,[3] it does not tell the whole story of how *South Park*, for a time, "seized pole position in the culture industry" (Norris 1998: 66).

The tremendous concern and fascination with *South Park*'s "no-brow" humor (Wild 1998: 32) has largely deflected attention away from an equally interesting and significant factor in the show's history and status as a cultural artifact. From the very start, *South Park* has been closely tied to the culture of the Internet. In 1995, FOX TV executive Brian Graden hired Trey Parker and Matt Stone to create an electronic Christmas card (see McDonald 1997: 29; Span 1997: G8). The result was a five-minute animated video called, "The Spirit of Christmas," in which Jesus Christ and Santa Claus square off in a Mortal Kombat-style fight with the children of South Park looking on. As the e-card circulated in Los Angeles, it "became something of an underground legend, particularly on the Internet" (Cobb 1998: D1). A few weeks after learning about the video card, executives at Comedy Central struck a deal with Parker and Stone to make thirteen episodes based on the characters in the e-card and *South Park* was born. Since the Internet buzz surrounding *South Park* preceded rather than followed the show's production, by the time it aired in 1997 there were already "more than 250 unofficial Web sites ... devoted to news, gossip, and general worship" (Marin 1998: 59). From the start, Comedy Central encouraged these fan-sites to circulate audio and video from the series, eventually even distributing digital clips on the official *South Park* Web site.[4] A digitally created program with stop-motion style, *South Park* is low bandwidth and ideal for download. The Internet, then, was influential not only in the show's creation, but also in Comedy Central's subsequent marketing of it.[5] As 15-year-old Oskar Horyd told *Newsweek*, "Without the Internet I doubt I would have ever even heard about it" (Marin 1998: 59–60).

This essay is about *South Park*'s online fans – fans such as 14-year-old Austin Heap and 15-year-old Matt Lennen whose jointly operated *South Park* Web site was averaging 10,000 visitors a day in 1998 (Weise 1998: D1), fans whose interest in the show is connected to, mediated by, and played out on the Internet. Seeking to understand more fully the relationship of the television series *South Park* to its online fandom, I undertake an examination of *South Park*'s spirited Internet following.[6] Though the Internet provides users with a multitude of ways to interact, everything from e-mail and chat rooms to listservs and multi-user domains, this study is limited primarily to "home pages" or personally authored Web sites. In the decentered, hypertextual, multimedia environment of the World Wide Web, homepages serve as the idiom for constructing "home" identities (Turkle 1995: 258). They reflect, according to Esders, "deep-seated desires to construct personal presentations of the self and hence one's chosen identity"

(2000: 80). As such, a critical examination of *South Park*-themed home pages affords a revealing snapshot of how their creators view themselves and their relation to others. Based on an analysis of these sites, I argue that *South Park*'s online fans enact a postmodern sensibility consistent with the underlying logic of the television series. That is, *South Park* supplies a model for the crafting of identity and the production of distinction in a semiotically rich (i.e., information laden) landscape. Before turning to this analysis, however, I would first like to address briefly the importance of the Web as an object of study, to review several of the unique challenges it poses for scholars, and to describe my overall approach.

Web research: surfing as a mode of enquiry

The study of online community is certainly not novel. Numerous scholars (Catalfo 1993; Dibbell 1999; Rheingold 1993; Tepper 1997) have examined the electronic exchange of messages among Internet users with shared interests, and several studies (Baym 2000; Jenkins 1995) have suggested that media products such as television programs may furnish the common interest that unites a community. However, as Gauntlett argues:

> Most of the studies of virtual communities are about groups exchanging messages on newsgroups and e-mail discussion lists, or groups who often meet in the same chat rooms. These studies seem, so far, to have ignored the communities that develop amongst similarly themed websites and their creators, which in many ways may be stronger and more permanent. Participants in chatting groups may come and go, whereas the bonds of friendship and interdependence which the Web, by its interconnected nature, breeds amongst web site creators – expressed in public links and personal e-mails – may be more compelling.
>
> (Gauntlett 2000: 14)

To the extent that Web sites offer a particularly complex picture of how users negotiate their identities (Cheung 2000: 44–5), it is vital that communication scholars carefully attend to the rhetorical choices made by Web authors.

Studying the Web poses a number of challenges to traditional models of textual analysis – not the least of all by disrupting what is meant by a "unified" text (Landow 1997: 33, 64). As a hypertextual medium, the World Wide Web is nonlinear, dynamic, and indeterminate (Aarseth 1994: 59–61). Nonlinearity indicates that there is no fixed sequence dictating how the text should be read. There is no prescribed beginning, middle, or end, and users can enter the text at any point. Dynamic means that the World Wide Web is never finished and static, as new Webpages are continuously being added and others deleted. Likewise, the content of even a single Web site is often in flux, as Web authors forever expand, cut, and rearrange the content of their pages. Indeterminacy highlights that the traversal function between Webpages (i.e., the link) is also marked by instability. Web authors routinely update hyperlinks, deleting some and adding others, thereby altering the relationship among pages. Therefore, no two people could ever have precisely the same experience "reading" the Web. Given these challenges, using a scientific standard for selecting which Webpages in a community to analyze, such as popularity measured in page hits, hardly makes sense.

I propose, instead, an approach based on "surfing" or following self-appealing hyperlinks from one site to another. Despite its rather obvious unscientific character, this approach mirrors in form the experience of the individuals under study. Although not comprehensive – it would be impossible to follow every link on every site – it is also not entirely random, as movement through the community is limited (structured) by the links provided. My point of entry for this study was Beef-Cake.com, which when I began this study in 1998 was, according to *Newsweek* magazine, "The largest [*South Park*] site" (Marin 1998: 59). From there, I surfed into thirty other *South Park*-themed Web sites (identified at the end of this chapter), all the while cataloging content similarities and differences and charting underlying formal patterns (i.e., aesthetic and technical choices made by Web authors). Since the Web is a dynamic medium, I also decided to introduce a longitudinal component into the study, and in May 2001, I returned to the sites I had initially studied in 1998 to see what, if anything, had changed. Of the thirty-one Web sites in my original study, twelve no longer existed, one (Mr. Hat's Hell Hole) had moved to a new URL, one (Beef-Cake.com) was undergoing revision and was temporarily offline, and the remaining sites had all been substantially revised – with several of the pages no longer dedicated solely to *South Park*. The text, artifact, object of this study, then, is scarcely any of these things, and although it exists only in my experience, I remain convinced that it has much to teach us.

Travels in the *South Park* Cybercommunity

An analysis of the formal and content characteristics of thirty-one *South Park*-themed Web sites conducted over a three-year period (1998–2001) highlights seven key principles: connectivity, interactivity, originality, mastery, iconicity, marketability, and adaptability. In this chapter, I describe each of these characteristics and analyze how – through their enactment – *South Park* Web authors negotiate their individual and collective identities and adapt to the conditions of an increasingly postmodern landscape.

Connectivity

Perhaps the single most significant feature of contemporary cultural life is the radical explosion of information (Wurman 1989). As new electronic technologies have expanded the production and flow of information, cultural life has become inundated with what has alternatively been called "data glut" (Shenk 1998), "semiotic excess" (Collins 1995), and "radical semiurgy" (Best and Kellner 1991) – a seemingly endless and unmanageable array of signs.[7] One key consequence of the information explosion has been that information itself has become ever-more specialized. The increasing specialization of information and knowledge contributes, in turn, to cultural fragmentation, to the rise of modern alienation and disconnection, and to the dissolution of traditional community (Harvey 1990). Prior to the advent of electronic media, the flow of information was stringently tied to geography. Information was transmitted locally, primarily by word of mouth, and what people knew was shaped by where people were. Community then, which depends upon a sharing of information (and interests), was also bound geographically (Vitanza 1999: 60). But in a media-rich landscape, the sources of information are so varied and pervasive that physical place is no longer as central a predictor of what people know, and subsequently no longer a guarantee of community.

With the flow of information no longer closely tied to geography, culture's inhabitants – especially those reared on the new information technologies of television and computers – consume ever-more specialized data, contributing to the difficulty of connecting with others who share *only* a common geography. Through the Internet, however, individuals can "connect" with others who share their distinctive interests, no matter where those with similar interests may be located. As Healy explains, "the Internet, as the name suggests, is not about escape into isolation, but rather an ongoing and outgoing exercise in connectedness" (1997: 57). With television being consumed almost exclusively in the home and the medium itself transgressing geographic boundaries, *South Park* fandom does lend itself well to place-centered models of community. This is especially true of *South Park* fans, who are primarily adolescent boys and have no means of traveling long distances in order to interact.[8] Not surprisingly, then, die-hard fans of the series use the Internet, and specifically the World Wide Web, to articulate their sense of community. Precisely how *South Park*'s fans use the Web to "come together," to forge meaningful relationships, and to build (cyber)community is the concern of the remainder of this section.[9]

The most obvious level at which *South Park*'s online fans enact a communal identity and demonstrate the principle of connectivity is through shared content. Without exception, the thirty-one Web sites I examined in 1998 featured images, audio, and often video from the television series. On the vast majority of Web sites, digital material from the show was organized and presented within a specially designated section of the overall site generally titled, "SP Downloads" or "audio and video." It is not simply the *display* of common content on *South Park* Web sites that fosters connectivity, but the actual *sharing* of that content. When the series began production in 1997, Comedy Central was not yet distributing audio and video clips on the official *South Park* site. Hence, the digital material that was circulating on the Internet prior to 1999 – when Comedy Central began providing material – had been captured and digitized by fans. Since this practice requires special computer equipment and software that most fans would not have had at the time, the ubiquity of *South Park* images, audio, and video testifies to its circulation among fans. Just as some fandom communities share perceptions and analysis of the texts they follow (Baym 2000; Jenkins 1995), *South Park's* fans share the text itself. During the show's first season, many fans did not have access to the show through their cable provider, and they had to utilize other means to pursue their interest. The sharing of information, multimedia in this case, was central, then, to the emergence of community.

South Park-themed Web sites also embody the principle of connectivity at the structural level of hypertextual links. Hyperlinks are "relational" as much as they are "functional." In addition to providing a mechanism to move from one site to another, they publicly express an association between the self and others. Explains Shields:

> In a network, then, the status of individual elements is determined by their connections.... The [Web]page takes some of its identity from this participation in a network. First, its identity is relational; it is not self-contained, but depends on its relationship with other elements.... Beyond being partly relational, the identity of elements depends on the substantive identity and character of the elements to which it is linked.
>
> (2000: 150)

Although the *general* practice of hyperlinking (and thus the principle of connectivity) is plainly not unique to *South Park* Web sites, the *specific* practices of hyperlinking used in these Web sites are distinctive (although certainly not exclusive). The *South Park* Web sites I examined operate as part of a "webring" – a specially designed hyperlink protocol that connects a large series of (similarly themed) Web sites in a virtual circle. Each Webring member displays a common "banner" at the bottom of his/her site that allows visitors to interact with subsequent ring members (to follow the circle) by selecting the "view next site" hyperlink. The *South Park* Webring, which re-inforces solidarity by creating a virtual boundary of inclusion and exclusion, was founded on 31 December 1996 (before the show premiered) and listed 247 sites in 1998. Thus, the hyperlinking practices of the Web sites in this study function as an articulation of communal identity, and promote connectivity among a particular group of Internet users: in this instance, *South Park* fans. Through the *sharing* of information and the *linking* of Web sites, *South Park* fans have created a "living network" of social relations that transcends geography.

Interactivity

Wynn and Katz (1998) contend that personal Webpages are "unilateral presentations of self, because [social] conventions are less well established [in cyberspace where the audience is unknown]." Though this may be true of *many* personal Web sites, it does not appear to be the case for *all* such sites. That the *potential* audience for Web sites is, of course, limitless and unknown does not take into account that the *actual* audience for similarly themed, fan-based Web sites is primarily fans. Far from *South Park*'s Web authors creating a one-way message to an unknown audience, they must continually negotiate the Web authoring norms and conventions established and policed by fans. The principal way that conventions are regulated in the *South Park* cybercommunity is through the presence of electronic guestbooks – interactive, public registries that allow visitors to furnish Web authors with feedback about their sites. Fully 85 percent of the Web sites that I examined in 1998 featured guestbooks, which function to privilege participation and to heighten the sense of communal involvement. That any visitor can review and respond directly to any Web site with a guestbook works to decentralize communal authority, and to transform text construction into a collaborative process.

Collaboration occurs on two levels – by altering the content of the Web site one is responding to, and by providing feedback for revision to the site's author. Because of the way electronic guestbooks are set up, comments posted to guestbooks by visitors are automatically recorded in the guestbook registry, where they are available for all future visitors to view. This means that the comments posted to a guestbook literally become part of that Web site's content. At this level, individual Web sites are multiply authored. Collaboration is also exercised through advice giving, as visitors to guestbooks may suggest design elements such as new color combinations or technical elements such as HTML coding tricks to make a site more appealing or user-friendly. At South Park Forum – a Web site designed for chatting about topics related to *South Park* – three of the eleven chat rooms are dedicated to Web authoring (see www.gotimmygo.com/gtg, accessed 25 September 2002). One room offers general Web authoring advice, another offers advice on 3-D modeling programs for creating graphics, and a third the URLs for new *South Park* sites. The centrality of guestbooks, as well as chatrooms, in the *South Park* cybercommunity suggests that the construction of Web sites is a much less unilateral and a much more interactive and collaborative process than indicated by Wynn and Katz.

The principle of interactivity is further re-inforced by the Web's underlying organizational structure: hypertext. According to Landow, hypertext is "text composed of blocks of words (or images) linked electronically by multiple paths, chains, or trails in an open-ended, perpetually unfinished textuality" (1997: 3). Unlike more traditional forms of textuality, such as novels in which the author imposes direction (and to a great extent meaning) on the reader, hypertextuality provides the reader with more control. A Web site cannot be read from left to right or top to bottom because its structure is continually interrupted by links (jumps) either to external pages or to other points on the same page. The reader must take an active role in the process of reading, continually making choices about which direction to follow, for how long, and whether or not to return to previous points. In some senses, the reader becomes the author, weaving together textual fragments into a meaningful whole through the act of surfing, a process known as, "bricolage" (see Hebdige 1987: 103). The structure of the TV series *South Park* is, in many ways, the tele-visual equivalent of hypertextuality. According to Ott and Walter (2000: 437), *South Park* is intensely "intertextual" and gestures endlessly to "cheesy popular culture" (Collins 1998: 76). With *South Park*, viewers do not so much *follow* the narrative (which is usually simplistic and often nonsensical) as "surf" for the next popular allusion, the next opportunity to move outside the text. Viewers *author* the show more than they *watch* it.[10] After all, the series scarcely makes any sense if one does not possess the ability to move back and forth between the show and its popular allusions.

Originality

Fan communities are cultural producers (Bacon-Smith 1992; Baym 2000; Jenkins 1995; Pullen 2000). Episode guides, character biographies, production sched-ules, fanzines, fiction, and artwork represent just a few of their varied products. *South Park*'s online fans are no exception, and their Web sites feature everything from self-created games and cookbooks to character diaries and drawing tuto-rials. In generating these cultural products, a premium is placed on originality. Since images, audio, and video from the television show are widely available (thanks to Comedy Central's unusual sanctioning of their circulation), fans must find alternative ways to distinguish their sites from the hundreds of others in the community. This section probes how the principle of originality is defined and policed by *South Park*'s online fans.

Among the most common forms of "original" content on *South Park* Web sites is what fans term "parodies." Mr. Hat's Hell Hole, for instance, features an array of image, song, fiction, and video parodies (www.mrhatshellhole.com/paro-dies/) that situate the characters of *South Park* in well-known movies, television

227

shows, advertisements, and musical groups. In 2001, this Web site featured eight complete movie scripts, including a spoof on the Hollywood blockbuster *Jurassic Park* titled *Your Asskicked Park*, and a spin-off of *Austin Powers: The Spy Who Shagged Me*, titled *Austin Powers: The Spy Who Barfed On Me*. The song parodies featured lyrical revisions of The Beatles' "Nowhere Man," titled "Beefcake Man," Nirvana's "Smells Like Teen Spirit," titled "Smells Like Terrance and Phillip," Aerosmith's "Janie's Got a Gun," titled "Kenny's Bought a Gun," and dozens of others. Similarly, at sweeet.com, the site's Web author employs a professional 3-D computer-modeling program (3D Studio Max r2) to create parodies of popular movie posters (see Figure 12.1).

The Web authors at Comedy Matrix (formerly Babylon Park) write and produce digital cartoons that combine *South Park* with various other media texts. In 1998, a simple Internet joke, "Oh my God, They killed Koshi!" gave birth to the sci-fi spoof *Babylon Park*, which in the words of its creators, "is the ultimate crossover epic, blending the labyrinthine story line of *Babylon 5* and the limitless fart jokes of *South Park*" (www.infinicorp.com/babylonpark/). The first two episodes of *Babylon Park* – "Spoohunter" and "Episode 000" – were both available free for download as RealVideo in 1998. Within a year, *Babylon Park* became so popular that the authors released "Frightspace," a spoof of the

Figure 12.1 Sweeet.com

Babylon 5 made-for-TV-movie, "Thirdspace." "Frightspace," which could be purchased on VHS for $24.95, sold out quickly, and the authors created still other videos, such as the recent title "Grudgematch," which, for a mere $21.95, pits the crew of *Drek Trek: Forager* against the characters of *Babylon Park*. The characters in the "Grudgematch" video are a cross between the flesh and blood actors from the sci-fi television series *Star Trek: Voyager* and *Babylon 5* and the characters of *South Park*; the videos are animated in the crude stop-motion "style" of *South Park*.

In the strict literary sense of the term, the fan-created texts found at Mr. Hat's Hell Hole, sweeet.com, and Comedy Matrix are not parodies. In most instances, the texts do not satirize or comment critically on the media texts they imitate or gesture to, and in the case of several of the image- and video-based products (especially at Mr. Hat's Hell Hole), they do not even caricature the texts they steal from. Rather than simply *resembling* other media texts, fan-generated images *reproduce* them, placing *South Park*'s characters in a new context with the aid of graphics editing software such as Photoshop. In one image from Mr. Hat's Hell Hole, for instance, the faces of characters from the 1980s television series *The A-Team* are digitally replaced with the faces of *South Park* characters to create *The SP Team* (www.mrhatshellhole.com/parodies /ateam.htm). Lacking the "ulterior motive" characteristic of parody, the fans' combination of *South Park* with other media texts is better described as "pastiche" – a neutral practice of compilation (Jameson 1994: 17) – than parody. Notably, pastiche may also be the preferred narrative mode of the television series *South Park*, which frequently places the characters in the context of other media events or introduces the characters to media celebrities (Blivess 1999). Thus, fans may simply be replicating the mode of textual production that they observe in the series in their own textual creations. Since fans invent neither the characters, nor the contexts used in their productions, the principal claim to "originality" in such productions concerns the technical skill needed to create the particular character/context combinations.

On *South Park*-themed Web sites, then, originality often has more to do with "origins" (being the *first* to do something) than with innovation, inventiveness, or imagination (being artistically creative and provocative).[11] The extreme value placed on being "first" to create a new image or graphic also extends to the content and design of the Web sites themselves. On the Internet, where images, information, and even HTML code can be pirated with a few, simple mouse clicks, the *South Park* cybercommunity is decidedly critical of stolen ideas and materials, and a lack of originality is often strongly and publicly denounced in visitor guestbooks. The following three comments posted to the guestbook at South Park Addict illustrate the community's commitment to ensuring original material:

Stop trying to blame Snow Calico for stealing your ideas. Her site was first to have them and you're just jealous. (record 127)

hey why do you always brag about how original your site is? I think your site sucks, I got here from southparkspot, which is way better than your site. SP Addict is a piece of shit, so quit bragging on how original it is! (record 162)

um…i was just wondering if the person that made this site had any skill…or did he just copy stuff from peoples sites reading your contests page sort of got me mad…you want the persons originiallity [sic] and not your own…i say u do the stuff your self. (record 246)

As originality is largely divested of the creative, inventive process in favor of origins, the concept of "authorship" is similarly transformed into a set of chiefly technical skills. The Web authors at Mr. Hat's Hell Hole, for instance, display the following warning on their site: "South Park, it's [sic] characters, images, and any other related items are registered trademarks and/or copyrights of Comedy Central.… This page and its authors are not affiliated with Comedy Central. All original content, both graphical and textual, is the intellectual property of Vin Casale and Matt Godfroy. None of the content of this page may be used without permission." Since the Web site is comprised of images of *South Park*'s characters drawn by Casale and Godfroy (but utterly indistinguishable from the show's images), the warning at the bottom of the page suggests that, at least, these two fans conceptualize authorship as involving the technical skills needed to draw or to animate the characters, but not the creative skills needed to invent the characters. Fans' desire to "protect" the *South Park* images they generate suggests further that technical skill, and in particular graphic proficiency, carries cultural currency in the *South Park* cybercommunity, and translates into power via reputation.

Mastery

Sometimes the *conspicuous absences* – the practices one would expect to find, but does not – in a culture are as central to understanding that culture as are the manifested practices. Previous research indicates that exegesis, or sustained analysis of an artifact's meanings, is a prominent feature of many fan-based communities (Baym 2000; Jenkins 1995). In the *South Park* cybercommunity, however, fans do not engage in analysis of character motivations or plot developments, and there is seemingly no interest in the *meanings* of the original televisual text. The near total absence of interpretive work by fans may be related to the show's structure, which according to Norris is about, "style and form more than content" (1998: 68). Comprised primarily of intertextual allusions and sound bites, *South Park* does not invite in-depth plot or character analysis. In fact, the "conclusions" to episodes are rarely logical, necessary, or even outcomes related to preceding events. Meaning appears to be entirely secondary to the pleasure of consumption, to "getting" all of the intertextual allusions and self-reflective references. In fact, there exists quite a bit of competition within the community to display the most obscure and detailed knowledge of the show.

Web authors illustrate their knowledge of the show in a wide variety of ways, ranging from listing the magazines that have featured *South Park* on their covers to a compilation of Kenny's quotations – no small task, since Kenny's statements are muffled by the hood of his coat.[12] The trivia that comprises these lists is detailed and comprehensive, since to gloss-over or misreport information is to risk public criticism. Observes a visitor to the guestbook at South Park Addict: "On your secret thing [Webpage] you left out that cartman said in scuzzlebutts [sic] right hand is celery but when scuzzlebutt comes it is in his left hand" (record 160). This visitor is critical of the author, not for being incorrect, but merely for being insufficiently detailed. The most serious offense, though, is misreporting facts, as this post to the guestbook at Goin' Down to South Park indicates: "Hey, I just wanted to tell you that you had a somewhat cool site, however you made one major mistake. In [the episode] 'The Zoo,' you said the elephant was Stan's pet. That is so off. It's KYLE'S ELEPHANT!! Just saying. Hope for your sake you take the time to correct it" (record 249). This visitor treats the mistake as a profound shortcoming of the Web site and warns that such an error could have negative consequences for the author. The unstated consequence is a loss of prestige. Since knowledge equals prestige within the informational economy of the Net (Jenkins 1995: 59), there is a desire to demonstrate it. Some fans illustrate their knowledge (and thus superiority) by pointing out errors. Others demonstrate it by constructing *South Park* quizzes that test a visitor's knowledge of the show.[13] And some simply claim it, as this comment at South Park Addict highlights: "I AM THE ABSOLUTE BIGGEST SOUTH PARK FAN! I KNOW EVERY SECRET ABOUT SOUTH PARK AND I HAVE SEEN EVERY EPESODE [sic] 20 TIMES" (record 128). In each of these instances, mastery of the text is demonstrated not through interpretation or analysis, but through detail and comprehensiveness. The "true" *South Park* fan is one who consumes all and knows all.

Iconicity

In a previous section of this chapter, I explored how the practices of *South Park*'s online fans generate a sense of connectivity in an increasingly fragmented world. That fragmentation is due in part, I suggested, to the radical explosion of information. In this section, I want to consider how another common practice of the show's online fans may assist individuals in negotiating the endless (re)circulation of images and text (i.e., in processing information). *South Park*-themed Web sites make consistent use of icons – symbols whose form suggests meanings or functions that are considerably more complex than the symbols themselves. Most computer users are familiar with icons because they are the basis for executing functions in Windows-based environments. The "trash can" icon located on most computer desktops, for instance, signals a mechanism for discarding an unwanted file. In the *South Park* cybercommunity, icons such as Webring banners encapsulate a range of complex social relations, and serve to identify a set of shared norms without actually naming them. Award logos also function iconically by conveying quickly a set of traits embodied by a Web site. Additionally, twenty-nine of the original thirty-one Web sites studied utilized a simple, self-created graphic at the top of the main page to distinguish the site and make it easily recognizable. *South Park*-themed Web sites commonly reduce these graphics to smaller images, and employ them as active hyperlinks to those sites. Since icons create meaning through visual metonymy, their repeated use privileges a logic of reduction (and immediate assessment) over extended exposition (Brummett 1994: 64, 101).

For *South Park*'s online fans, the logic of reduction is evident in the near instantaneous appraisal of Web sites as "cool" or "sucks." These "snap" or binaristic judgments are the most common comments posted to guestbooks, and they may serve to reduce information anxiety by allowing users to process huge volumes of information more quickly. In reacting to *South Park* Web sites, visitors tend not to offer explanations of their judgments, regardless of whether the assessments are positive, "kenny kicks ass and so does this page" (ParkSouth, record 233), or negative, "Your Site Suck [sic] Like Shit" (Goin' Down to South Park, record 248). The comments posted to electronic guestbooks share the underlying logic not only of the Web, which reflects a binaristic either/or mentality,[14] but also that of the television show. *South Park* is itself iconic in its portrayal of characters and story lines. The characters are decidedly flat, two-dimensional. I am referring not just to the way they are animated (as cartoons), but to the way they (inter)act. The characters, who endlessly fling epithets at one another, lead two-dimensional lives; they are either for or against the latest political cause sweeping their town. The show is not a complex investigation of or critical commentary on any of the issues it raises. Rather, the issues merely serve as a basis for its allusions to outside media events and celebrities. The show surfs the media landscape of which it is a part, reducing political causes and social issues to a series of crude caricatures, much like the fans surf the *South Park* cybercommunity of which they are a part, passing decisive judgment as they negotiate the tide of images.[15]

Marketability

Two years before the Internet buzz about *The Blair Witch Project* (1999) transformed a relatively low-budget film into a financial blockbuster, *South Park* was
already demonstrating the tremendous marketing potential of a decentralized
communication network. Within any network, but especially one as colossal as the
Internet, buzz is largely about visibility, about being seen. As noted in the introduction to this chapter, Comedy Central actively fueled *South Park*'s online
fandom by encouraging the digital circulation of images, audio, and video from
the series. With the resources for constructing elaborate multimedia Web sites
readily available, the Web witnessed an explosion of *South Park*-themed Web sites.
Ubiquity alone is no guarantee of visibility in a decentered network, however.
Sites still have to be found, and being found on the Web requires being *indexed*. An
index is a device that directs users to a specific point within a larger landscape. In
the digital expanse of cyberspace, search engines serve an indexing function as do
other Web sites. But how does an independent Web author encourage other sites
to index (i.e., hyperlink to) his/her Web site? As with commercial Web sites, this
is done through promotion. *South Park*'s online fans actively promote their Web
sites through guestbook commentary and the display of Web awards. Many Web
authors surf to other *South Park* Web sites where they solicit fans to visit their sites.
Posts one visitor to South Park Society's guestbook, for instance, "Please visit my
site it took me a very long time to make" (record 87).

Since linking to other sites is, in part, an articulation of one's own virtual
identity, there is a compulsion to link to *quality* sites.[16] Quality is defined primarily in terms of originality, technical sophistication, and aesthetic attractiveness.
Not surprisingly, then, many *South Park* Webpages are digital monoliths of elaborate design, multimedia integration, and advanced programming, and often, they
rival commercial sites in sophistication, interactivity, and overall aesthetic appeal.
While amateur Web sites tend to be flat and static, *South Park*-themed sites
employ self-designed and self-generated animation, MP3 audio formatting,
streaming video, and JavaScripting – a computer language that simulates animation by building on existing HTML (hypertext markup language) – to give their
pages a more 3D and dynamic feel. The prevalent use of navigational frames and
feedback mechanisms, such as guestbooks, heightens the sense of interactivity
and testifies to advanced programming skill. But the pages are not just about
glitz, as they utilize basic design principles such as contrast, repetition, align-
ment, and proximity (Williams 1994) to make them more user-friendly and
aesthetically pleasing. Sites that embody these elements commonly earn praise
from community members. As a visitor to the guestbook at *South Park* Society
comments: "Awesome site! I can tell you have far too much time on your hands!
LOL Good Job! Dan." (record 88). Although, at first glance, it appears this
visitor is suggesting the author's efforts are a waste of time, "LOL" (or laugh out

loud) indicates that the comment is intended ironically, and that the visitor truly appreciates the effort that went into making the site.

Another mechanism for promoting Web sites is the display of "Web awards" – individually authored graphics (like logos) that celebrate some aspect of Web site design and are distributed by their creators. The Kicked Baby Award, which references an event from *South Park*'s premiere episode, is, for instance, specifically designed to reward original content in *South Park* Web sites. Writes the creator of the Kicked Baby Award:

> This award is given out to sites with great original material, lots of information, and a generally all-around great site! Ike doesn't like: only links, borrowed stuff (unless it's credited) and boring material. After all, babies have a short attention span! Ike likes: Lots of information, cool features, interactive sites, and easy navigation.
>
> (parksouth.simplenet.com/award/)

Through award logos, which are "proportionately sized for display" (Elmer 2000: 166), a Web site simultaneously promotes itself and the Web site that gives the award, which is usually hyperlinked through the award itself. Hence, "Web site awards," argues Elmer, "speak to a hypertextual politics of finding and being found – that is to say a means of Networking and promoting a hypertextually linked community of like-minded resources and interests outside of the economically powerful yet simply index or subject-based default portal, search engine, or Net guide" (2000: 166).

Adaptability

On the fast-paced information superhighway, stagnancy is a virtual guarantee that a Web site will become electronic road kill. With microprocessors doubling in performance every eighteen months (Pritchett 1996) and connection speeds jumping dramatically in recent years from 56 kilobytes of data per second to 1.5 megabytes of data per second (with cable connections), the Web is a dynamic, ever-changing landscape. Thanks to increases in computing power, changes in infrastructure and networking such as fiber optics, and user-friendly animation software such as Flash, the Web has become a significantly more graphic-intense environment than it was a mere five years ago. To keep pace with changes in technology and to remain stylistically fresh, Web authors must continually revise and update the design and content of their sites. When I first surfed into the *South Park* cybercommunity in 1998, one-third of the sites that I visited openly advertised that they were "under construction." I suspect that the number of sites that were actually being revised on a routine basis was significantly higher, but that they simply did not publicize it. With new episodes of the television series

South Park being produced on a regular basis, Web authors had, at the very least, to regularly update their episode guides and download offerings if they wanted to continue to attract visitors. By all appearances, Web site authors were investing tremendous time resources in adapting their sites to the demands of both emerging technologies and the ongoing production of episodes. In fact, upon returning to the Web sites I had originally studied in 1998, I discovered that all nineteen of the initial thirty-one sites that remained had undergone substantial revision.

Individual Web sites were not the only thing that had experienced change in the *South Park* cybercommunity however. A visit to the *South Park* Webring on 31 May 2001 revealed that the total number of Web sites in the ring had declined from 247 just three years earlier to 67. This shift signals that the interconnections marking the boundaries of the community had changed dramatically. Although there are likely a number of factors that contributed to this decline, I wish to speculate about three in particular. The same time period that witnessed a decline in Webring membership saw a decline in the popularity of the television series. Vitality of online fan communities may be linked to vitality of the media text that fans follow. Some media scholars (see especially Kellner 1995: 233–47) have argued that identity in a postmodern world is fluid and closely tied to circulation of images and styles in the culture industry. Many of *South Park*'s fans may have found a more recent and popular media text from which to derive a sense of community. A second, related factor that may have contributed to declining membership in the Webring is the composition of the membership. In the initial study, twenty-three of the Web authors were self-identified as adolescent boys, two as adolescent girls, and seven were unknown. Thus, it may be that as the Web sites' authors grew older, their tastes and priorities shifted. With the show no longer as popular in 2001 as it was in 1998, new fans were not replacing the fans that had left. It is possible also that some Web authors "closed" their Web sites because they proved too time-consuming or because they could not compete (technically) with more elaborate and advanced Web sites, which were more communally prestigious.

Postscript, postmodern, postmodern script

This chapter has been a long time in the (un)making. I have been thinking, speaking, and writing about – as well as "surfing" through – the *South Park* cybercommunity for nearly four years now. And each time I engage in these activities, I discover something new, something unseen in my previous engagements. This endless sense of discovery has made describing my experiences particularly challenging, and this chapter reflects my fourth (hence v4.0 in the title) attempt to grapple with what those experiences mean and what they can teach us. So, rather than merely summarizing what I have said up to this point and imposing a strong and tidy sense of closure, which my object of study has itself consistently resisted, I would like to spend a few moments reflecting on the process of writing this chapter, and then to speculate about what some of the difficulties I faced may mean for critics generally, and for the way we study postmodern media such as the Web in particular.

When I use the phrase "*South Park* cybercommunity," it conveys a sense of boundaries and borders, a sense of a relatively discrete, coherent, and unified object of study. That *sense* arises I believe, in large part, from the fact that the practices of that community are indeed textualized in its Web sites. But as much as *South Park*-themed Web sites may *feel* like a discrete, coherent, and unified text, they constitute a far more dynamic, dispersed, and fleeting text than the media texts (such as film) critics traditionally have studied. The formal properties of Web-based textuality, namely hypertextuality, are profoundly different from the formal properties of traditional, single-authored, linear, stable, bounded textuality (Aarseth 1994: 51–86; Heim 1993: 29–40; Landow 1997: 33–48; Levinson 1997: 136–47). Those differences are important not only for the authors of texts, but for readers and critics as well. Describing the unique challenges that hypertext poses for critics, Landow writes:

> Hypertext, which permits readers to choose their own paths through a set of possibilities, dissolves the fundamental fixity that provides the foundation of our critical theory and practice…. The critic has to give up not only the idea of mastery but also that of a single text at all as the mastery and mastered object disappear. In this admission of a relatively weaker, less authoritative position in relation to both text and reader (other readers), the critic, whatever he or she may become, in two ways becomes more like a scientist, who admits that his or her conclusions take the form, inevitably, of mere samples. Like the physicist dipping into a million trillion events, like the drama reviewer discussing only some of the many performances, the critic explicitly samples and *only* samples, one must add, by actively participating in text production in a far more active way than ever before.
>
> (Landow 1994: 33, 35)

Because critics who study Web-based phenomena are involved in the production of the text or object of enquiry that they are studying, the text militates against traditional modes of argument. Hypertextual artifacts, for instance, resist universalizing claims, especially regarding meaning, as well as linear arguments. Since linear argument unfolds temporally, the succession of claims implies more or less causal relationships among ideas.

Linear argument, which most academic writing is, does not lend itself well to describing or analyzing new forms of textuality such as hypertext, as it is ill-equipped to capture the complexity and multiplicity of relationships that exist within a hypertextual artifact. From this perspective, my experiences in the *South Park* cybercommunity are probably best suited for hypertextual presentation. Since that was not an option in this case, however, I tried to cheat the difference between hypertext and the more traditional modes of textuality that are typically found in books. This chapter is written in fragments, each of which stands, in large part, on its own – meaning that to understand the seven principles (logics) I identify, the reader does not "necessarily" have to read them in the order they are currently arranged. Indeed, in crafting this chapter, I experimented with different arrangements of the principles. As I re-arranged them, the juxtapositions resulted in new insights, which often did not "fit" anywhere. Actually, I started with only five principles, and two others emerged as a result of my organizational experiments. So, I offer the principles of connectivity, interactivity, originality, mastery, iconicity, marketability, and adaptability not as a linear argument, but as a collection of fragments, a sampling of my experiences in the *South Park* cybercommunity. My hope is that collectively these fragments add up to something more than what they represent individually, that they form a mosaic – one that is neither stable nor complete. Further, my hope is that the text (of this essay) invites readers to extend and modify it just as *South Park*'s online fans extend and modify *South Park*.

On that note, if I were to change one thing about this chapter, it would be the way I talk about the *South Park* cybercommunity as somehow distinct from the television series *South Park*.[17] This perspective perpetuates a fictional, fabricated border. *South Park*, in all its manifestations, embodies a new form of textuality and perhaps more than most contemporary media texts elides existing classification and boundaries. The television show and its online fan following are intricately interwoven, neither one existing "outside" or "before" the other. They simultaneously function to cross-promote and cross-animate one another. As the header at Mr. Hat's Hell Hole exclaims: "We ARE South Park: For the fans, by the fans." Critics who study postmodern forms such as the Web need to take seriously the ways that media texts – thanks to technological convergence and the decentering of the author – are increasingly mutable, boundless, and dispersed.

Because this paragraph is located at the bottom of the last page of this essay, it will likely be read as a conclusion, or even more unfortunately as *the* conclusion. The compulsion to read this paragraph as a conclusion, as well as the feeling that one has "arrived" here suggests just how powerful textual form is in shaping our perceptions and structuring our experiences. The whole notion of an ending, of closure, however, is decidedly antithetical to the form of postmodern media and to Web-based texts in particular. In a postmodern sense, the "text" does not exist independent of the activities of the reader, and beginnings and endings are simply self-fashioned portals that mark individualized experiences. Members of and visitors to the *South Park* cybercommunity create their own entrances and exits, and once inside, the paths they follow and the activities they engage in are many and varied. Some come for a sense of connection; others for a sense of self-worth. Some come to illustrate their technical abilities; others to learn those skills. Some come to sell their creations; others to buy them. Some come just for fun, to escape the social responsibilities they bear; others to fulfill those responsibilities, and to write academic essays. Or, at least, that was my experience.

Notes

1 An earlier version of this essay was presented at the 1999 Western States Communication Association annual convention, Vancouver, BC, February 19–23.
2 Ratings translate to advertising dollars. "Blue-chip advertisers like AT&T, Calvin Klein and Snapple are paying as much as $80,000 for a 30-second spot, 20 times the network's original rate card cost" (Marin 1998: 58).
3 For merchandising data, see Johnson (1998: 10F); Ross (1998: 38); and Kloer (1998: L3).
4 The official *South Park* Web site is a fan favorite. In fact, "Some 40% of the traffic to Comedy Central's Web site visits the 'South Park' Area" (Ross 1998: 38). It was not until the show's second season, however, that the site began to distribute *South Park* clips.
5 Betsy McLaughlin, senior vice-president of merchandising for the California-based Hot topic chain, "credits [the Internet] with helping to drive interest in both the show and licensed product" (Johnson 1998: 10F).
6 I describe the online fans as "spirited" because when the show's producers promised to answer the frequently debated question "Who is Cartman's Father?" in 1998 and then did not as part of an April Fool's joke, online fans organized an e-mail campaign that prompted Comedy Central to alter the scheduled production order of the series' episodes (see Glaser 1998: 48).
7 The information explosion is a consequence of changes in both the production and flow of information. By *production*, I mean the generation of "new" data. Inexpensive word processors, desktop publishing tools, video recorders, and the Internet allow more people to produce more information than at any time in history. "Since 1990," reports Biocca, "the size of the Internet has approximately doubled every year.... By one conservative estimate, there are more than 8 billion [Web]pages.... Although already enormous, the current cyberspace information volume may be <5% of the information that will eventually appear" (2000: 23). Wurman estimates that, "More new information has been produced in the last 30 years than in the previous 5,000" (1989: 35). By *flow*, I mean the storage, retrieval, and transmission of "old" information. Networked computers, CDs, digital recording devices, and cable television contribute significantly to an endless recirculation of existing information.
8 Some other fan-based communities, who are older, do physically come together to share information (see Bacon-Smith 1992).
9 Since definitions of community are always political (involved with power relationships), there is significant debate in academic circles about precisely what constitutes an "electronic community" (Baym 1998; Catalfo 1993; Foster 1997; Jones 1998; Rheingold 1993; Tepper 1997; Wilbur 1997). Because this essay is not specifically concerned with the philosophical debates about community, and because the definitions adopted are often elitist, this essay will employ a somewhat more general understanding of the concept as a group marked by shared interests, shared norms, and a sense of commitment (Stacey 1974). Based on this definition, I will be treating *South Park*'s online fans as a community. That is not to say that the *South Park* cybercommunity does not have its limitations. As Licklider and Taylor noted as early as 1968,

electronic communities tend to attract like-minded individuals. The audio files, images, links, IP addresses, and guestbook commentary in the *South Park* cybercommunity suggest, for instance, that sexism and homophobia are widely accepted.

10 The show validates viewers' associative jumps much as the Web validates users' personal navigation through the endless array of signs – a process that symbolically alleviates information anxiety. By fostering a "literacy that is prompted by jumps of intuition and association," Heim explains, "Hypertext helps us navigate the tide of information" (1993: 30, 40). For more on the associative logic of the link and hypertext, see Cali (2000).

11 The two notable exceptions to this claim in my sample would be the images at sweeet.com and the videos at Comedy Matrix. These products – although still better classified as pastiche than parody – demonstrate a greater level of sophistication and creativity than most of the products generated by *South Park*'s online fans.

12 The show's producers intentionally garble Kenny's statements to get them past television's censors. Kenny frequently employs profanity and his favorite topics are genitalia and sex toys. For a list of "What Kenny Says," see Kenny's Kingdom at www.kennyskingdom.com.

13 Questions usually refer to specific statements made by characters, or to images that appear in the background of scenes. Sample questions include, "How much does Jesus weigh?" "If you were to spank Mr. Garrison's ass, what should you call him?" and "What phrase is written on Officer Barbrady's police car?" The answers, incidentally, are "135 lb. 1 oz.," "Charlie," and "To Patronize and Annoy," respectively.

14 At its most basic level, digital data is comprised of bits. "A bit is a state of being: on or off, true or false, in or out, black or white. For practical purposes we consider a bit to be a 1 or a 0" (Negroponte 1995: 14). Hence, all digital media operate on a binary logic.

15 For a more extended discussion of how postmodern media provide symbolic resources for navigating semiotic excess, see Rushkoff (1996).

16 The exception to this rule is those Web sites that pride themselves on "comprehensiveness" and attempt to link to as many related sites as possible. Indiscriminate linking is the exception, however, and most fan sites link selectively.

17 By nearly any standard of academic writing, this paragraph is an odd one. Why, you might be wondering, would the author identify something he wishes to change in the essay and not simply make that change? Is he lazy? Sometimes, but not in this case. In this section of the essay, I am trying to convey a sense of textual openness, to demonstrate how even this essay, which is now in print, is not finished or closed to writing. I am trying to get the reader to think about what it means to say a text is perpetually unfinished. Hopefully, this helps to convey a sense of the open character of textuality on the Web. For a related discussion, see Barthes (1988: 155–64).

Bibliography

Aarseth, E. (1994) "Nonlinearity and Literary Theory," in G. Landow (ed.), *Hyper/Text/Theory*, Baltimore: Johns Hopkins University Press.

Bacon-Smith, C. (1992) *Enterprising Women: Television Fandom and the Creation of Popular Myth*, Philadelphia: University of Pennsylvania Press.

Bark, E. (1998) "'Chicago Hope' Bares the Needle, Pokes Fun in 'Cheek'," *The Denver Post*, 6 November: 9F.

Barthes, R. (1988) *Image, Music, Text*, New York: Noonday Press.

Baym, N. (2000) *Tune In, Log On: Soaps, Fandom, and Online Community*, Thousand Oaks, CA: Sage.

——— (1998) "The Emergence of On-Line Community," in S. Jones (ed.), *Cybersociety 2.0: Revisiting Computer-Mediated Communication and Community*, Thousand Oaks, CA: Sage.

Best, S. and D. Kellner (1991) *Postmodern Theory: Critical Interrogations*, New York: Guilford Press.

Biocca, F. (2000) "New Media Technology and Youth: Trends in the Evolution of New Media," *Journal of Adolescent Health*, Volume 27: 22–9.

Blivess, S. (1999) "Mapping *South Park*: Social Satire or Postmodern Parody," paper presented at the meeting of the Western States Communication Association, Vancouver, BC, February.

Brummett, B. (1994) *Rhetoric in Popular Culture*, New York: St. Martin's Press.

Cali, D. (2000) "The Logic of the Link: The Associative Paradigm in Communication Criticism," *Critical Studies in Media Communication*, Volume 17: 397–408.

Catalfo, P. (1993) "America, Online," in S. Walker (ed.), *Changing Community: The Graywolf Annual Ten*, St. Paul, MN: Graywolf Press.

Cheung, C. (2000) "A Home on the Web: Presentations of Self on Personal Homepages," in D. Gauntlett (ed.), *Web.Studies: Rewiring Media Studies for the Digital Age*, New York: Oxford University Press.

Cobb, N. (1998) "'South Park' – It's a Gas, Creative, Crass, Obsessed with Bodily Functions, Cable's New Cartoon, Nurtured by the Net, has Grown into a Cult Phenomenon," *Boston Globe*, 28 January: D11.

Collins, J. (1998) "Gross and Grosser," *Time*, 23 March: 75–6.

—— (1995) *Architectures of Excess: Cultural Life in the Information Age*, New York: Routledge.

Dibbell, J. (1999) "A Rape in Cyberspace," in V. Vitanza (ed.), *Cyberreader*, Boston: Allyn & Bacon.

Elmer, G. (2000) "The Economy of Cyberpromotion: Awards on the World Wide Web," in A. Herman and T. Swiss (eds.), *The World Wide Web and Contemporary Cultural Theory*, New York: Routledge.

Esders, K. (2000) "(The) Playing Author: Narrativity and Identity in Literature and Interactive Media," in E. Kraus and C. Auer (eds.), *Simulacrum America: The USA and the Popular Media*, Rochester, NY: Camden House.

Foster, D. (1997) "Community and Identity in the Electronic Village," in D. Porter (ed.), *Internet Culture*, New York: Routledge.

Gauntlett, D. (ed.) (2000) *Web.studies: Rewiring Media Studies for the Digital Age*, New York: Oxford University Press.

Glaser, M. (1998) "Love 'em or Hate 'em, 'South Park' and its Antics Set the Web Abuzz," *Los Angeles Times*, 9 April, Section CAL: 48.

Harris, L. (1998) "'South Park': Educators Not Amused," *The Atlanta Journal-Constitution*, 4 March: C1–2.

Harvey, D. (1990) *The Condition of Postmodernity: An Enquiry into the Origins of Cultural Change*, Cambridge, MA: Blackwell.

Healy, D. (1997) "Cyberspace and Place: The Internet as Middle Landscape on the Electronic Frontier," in D. Porter (ed.), *Internet culture*, New York: Routledge.

Hebdige, D. (1987) *Subculture: The Meaning of Style*, New York: Routledge.

Heim, M. (1993) *The Metaphysics of Virtual Reality*, New York: Oxford University Press.

Jameson, F. (1994) *Postmodernism, or, the Cultural Logic of Late Capitalism*, Durham, NC: Duke University Press.

Jenkins, H. (1995) "'Do You Enjoy Making the Rest of Us Feel Stupid?' alt.tv.twinpeaks, the Trickster Author, and Viewer Mastery," in D. Lavery (ed.), *Full of Secrets: Critical Approaches to Twin Peaks*, Detroit: Wayne State University Press.

Johnson, G. (1998) "'South Park' Products Move into Big Chains," *The Denver Post*, 16 November: 10F.

Jones, S. (1998) "Information, Internet, and Community: Notes Toward an Understanding of Community in the Information Age," in S. Jones (ed.), *Cybersociety 2.0: Revisiting Computer-Mediated Communication and Community*, Thousand Oaks, CA: Sage.

Kellner, D. (1995) *Media Culture: Cultural Studies, Identity and Politics Between the Modern and the Post-modern*, New York: Routledge.

Kloer, P. (1998) "'Beavis' Who? Meet Cable TV's New 'Butt-heads'," *Atlanta Journal and Constitution*, 8 February, P: L3.

Landow, G. (1997) *Hypertext 2.0: The Convergence of Contemporary Critical Theory and Technology*, Baltimore: Johns Hopkins University Press.

—— (1994) "What's a Critic to Do? Critical Theory in the Age of Hypertext," in G. Landow (ed.), *Hyper/Text/Theory*, Baltimore: Johns Hopkins University Press.

Levinson, P. (1997) *The Soft Edge: A Natural History of the Information Revolution*, New York: Routledge.

Licklider, J. and R. Taylor (1968) "The Computer as Communication Device," *Science and Technology*, 76: 21–31.

Marin, R. (1998) "The Rude Tube," *Newsweek*, 23 March: 56–62.

McDonald, S. (1997) "Tales from the Park Side," *TV Guide*, 18 October: 28–30.

Negroponte, N. (1995) *Being Digital*, New York: Vintage Books.

Norris, C. (1998) "Welcome to South Park ... Fat-Ass," *Spin*, March: 66–8.

Ott, B. and C. Walter (2000) "Intertextuality: Interpretive Practice and Textual Strategy," *Critical Studies in Media Communication*, Volume 17: 429–46.

Pritchett, P. (1996) *Resistance: Moving Beyond the Barriers to Change*, Dallas: Pritchett & Associates.

Pullen, K. (2000) "I-love-Xena.com: Creating Online Fan Communities," in D. Gauntlett (ed.), *Web.studies: Rewiring Media Studies for the Digital Age*, New York: Oxford University Press.

Rheingold, H. (1993) *The Virtual Community: Homesteading on the Electronic Frontier*, Reading, MA: Addison-Wesley.

Ross, C. (1998) "Advertisers Flock to Comedy Central's Racy 'South Park'," *Advertising Age*, 12 January: 3, 38.

Rushkoff, D. (1996) *Playing the Future: How Kids' Culture Can Teach us to Thrive in an Age of Chaos*, New York: HarperCollins.

Shenk, D. (1998) *Data Smog: Surviving the Information Glut*, San Francisco, CA: Harper.

Shields, R. (2000) "Hypertext Links: The Ethic of the Index and its Space–Time Effects," in A. Herman and T. Swiss (eds.), *The World Wide Web and Contemporary Cultural Theory*, New York: Routledge.

Span, P. (1997) "'South Park' Pushes the Taste Envelope," *Washington Post*, 14 September: G8.

Stacey, M. (1974) "The Myth of Community Studies," in C. Bell and H. Newby (eds.), *The Sociology of Community*, London: Frank Cass & Company, Ltd.

Tepper, M. (1997) "Usenet Communities and the Cultural Politics of Information," in D. Porter (ed.), *Internet Culture*, New York: Routledge.

Turkle, S. (1995) *Life on the Screen: Identity in the Age of the Internet*, New York: Touchstone.

Vitanza, V. (1999) *Cyberreader*, Boston: Allyn & Bacon.

Weise, E. (1998) "'South Park' Kids Find Home on Web but Comedy Central's Not Laughing," *USA Today*, 27 February: D1.

Wilbur, S. (1997) "An Archaeology of Cyberspaces: Virtuality, Community, Identity," in D. Porter (ed.), *Internet Culture*, New York: Routledge.

Wild, D. (1998) "South Park's Evil Geniuses and the Triumph of No-Brow Culture," *Rolling Stone*, 19 February: 32–7.

Williams, R. (1994) *The Non-Designer's Design Book: Design and Typographic Principles for the Visual Novice*, Berkeley, CA: Peachpit Press.

Wurman, R. (1989) *Information Anxiety*, New York: Doubleday.

Wynn, E. and J. E. Katz (1998) "Hyperbole over Cyberspace: Self-Presentation and Social Boundaries in Internet Home Pages and Discourse," *The Information Society*. Available at: http//www.slis.indiana.edu/TIS/articles/hyperbole.html (accessed 28 May 2001).

South Park Web sites (accessed 1998)

ADEQUATE.com's South Park: http://www.adequate.com/SouthPark/
Aliens Stuck Things Up Your Butt! http://wso.williams.edu/~cfairban/s_park.html
Babylon Park: http://www.infinicorp.com/babylonpark/
Beef-Cake.com: http://www.beef-cake.com
The Cheesy Poof Factory: http://members.aol.com/spstan98/cheesypoof.html
Crack Whore Magazine: http://come.to/crackwhoremagazine
Goin' Down to South Park: http://members.tripod.com/~user100/main.html
Ike's World: http://www.msc.net/cory.stahl/default.htm
Juice's South Park Spot: http://www.southparkspot.com
Kenny Kombat: http://vinnie.mannino.com
Kenny's Kingdom: http://www.kennyskingdom.com/
mmmkay.com: http://www.mmmkay.com
Mr. Hat's Hell Hole: http://mrhat.simplenet.com
ParkSouth: http://parksouth.simplenet.com/
South Park: http://www.comedycentral.com/southpark/
South Park Addict: http://www.spaddict.com/
South Park Central: http://www.fandom.com/south_park/
South Park Cows: http://www.southparkcows.com
South Park Exchange Network: http://exchange.sparchive.com/
South Park Files: http://spfiles.simplenet.com
South Park Online: http://www.spnews.com
South Park Rangerstation: http://www.rangerstation.com
The South Park Sanctuary: http://sps.cjb.net
South Park Society: http://come.to/spsociety
South Park Underground: http://members.aol.com/Obsiddia/
South Park: We Speak the Language: http://members.aol.com/Yoda591/
The South Park Webring: http://www.geocities.com/TelevisionCity/8940/index.html
Surf Park: http://members.aol.com/Scream2Now/sp.html
sweeet.com: http://www.sweeet.com/
Sweetypops.com: http://www.sweetypops.com
Weightgain 4000: http://www.weightgain4000.com

Index

References to illustrations are in *italics;* those for notes are followed by n